Supporting Your Teen's Mental Health

Supporting Your Teen's Mental Health

Science-Based Parenting Strategies for Repairing Relationships and Helping Young People Thrive

ANDREA TEMKIN-YU

Oxford University Press is a department of the University of Oxford.
It furthers the University's objective of excellence in research, scholarship,
and education by publishing worldwide. Oxford is a registered trade mark of
Oxford University Press in the UK and in certain other countries.

Published in the United States of America by Oxford University Press
198 Madison Avenue, New York, NY 10016, United States of America.

© Oxford University Press 2025

All rights reserved. No part of this publication may be reproduced, stored in a retrieval system, transmitted, used for text and data mining, or used for training artificial intelligence, in any form or by any means, without the prior permission in writing of Oxford University Press, or as expressly permitted by law, by license or under terms agreed with the appropriate reprographics rights organization. Inquiries concerning reproduction outside the scope of the above should be sent to the Rights Department, Oxford University Press, at the address above.

You must not circulate this work in any other form
and you must impose this same condition on any acquirer

CIP data is on file at the Library of Congress

ISBN 9780197768617

DOI: 10.1093/oso/9780197768617.001.0001

Printed by Sheridan Books, Inc., United States of America

The manufacturer's authorised representative in the EU for
product safety is Oxford University Press España S.A. of el Parque
Empresarial San Fernando de Henares, Avenida de Castilla,
2 – 28830 Madrid (www.oup.es/en).

CONTENTS

1 Getting Started with This Workbook 1

2 The Basic Principles of Parent Work 8

3 Caregiver Coping 12

4 Making Sense of Behavior 31

5 Selective Attention 56

6 Validation 104

7 Building Meaningful Routines 124

8 Helpful Support versus Unhelpful Accommodation 148

9 How to Set Up Consequences That Work 171

10 De-Escalation 206

11 Putting It All Together 249

12 Maintaining Skills and Seeking Professional Support 272

Acknowledgments 291
Index 292

1

Getting Started with This Workbook

INTRODUCTION

Over the last few years, I have felt a growing pull to write a book for parents and caregivers who are trying to support their kids' mental health. This urge has stemmed from two places: my work as a clinical psychologist and my role as a mom. At my job, I specialize in working with children and young adults who are struggling with their mental health. While I have greatly enjoyed meeting one on one with kids themselves, I have found a real love for helping parents and caregivers behind the scenes. It has been especially valuable to work with parents of teens, who can easily feel stuck between their child's independence and the bigger, scarier problems of adolescence. My work gives me the opportunity to watch kids conquer obstacles with the support of their caregivers, and I get to help parents learn how to support the people they love most in the world.

As a mom, I know the overwhelming love parents have for their children, as well as the deep drive to care for and help them. Our kids' joy can feel like pure bliss. Even their smallest wins can make your heart swell. But it is also painful to see their pain, and heartbreaking to watch as confusion, embarrassment, or worry cross their faces. This can be especially hard if there is not a clear fix for the problem in front of them. It is one thing to kiss a scraped knee or run after them with the lunch they forgot on the counter. But what about when they are being bullied? How about when their hearts are broken, or when unexplained sadness keeps them from getting out of bed in the morning? What is the playbook for when your teen is too scared to try a hobby, or too full of doubt to say hi to somebody new? Or when they just can't seem to figure out how to navigate school, despite how bright they are? As kids shift into adolescence, the problems get bigger and more complicated. This is true for most teens, but it can be especially hard for those with mental health concerns such as anxiety, depression, and Attention Deficit Hyperactivity Disorder (ADHD). The difference between typical teen growing pains and true mental health disorders is muddy, and it can be scary and confusing for parents.

As a mom who is also a psychologist, I feel unusually lucky to have certain parenting tools in my toolbox that I know can be useful in supporting my kids. At the same time, it feels immensely unfair that these tools are not available to everybody else. Therapy is expensive, and waitlists are long. Podcasts and webinars are useful, but a few 30-minute videos or social media posts cannot possibly cover everything that parents need. Books on this topic exist, but many focus on specific issues and do not offer ways to practice what is being taught. Practice is key, and without it the best skills in the world can fall flat. All of these factors have led to this book.

MEETING THE GROWING NEEDS OF TEENS AND THEIR PARENTS

Adolescent mental health difficulties are on the rise. Rates of depression seem to be growing with younger generations, along with other diagnoses like anxiety and Autism Spectrum Disorder. In fact, more than half of all mental health diagnoses are made in those 14 and younger. Other concerns, such as substance abuse and ADHD, have rates of approximately 12.5% and 10% among teens, respectively. Difficulties such as eating disorders, bipolar disorder, and psychosis are less common, but can have huge impacts on teens and their families. There seems to be a growing web of factors that, all together, are increasingly harmful for today's teens. This topic could be a whole book on its own, but I will note a few of them below.

- *The internet and social media.* The rise in internet use and social media has created an entire online world where teens interact. Some of this leads to amazing growth and connection. It also enables constant comparisons between peers and brutal cyberbullying. Many schools rely on technology to help with learning, but kids often struggle to balance schoolwork with the pull to spend more time on social media.
- *Academic pressure.* On top of this, academic competition is greater than ever, with students feeling the pressure to overachieve inside and outside the classroom. Teens believe that to succeed, they must join multiple clubs, become skilled in art or music, and volunteer their time. All this while getting great grades and acing tests. This is already an impossible task for most teenagers, but especially those with limited resources. Not all families can afford club fees and tutors; some teens may need to help out with younger siblings at home, or have to work after school.
- *Substance use.* Another scary shift has been expanding access to substances, which can be a minefield for kids to navigate. The opioid epidemic has not spared teens, leading to overdoses across the United States. Other substances, such as nicotine and marijuana, have seen an uptick in popularity with the legalization of marijuana in many states, and the introduction of odorless vapes that make it easy for teens to use without being noticed.
- *Global instability.* Global factors influencing teens also started to play a more significant role in the mid-late 2010s. Starting in the early 2020s, rates of mass shootings skyrocketed, leading to a heightened sense of anxiety for teens and their families. Prompted by gun violence in school and climate disasters, many young people are becoming more involved in politics. Though important and meaningful, the higher rates of activism overlap with increasing political division, meaning more teens are aware of political roadblocks and feeling the stress of them.
- *The pandemic.* On an international scale, the start of the COVID-19 pandemic in 2020 led to great change for youth and families. There were concerns for physical well-being: sickness and loss of life for individuals and their families, preexisting illnesses made worse by COVID, long COVID, and an increase in domestic violence. There were also hits to basic needs, including food and housing, job loss and financial stress, and product shortages. As parents and caregivers are well aware, teens also had to cope with school closures, loss of learning supports, and overstretched school systems. Social isolation took a major toll, particularly for adolescents, because peers are key.
- *Inequality and racism.* During this unraveling of day-to-day living came the global spotlight on systemic racism. This, along with the unequal impact of COVID on BIPOC populations, forced people to pay closer attention to the significant inequality that exists in society. While greater awareness of this problem is critical, it has also highlighted an immense sense of grief and worry. On top of that, there

are major battles over the rights afforded to LGBTQ+ individuals, fights over what books are appropriate for teens to read, and changing policies around peoples' rights to make decisions over their bodies.

I mention these factors because they are very real to teenagers. Over the last several years, each of these topics has been brought up time and time again in my sessions with teens. Teenagers today are thinking about these issues and feeling anxious, sad, and helpless. These concerns have led to an overall increase in peoples' baseline levels of stress. *Nobody* is starting out at a perfect 0 anymore. These stressors feel particularly unfair to teenagers, who are hugely impacted by their environment but do not have the same amount of control to change it as adults. Depression and anxiety in young people have significantly increased as a result of all of these difficulties, as have rates of suicide. There is a very real crisis in youth mental health that is chilling to watch unfold, and will likely get worse in the coming years.

A PATHWAY FORWARD

The potential risks for adolescents of today are probably all too obvious to parents and caregivers. It is likely that your child, or one of their friends, has faced significant mental health challenges. Many parents are doing their absolute best to help their teenagers, but parenting is hard. It is *so* hard. Some caregivers feel like they have zero clue how to help a struggling teen. Others may feel that the parenting they themselves had growing up was less than great, even harmful in some way, and worry about repeating negative patterns. A lot of families have good ideas about what to do, but struggle to follow through. Many parents ping-pong back and forth between strategies, torn about the best option and swayed by emotions, outside influence, or sheer desperation. Many families are actually doing 85% of the "right" things, but need a few tweaks to get across the finish line.

Whatever category you fall into, having the right tools will make your job much, much easier. My hope is that this book gives parents and caregivers a clear pathway to support teens who are struggling with their mental health (though it describes parenting skills that can be useful with any teenager). These skills are evidence-based, meaning that research has shown they are useful in supporting teens, and they will help you strengthen your relationship with your child while managing conflict and encouraging more skillful choices. There is no one skill in this book that will be the perfect solution to all of your teen's struggles, but each skill has a very important purpose, and when you combine them, you will have a powerful set of tools.

In addition to helping you support your child and encourage them to make good and informed choices, a primary goal of this book is to help you feel more confident in your parenting decisions. It will not get rid of all of your teen's problems forever—that's impossible, as teenagers are still teenagers, after all. However, when problems do come up with your teenager, you will have the skills to make thoughtful parenting choices that reflect your values. This tends to be more effective—and feel better!—than scrambling to react to your kid's latest problem behavior. This workbook is designed to give you the information and the practice you need to master each of the skills I will discuss.

WHAT TO EXPECT IN THIS WORKBOOK

Notice that I use the terms "parents" and "caregivers" throughout this chapter. This continues throughout the chapters, but most examples refer to "parents" to help with consistency and ease of reading. Still, for the purposes of this workbook, the terms are interchangeable. The skills are useful and important for anyone who wants to feel more confident in supporting the teenager in their life, regardless of how they are related.

A few other terms you will see frequently are "dysregulation" and "skillful versus unskillful behavior." By dysregulation, I mean an emotional or behavioral reaction that seems to be out of control or out of proportion to the situation. For example, a teen who gets a C on a grade and curses out the teacher in the middle of class could be referred to as dysregulated. Somebody who has their first break-up and sobs all week without being able to eat, drink, or get out of bed may also be dysregulated. Along the same lines, unskillful behaviors are actions that tend to do more harm than good, whereas skillful behavior are choices that generally help the teen move forward. Unskillful behavior after a break-up may be social media stalking an ex. It's not that this behavior is "bad" or "wrong," it just is not that helpful. On the flip side, skillful behavior may be venting to a friend while taking a walk. This does not necessarily make everything better, but it's a social interaction that got the teen up and out of bed. Globally, that is a useful step to take.

Each chapter in this book describes different concepts or skills that caregivers can use to support their teen's mental health. The early chapters focus on strategies designed to help parents strengthen their bond with their teens. This way, families can build a really strong relationship and communication foundation before getting to more challenging skills that may lead to conflict (like rewards and consequences). Strengthening your relationship will make the later tools easier for you and a little more acceptable to your teen. The later chapters also cover tools to help your teen decrease inappropriate behavior and increase skillful choices. It will also include ways for parents to respond to outbursts or dysregulation in their teens.

Throughout the book, I offer many examples of typical parent–teen scenarios, particularly those that come up often for kids with symptoms of anxiety, low mood, or ADHD. These are very common mental health concerns, and I think it can be useful for parents to get a clear picture of what problem behaviors may occur with different groups of symptoms. You can certainly use these skills even if your child does not have a mental health diagnosis. (In fact, I would love it if every parent had access to these strategies from the time their children were little, because I think they can be helpful for everyone.) I do not include specific examples of other types of mental health issues, such as substance use, disordered eating, or serious mental illness. Many of these parenting tools can still be helpful in the presence of these concerns, but these conditions often require more individualized support of a mental health professional (see Chapter 12 for additional details).

Most chapters follow the same format:

- *Background and information about a parenting skill*: Explains each tool and why it's important.
- *Stuck points*: Highlights common ways in which parents can veer off course when trying to use certain skills.
- *Test your knowledge and test your skills*: Exercises that will help you to remember details about each skill and give them a try yourself. Answer keys will allow you to

check how you did, in hopes of helping you learn the skills inside and out and get more comfortable using them in real life. The more you practice, the more automatic each skill will become when you're interacting with your teen.
- *Try it out*: Worksheets asking you to plan out skill practice during the week. Nobody else is going to see your answers, but you will be more likely to keep up with the practice if you take some notes for yourself. If you hate writing, feel free to record your answers in a voice note or video!

MAKING THIS WORKBOOK WORK FOR YOU

Read through the recommendations below to help you make the most of the many skills you will learn in this workbook.

Set Appropriate Expectations

There is lots of evidence to suggest that the skills in this book can support growth for families, especially when used together. That said, there is no perfect skill that works for every situation or is 100% effective. That is okay. Look for ways that skills can help improve situations, rather than solve them completely. There are no quick fixes in parenting, and it will take time for you to get comfortable with the skills and see results. I encourage you to have patience with yourself and the tools, especially when you find yourself tempted to skip over a skill that seems weird or too difficult. Once you have practiced everything, you can take the tools in front of you and find the combination that works best for your family.

Consider Your Goals and Family Patterns

Different skills are good for different things. Here is a sample of some of the goals different tools in this book have:

- building empathy for your teen
- increasing your understanding of behavior
- helping your child feel comfortable with their emotions
- building trust in the parent–child relationship
- increasing your child's self-esteem
- building your teen's independence
- encouraging smart choices and decreasing unhelpful choices
- helping your teen think ahead
- making conflict less frequent or less intense.

This is a lot, and there are more! As you read through the chapters, consider what goals are most important to you—including long-term goals. Do you care more about your teen's independence right now, or five years from now? Are you more focused on stopping problem behaviors this month, or building trust in the parent–child relationship over the next decade? There is no right or wrong answer, but keeping your goals clear will help give you a north star in terms of what skills may be most useful for you.

Your relationship with your teen will also play a role in what skills you focus on most. If you have a close relationship that is filled with warmth and support, you probably have a little more wiggle room to use more conflict and behavior change strategies sooner. If your relationship is strained, mastering the earlier skills to build a strong relationship foundation may be your first step. At the start of each chapter, do a quick check in with yourself to see if your goals have shifted and if the relationship is where you want it to be.

Think About Who Else Needs to Know About These Skills

If you have a coparent or caregiver for your child and have a good relationship with them, try to make your way through this workbook together. Having adults on the same page can help your teen's brain adjust to the changes you are making more quickly. It is also helpful for you because you will have a partner to practice skills with and keep each other accountable.

Sometimes coparents are fine with how things are going and do not really want to learn from a workbook. After all, it's work! You have a few choices. If the relationship with this person is solid and you feel comfortable having a conversation with them, do it! A few points you could make are that:

1) a united approach will be less confusing for your teen and lead to faster change;
2) reading a workbook is one of the least intensive ways to try to make parenting changes, and things will get much more intense if problems worsen to the point of needing professional help;
3) you respect your coparent and would value their opinions on the skills in this book; and
4) their willingness to learn this information shows both you and your child how much they care.

If you are not comfortable speaking to another caregiver for whatever reason, that is okay too! You can make your way through this workbook on your own and absolutely still see positive change. Some skills may take longer to sink in, but you can certainly still help your teen by being mindful about how you relate and respond to them. Also remember that brains are clever! Your teen will start to learn the difference between different places and situations. They will know what behavior is expected around you versus others. It can be frustrating when problems arise when you are not around. But this is outside of your control, and you can still have a positive influence when you are involved. For your own sake, it might be helpful to check in with a friend or family member about what you are learning. This certainly is not required, but adjusting parenting patterns is a lot of work, and having support can be helpful.

This goes for single parents, too. These skills are still effective, and you will not have to worry about inconsistency across partners. Think about what systems or check-ins you could put in place to help you feel supported and stay motivated. If nothing comes to mind, this workbook is full of ideas to help you keep moving forward!

YOU GOT THIS

Parenting a teen is hard—and amazing, and scary, and frustrating, and full of surprises, and so much more—and if you are reading this, then you know things can get much more intense if your teen has mental health challenges. This workbook is here to give you core parenting strategies that will help you work through the difficulties you and your child will face throughout their adolescence. Each chapter is filled with strategies that are backed by science, and that have been designed to support kids who are struggling. The workbook gives you clear tools and enough practice to feel comfortable using them in your everyday life. There may not be a cure-all for teen angst, but this workbook is here to help. You got this.

2

The Basic Principles of Parent Work

WHAT ARE THE BASIC PRINCIPLES OF PARENT WORK?

Before jumping into the skill chapters in this workbook, there are a few general parenting fundamentals that are useful to keep in mind. These include prioritizing your relationship, slowing down the pace of change, being consistent, being specific, and being neutral. These will help you better support your teen as they overcome challenges and build more skillful behavior.

CHANGE IS GOOD, BUT YOUR RELATIONSHIP COMES FIRST

It is important to think about how to help your child make changes while also holding onto a strong bond with them. This can be a tricky balance—whether they are overcome with anxiety in a crowd, unable to get out of bed because of depression, or falling behind in school because of their ADHD. As parents, we're eager for our children to push through hard times by problem-solving or making better choices. This is completely understandable—you care for your child and want what is best for them. Sometimes when problems happen, parents are pulled to try harsher methods, including yelling, criticizing, dismissing concerns, demanding big changes right away, or using really big punishments. It feels like if you can say *just the right thing* or threaten the exact right punishment, you will get your kid to see the light. Unfortunately, all of these strategies can backfire. If your teen is not ready or able to make a better choice, taking a hard line will only make them more stressed out or self-blaming. On top of that, they will likely feel misunderstood or criticized by you, which is going to take a toll on your relationship.

You may feel that it is okay for the parent–child relationship to take a back seat as long as it helps your kid to do better in other ways (like getting their homework in or showing up to their summer job on time). This is a fair viewpoint. It's not your job to be your child's best friend *or* to avoid making them upset at all costs. But this way of thinking can accidentally lead to more problems down the road if it causes your teen to lose interest or respect in your relationship.

As a parent of a teen, you're probably already seeing how much parents lose control over their kids as they get older. Long gone are the toddler days when you could pick them up and move them into a different room or quickly swipe a toy out of their hands (not that it was so easy back then, either). But as teenagers? There's no chance. Teens are much more independent. They can get places on their own and make decisions without telling you. Some may even have jobs and money to spend on what they choose to. This independence increases once they turn 18, and certainly when they move out of the house. Given this, it is important to start letting go of the idea that you can or should be making decisions for your kid, because any control you have right now is just temporary (an understandably scary thought).

Instead, think about how you can continue to *influence* your teen's life. Kids who feel close with their parents will be more likely to share about their lives, talk to them about problems, and listen to their advice. They will care about what you think of their choices and keep it in mind when making decisions. It doesn't mean they'll always do what you want, but your voice will have a much larger and more enduring place in their heads if you keep your relationship strong. So as you're thinking about helping your teen with the problems they have right now, do not completely sacrifice your bond for progress in *this* moment.

SLOW DOWN THE PACE OF CHANGE

One thing that can help you keep your parent–teen bond strong is to focus on slowly helping your child make progress instead of pushing for quicker change. This is called "shaping." Most people have done this at some point in their lives. For example, when somebody tries to get in shape they don't usually start off with a marathon. They might try walking, then move up to a jog, then make the workouts longer or faster until they finally reach the speed or distance they want to be at. The same idea applies for teen mental health, and there are few (if any) times when you would expect a teen to meet a mental health or behavioral goal the week they start working on it. Instead, parents can think about what sort of gradual steps they can take to build success over time. Shaping lowers conflict and disappointment that can come up when parents set a goal that is too high. Instead of everybody feeling demoralized when a teen doesn't measure up, everybody can feel proud and motivated by the smaller progress that happens each step of the way. This will keep interactions positive instead of negative and allow everybody to build momentum.

CONSISTENCY IS KEY

No matter what skill you are learning about in the rest of this book, consistency is a key ingredient to success. When parents react the same way each time a certain situation comes up, teens will have an easier time making the connection between their choices and the good or bad outcomes that come next. When parents are inconsistent, conflict grows and it takes much longer for kids to change their behavior. For example, say your teen has a habit of asking to stay out past curfew. On Friday you come home from work after a great day. You're in a good mood and have lots of patience, so when your teen asks to stay out 30 minutes later than usual, you say yes. Then on Saturday, you have a crummy day. Groceries were way too expensive, you got stuck in traffic, and you had a frustrating conversation with a family member. You are on your last nerve. In comes your kid asking to stay out an extra 30 minutes later, and you say: "Absolutely not! I don't know why you always try to stretch the rules." You can probably already see the problem. Your teen's behavior stayed the same, but yours changed. Now your kid is upset because it seems like you're always changing the rules or are saying no just to be mean. *You're* upset because you feel like your child is not respecting your boundaries. And on top of all this, your teen is still going to ask to extend curfew next Friday again. Why? Because if there is even a small chance you're going to say yes to something they really want, it is definitely worth the ask. Being consistent can be very hard, but it will amp up all the skills and help them work much faster.

BE SPECIFIC

Vague instructions or suggestions, such as "behave," "relax," or "calm down," leave too much to interpretation. For example, when you say behave at a restaurant, you might mean that your teen needs to keep their voice down and stop elbowing their brother. At school, behave means to show the teacher respect. At home, you tell your kid to behave when you need them to follow directions, but also when they need to speak without the attitude. The problem, of course, is that you cannot know for sure that your version of "behave" matches what your teen has in mind. It's a recipe for disaster. You as the parent get mad because they didn't follow directions, and they as the kid get mad because they actually remembered not to raise their voice at you, but all you can talk about is how they rolled their eyes. Being specific gets rid of the gray zone and lets everybody know what the expectations are.

Another added bonus of being specific is that it can make it easier for your kid to follow through on what you want. Sometimes kids with mental health difficulties like anxiety, depression, or ADHD can feel paralyzed. When you see your teen falling apart and you say "Take a moment to get yourself together" a teen might have no idea what they're really supposed to do next. Being clear gives them an exit ramp out of their emotional distress. For example:

- *How about you take a walk around the block*
- *Go get yourself a cold glass of water*
- *Listen to some music that makes you happy*

It removes the hurdles of having to think about possible next steps and then pick something to try, both of which can be challenging for teenagers in distress.

TONE DOWN BIG REACTIONS

The final overarching idea I want to convey is that you want to remain neutral in stressful moments with your teens. This is easier said than done (see Chapter 3 on caregiver coping). It is common for parents to become emotional or reactive when managing teens with anxiety, sadness, attentional difficulties, or other challenging behaviors. Unfortunately, parents' own emotions and reactions can play a role in raising the intensity of parent–teen conflict, and over time, chip away at the bond.

Being neutral means trying to keep your tone, volume, word choice, and body language as calm and unemotional as possible. If you're not quite sure what that would look like, picture the waiter who seats you at a restaurant:

> *Welcome, please take a seat. Here are some menus. Our specials for today are salmon and linguine.*

If that doesn't work, think about the flight attendant on an airplane giving the safety briefing:

> *Once the captain turns off the fasten seat belt sign, you are free to walk about the cabin. We recommend that you keep your seatbelts fastened at all times when you are seated.*

As you might be able to imagine in your head, the vibe is somewhat bland, informative, and maybe a tad pleasant. That is what you want to try to get to during stressful moments with your teen. This helps in a few ways. First, parents and teens with mental health difficulties often get into a spiral of one-upping each other. You ask your teen to do something, and they yell (or cry, or slam the door) to get you to back off. Sometimes that works, but eventually you end up having to yell (or lecture, or threaten) to get them to listen. That also works for a short time, until your teen gets sick of it and yells louder, cries more, or slams the door so hard the frame shakes. You amp up your response, and then the cycle repeats. Before you know it, everybody is now expecting the worst and conversations head straight into a fight.

In order to stop that cycle, somebody has to lower the volume. Spoiler alert: it's never going to be the kid. They have a *decade* left before their brain finishes developing. This is one of those frustrating parenting moments where you just have to be the adult and take one for the team. That means gaining control of your own emotions so that you can come in calm and collected even when your child is not meeting you halfway. This is not easy and it takes some time to create change, but parents staying neutral is the first step toward lowering the emotional baseline of the household. Doing so helps interrupt the negative cycle and makes it easier for teens to listen to what you are saying, instead of only reacting to your volume or tone.

The other common problem is that once a negative cycle sets in, the lesson that a teen learns is that "My parent doesn't really mean what they're saying until they're yelling, has that certain edge to their voice, or threatens." No parent means to send that message, and most parents don't want to have to do those things to get their point across. By staying neutral during moments of conflict, you can teach your kids that they need to respond simply because you are speaking, and not because of your volume or how red your face is getting. Once you create that reset, it becomes much easier to talk to your teens about what needs to happen in the household.

BOOKMARK THIS CHAPTER

As you read through the rest of the book, keep a bookmark in this chapter. Review it every so often to keep these guidelines fresh in your mind. If you find yourself getting stuck on a certain skill, returning to the basics is a great place to start.

3

Caregiver Coping

Help Yourself, Help Them

WHAT IS CAREGIVER COPING?

Caregiver (or parent) coping refers to the strategies you can use to better manage difficult emotions and situations. This includes building your overall well-being across time, as well as how to deal with particularly tricky moments in real time. Understandably, this topic may not be what most readers expect to see as the very first topic in this workbook. However, as a parent or caregiver, your ability to manage stress and take care of your well-being should not, and cannot, be an afterthought. For the reasons listed below, it is important to put this chapter before any other skill, so please take your time here before you skip ahead.

YOU ARE WORTHY

Caregiver coping is important for a few reasons. The first is that you have value as a person outside of your role as a parent. You, as a human, are worth the time and effort it takes to learn how to deal with stress and feel better. Now reread that sentence. There are some people who may roll their eyes because this seems cliché or silly to mention in a parenting book. Or, in the best case, they already know this to be true and are not sure why it needs to be said here. However, there are many caregivers who struggle with this and have gotten so used to putting everybody else first that learning to help themselves takes a back seat. Amid everything you have going on, please keep in mind that you do not need to justify taking time to prioritize your own well-being. You are reason enough.

HELP YOURSELF, HELP YOUR KIDS

If you need another reason to build up your own coping skills, here it is: parenting takes a toll. As great as it can be, parents spend their days jumping from one fire to the next. And of course, outside of your role as a caregiver, you have a whole bunch of other things to stay on top of (a long commute, paying bills, an annoying work call, lunch with friends, making weekend plans for your kids, picking up food for home, etc.). Because you are a human and not a robot, all of these moments—with your children, coworkers, family, and the world—impact you. That is not necessarily bad, and there are hopefully many great parts of your days and weeks. But it is easy to feel drained after spending your time, energy, effort, and resources to keep up with it all.

As much as you love your children and want to do what is best for them, it is hard to make skillful parenting choices if you have no physical or emotional reserves left. Most parents know this in their bones. Yet it can still be tricky to take care of yourself. This is especially true if spending time on yourself means temporarily putting your children (and everything else) second. If this sounds like you, remember the airplane safety guidelines: in the event of an emergency, put your own mask on first before you help anybody else with theirs. You cannot be of help to anybody if you do not get the oxygen your body so badly needs. In your day-to-day life, you cannot help your teens the way you want to if you are struggling to hold yourself together. So if you find it difficult to prioritize your well-being for yourself, think about how doing so might allow you to parent the way you want to.

PAVE THE WAY FOR SUCCESSFUL INTERACTIONS

In a much more immediate sense, caregiver coping is important because the way parents approach their kids will impact how the interaction goes. If your starting level of emotional distress is lower, you will likely be able to talk in a calmer, more supportive way. You are more likely to see your teen's point of view, work together, and think outside of the box. As you can guess, those kinds of interactions have a decent chance of going well. On the flip side, higher baseline stress may lead to raised voices, an edge to your tone or words, or less patience. Some parents are more likely to give into their teen's demands when they are stressed (because they don't have the energy to fight). Other times the opposite happens, and parents speak more harshly (because empathy and flexibility go down).

Not only will you be less able to use your skills, but a stressed-out parent may well lead to a stressed-out teen. This, of course, goes both ways. Imagine your teen bursting through the door and with an attitude. Immediately, your defenses go up and it's likely to be a rough conversation. The same is true for your child, and if they sense anger, judgment, or stress from you, they are likely to mirror it in their own behavior. To try to lessen this upward emotional spiral, somebody has to try to come in calm. Caregiver coping strategies are one way to make sure that you do not accidentally add fuel to a fire you had not meant to.

MODEL THE BEHAVIOR YOU WANT TO SEE

A final reason to prioritize caregiver coping is because children are sponges who soak up the things that their caregivers say and do. Because of this, caregiver coping can be a helpful way to show them skillful, effective behaviors. As the old saying goes, actions speak louder than words. Case in point: you may have told your teen a hundred times not to raise their voice or slam the door. Yet when you yourself raise your voice or slam the door, your teen's brain files those behaviors away. Never mind that you are an adult and may believe that you a) are old enough to do those things, and b) can tell the difference between times when this behavior is or is not okay. Your kid's brain skips those details and instead stores away that pattern of behavior to pull out in the future. That does not mean that your child will copy every behavior. And there are many other things that influence your child's actions. But children do learn from what they see around them, and parents who can show helpful tools to cope with stress can set the stage for how a teen reacts to tough moments.

There are two bonuses to this. The first is that using coping strategies in front of your teen can help decrease any shame or judgment they may have about their emotions. After all, coping is not about pretending like you never feel sad, angry, or anxious. Instead, it is about noticing those emotions and responding in a way that helps you more than it hurts you. When parents can label their emotions and then visibly take action to cope, they send the message that it's okay to have feelings and find appropriate ways to respond. No need to pretend the feelings don't exist, and no need to just grit your teeth and white-knuckle through it. What a supportive, shame-reducing message.

The second bonus is that parents who model coping skills show their teens that they do not have to "fix" problems by themselves. Many teenagers struggle to talk about their difficulties, or believe they should just "figure it out" on their own. This can happen when they think their problems are a burden to their families, take on blame for everybody's struggles, or worry about what parents may think. This puts a lot of unnecessary pressure on teens at a time when they should be actively getting support. Whatever the reason a teenager is hesitant to open up, active displays of caregiver coping shows that parents are willing to roll up their sleeves and do the work right along with their child. Not only is their child not alone, but parents are active participants in finding ways to make things go more smoothly. Even when it seems like your teenager couldn't care less about your opinion, they are aware of and impacted by your words and actions.

TAKING STOCK

If you made it through to this point in the chapter without skipping ahead—well done for taking some time to pour energy into your own cup. The very first task is to take stock of the areas of your life that impact your well-being. Set aside time to really think about the ways in which different areas of your life may be (or could be) adding meaning, value, and fuel to your life, and the ways in which they may be raising your stress level or worsening your physical, emotional, or behavioral health.

EXERCISE 3.1 IDENTIFY WHAT'S IMPORTANT FOR YOUR WELL-BEING

Exercise 3.1 includes a list of different areas that parents commonly say impact their well-being. In this exercise, read through the list and rate how much you think each domain impacts *your* well-being on a scale of 1 (plays no role) to 5 (plays a huge role). Some items may be really important to how you feel or act, while others have very little influence on your life. For anything you have rated a 3 or above, write out a few ways that domain impacts you in positive or negative ways. The first row includes an example. There is an empty box at the bottom for you to add in other parts of your life that are not already on the list.

Rating	Domain	Notes
4	**Sleep**	More sleep = more patient, productive, happy. Less sleep = less fun, active, creative, efficient, more easily annoyed
	Family (immediate or extended, children)	
	Romantic/aromantic partnerships	
	Social life	
	Job	
	Hobbies	
	Physical health	
	Mental health	
	Sleep	
	Environment (location, local activities, climate, etc.)	
	Chronic or systemic hurdles	
	Global events (politics, public health crises, economy, etc.)	

After completing Exercise 3.1, take a look at what you have written and think about which of these areas you may be able to make changes in, and which are entirely out of your control.

AREAS OUTSIDE OF YOUR CONTROL

For almost everybody, there are at least a few things (both big and small) that impact well-being but are completely out of your control. For example, you may be worn out by negative news cycles, increasing rent, or dismissive bosses. Maybe an ex refuses to follow the divorce settlement, or you can't find a doctor to see your teen, or you live in an area with dangerous climate events. It is likely that you have limited, if any, options to change these stressors. Even if you could, it should not be on you to fix a system in which you are ignored, dismissed, undermined, or systematically discriminated against. There is no expectation (at least not in this workbook) for you to magically come up with a solution for these problems. However, it is still important to be actively aware of the ways that they directly or indirectly get in the way of your well-being. Why? Because it is very easy to take personal responsibility for the impact these factors have on your life.

Many parents beat themselves up over how they just can't seem to master a parenting skill. Or they can't believe they yelled at their kid or forgot to praise or support their child the way they wanted to. They truly think they are just bad parents or have some fatal character flaw. That is a wholly unfair perspective. Most parents have a mountain of stressors they are living under. Their limited bandwidth to stay emotionally grounded and tackle every parenting skill to perfection has very little to do with them as individuals. It has a lot to do with the fact that parents are neither superhumans nor robots, and are, in fact, regular people with regular reactions to stressful situations.

So if you ever feel like you are failing as a parent, take a look back at that exercise you just completed. See how much you are pushing through despite powerful forces making it difficult. Remind yourself of what amazing thing you are doing every single day to simply keep putting in the time and energy. When the seeds of doubt start to creep in about how you just aren't doing a good enough job, please keep in mind that there are very real factors that are relevant to your life and your well-being, and it is not your fault that you are impacted by them.

Beyond cutting yourself some serious slack for the ways in which these stressors impact you, there is a second reason for acknowledging domains you do not have direct control over. While you may not be able to reshape the entire landscape of your life, you might have some ability to shift how you choose to approach it—and I don't mean this in a "toxic positivity" kind of way. Simply putting a smile on, minimizing the role of these stressors, or having a "better attitude" is likely not a helpful choice here. But some people do find meaningful ways to help them cope with these stressors. It may be through sharing struggles with others in a way that builds connection and community. It may be picking one small area to advocate for in a manner that helps you feel empowered. It could be speaking with a healthcare professional about strategies that give you greater control over the emotional responses you have to these factors. It is not your obligation to change your life because some larger, bigger force is making things hard, and it should not have to be your responsibility. But some people do want to consider this route and find that doing so can foster practical, helpful changes, or create a sense of empowerment and meaning that helps to lighten the load.

BUILDING YOUR RESERVES WITH WHAT YOU CAN CONTROL

Look at the above exercise and think about the areas you believe *are* within your control (at least to some extent). For example, there may be *some* external factors outside of your control that impact sleep (like your job or when your kids wake up in the morning), but you might have some ability to make changes in small ways (like limiting pre-bed screens to improve sleep quality). These areas are a good place to start making small changes to improve your overall well-being. Consider the following: meaningful and fulfilling activities help build up emotional reserves (e.g., patience, kindness, flexibility). Stressors use up your reserves. People with lots of positive moments will have a bigger reserve, while people who are more disconnected and disengaged will have a smaller one. When a concern arises—like your teenager sneaking out—people who have fewer reserves built up are going to have a harder time coping. All it takes is one too many problem behaviors for you to burst. Cue the yelling, screaming, shutting down, and so on. The aim of building your reserves as a parent is to create more buffer so that you can more easily ride out the conflicts and concerns that pop up day to day. If your overall wellness is a priority, you will have more of a reserve to draw on. This is key to being able to use the skills discussed in the rest of this book. No more running on empty.

EXERCISE 3.2 CREATE A PLAN TO INVEST IN YOUR WELL-BEING

With the above in mind, you're going to start to think about where there might be wiggle room to put resources (time, energy, emotion, etc.) toward your overall well-being. In Exercise 3.2, you will create a plan for how you can shift one area of your life in a way that helps you to build your reserves over time. Follow the steps below and write your responses in the chart. Take a look at some of the examples provided if you need ideas.

1. **Select the area you want to work on first**
   Choose one area of your life that is strongly tied to your wellness that you would like to start making a shift in. If more than one area comes to mind, get started with your top priority and add on over time. Some people want to begin with the area they think will be easiest to change (a reasonable choice). Some parents want to go for the area that they think most impacts their well-being (also fair). Look for a balance; select an area that feels impactful, motivating, *and* doable. If you pick a domain and immediately feel overwhelmed with the thought of trying to shift it—maybe put a pin in that for now and circle back later.
2. **Set your goalpost and work backward**
   Think about how you would like this area to look in the future. Be realistic and do not pick a goal so big that you cannot meet it. For example, if your domain is exercise but you have never run a day in your life, do not say you are going to run a marathon in six months. Pick a reasonable future goal, and then consider the steps you can take along the way to create success. If your longer-term goal is six months out, where would you like to be three months from now to help keep you on track? Then, where would you need to be one month from now?

   Pro tip: once you have created these medium- and long-term goalposts—forget about them! That is, let them fade from your day-to-day to-do list. Having to keep all these future plans in mind can be overwhelming, and that is not the point of this. The point is to have a series of rough benchmarks to look toward as you track your progress every few weeks and make sure you are on pace (or need to adjust). Beyond that, there is no need to hyperfocus on steps that are far off down the road.

3. **Identify concrete, weekly tasks for the next four weeks**
Having picked a one-month goal, list what small weekly steps you could work on this month. These should be brief, doable, meaningful steps in your process. You want to pick items that, over the course of 6–12 months, will help you reach your longer-term goal. One of the most common pitfalls is for parents to identify their one-month goal—and then try to hit it in one week. For example, the one-month goal is to exercise three days a week and the person tries to run three days in a row the very first week. However, building reserves is not a race, and you will serve yourself (and your well-being) better by pacing yourself.

With that in mind, think smaller. Pick weekly goals that help you tackle the road bumps you see coming. For example, maybe you struggle with 1) accountability, 2) finding the time, and 3) feeling motivated. In those instances, the week one task may be texting your friends to see who is interested in setting up an exercise buddy system. Week two is to sit down with your partner to compare schedules and agree on what needs to shift for you to make time for your exercise plan. Week three is to spend 20 minutes crafting the perfect workout playlist, or making a to-do list of equipment you need to keep in your car so you can hit the gym on the way home from work. These would all be great tasks for your first month and you haven't even broken a sweat yet. No sprinting here, just a steady pace toward meaningful, workable changes.

4. **Expect barriers and then problem-solve**
As mentioned in the previous step, one helpful and important part of building your reserves is to figure out what has been getting in the way. For many parents, it is a lack of time or emotional or physical bandwidth. It always feels like there are more important tasks or people that need your attention. If this sounds familiar, reread the start of this chapter on why caregiver coping is so crucial. Whatever the reason change has been hard for you, get specific on how the barriers actually play out. See if you can break it down and identify small solutions that make it just a tad easier for you.

For example, perhaps finding "me time" is hard specifically because your teen has tons of extracurricular activities that keep you busy from dawn to dusk. Or perhaps it is difficult because you spend so much time during the day managing childcare and household tasks that you need time in the evening to catch up on work. Whatever the case may be, label the problem and start to brainstorm possible solutions. No need to solve it all in one sitting, but do consider how to chip away at hurdles and start investing in yourself. The more you can plan for and troubleshoot barriers *before they occur*, the more likely you are to have success.

You may come across some barriers that you cannot solve. When this happens do your best to come up with creative solutions that lower the hurdle in some way. For example, maybe a barrier to you having "you time" is needing to be around to help your kids with homework. Perhaps you truly cannot afford extra help or a tutor, and school does not offer additional study sessions. Maybe the solution is to facetime a family member to provide some virtual assistance while you gain back twenty minutes. Or perhaps you tell your teens to circle any issues they have a major issue with and you'll do one general check at the end of the night instead of having to be on call as a question pops up every few minutes. If no creative solutions exist and you cannot find a way to get over the barrier, it is okay to pick another goal that is more achievable and circle back to this if anything changes.

5. **Establish supports**

   Of course, following through with your plan is easier said than done. Behavior change is really hard. To help make it somewhat easier, the next step is to try to identify what supports or rewards you can put in place. Supports may be logistical (like coordinating times with a partner or babysitter if either is possible for you) or emotional (such as asking a friend to check in on you and cheerlead your efforts). Humans are social creatures—use those social supports to your advantage here!

   There are also lots of ways to use rewards. You could start by creating a rewarding environment. For example, if your goal is to focus on your mental health and it's hard getting yourself to your weekly therapy appointment, perhaps you plan to take the scenic route through the park that you love. Rewards can also be tangible. Maybe each day you complete your therapy homework you put aside $1 to spend on something that makes you smile. You can also link preferred activities to whatever area you are working on: you only get to watch your favorite show after you've scheduled your next follow-up session.

   These additions are probably not going to be the magical cure that suddenly guarantees success in your quest to rebuild your reserves. That's okay. The aim is simply to set up a handful of strategies ahead of time to make the entire process *slightly* easier. A few proactive tools with a small impact can sometimes be enough to lift you over a hurdle and help build your momentum.

6. **Identify the larger value**

   One final task is to outline how the area you picked (and related goals) fits with your larger values. It isn't *just* about exercise, or socializing, or feeling less anxious, or whatever goal you picked for yourself. It is about how that goal fits within your overall well-being, and how your well-being serves what's important to you in life. Perhaps you are motivated because you want to feel happier each day, and that is meaningful to you. Maybe you want to show your teens how worthy they are as people, and you need to demonstrate that belief in yourself in order for them to follow your lead. Perhaps you want your household to be calmer, and that is only possible if you are more centered. Whatever it is, come up with a concrete statement about how these goals serve your larger values. Doing so shifts the entire frame of thinking. It's no longer a debate about whether you should sink into your couch after work as opposed to going to the gym. It's about the importance of relaxing in this moment versus what you want most, in the long term, for yourself and your family.

In Exercise 3.2, you will put these steps together. First, take a look at the examples to see how a parent could craft a plan that helps them make progress. Then, fill out your own plan to build reserves in the blank template that follows.

EXERCISE 3.2 EXAMPLE 1: BUILDING RESERVES THROUGH BETTER SLEEP

Area you selected	Sleep
Future goal	7 hours, 7 days per week
Medium-term goal	7 hours at least 4 nights per week
Short-term goal (1 month)	6 hours at least 4 nights per week
List of weekly tasks to meet short-term goal	• Set regular sleep time alarm • Wake up at a consistent time • Create bedtime routine • Eliminate screens 20 minutes before bed
Anticipate barriers and problem-solve barriers	• Kids needing late homework help ➜ agree to alternative parent duty with my partner • Staying up later than I "should" because it's the only time I have to myself ➜ set alarm on my phone reminding myself of my longer-term value; schedule "me time" earlier in the day • Trying to fit in all chores/work/etc. after kids go to bed ➜ remind myself that my own well-being is more important than the dishes being done; realign schedule to clean up dishes right after dinner and have backpacks packed up at the same time
Establish supports	• Talk with partner about realigning household/parenting duties to allow me more time in the evening after kids go to bed • Create a reward plan: Every night I put down my phone 20 minutes before my planned bedtime = my favorite smoothie on the way to work
Identify the larger values	I want to be a more patient, more relaxed parent. Sleep is the key to this goal.

EXERCISE 3.2 EXAMPLE 2: BUILDING RESERVES THROUGH MENTAL HEALTH

Area you selected	Managing my anxiety/mood
Future goal	Feel in control of my emotions so that I am in charge of my choices, instead of my anxiety/depression
Medium-term goal	Be able to name and practice several concrete tools to manage anxiety/mood
Short-term goal (1 month)	Establish a plan for taking care of my mental health
List of weekly tasks to meet short-term goal	• Talk to friends about their strategies to manage mental health • Check if insurance covers therapy sessions • Call 2–3 therapists or psychiatrists to ask about openings • Search online and create a list of free virtual or in-person support groups

| Anticipate barriers and problem-solve | - Treatment is expensive → going to look through insurance, look online for free services, and ask clinics about sliding scale or low fee options
- I hate making phone calls → will check if therapists have an email I can reach out to first, and then will ask my friend to make the call with me if I need to
- It's really hard to find time to focus on my well-being → will prioritize finding virtual support options so I do not need to worry about commute time |
|---|---|
| Establish supports | Reach out to friends to help with the tasks listed above. |
| Identify the larger values | I want to feel like a happier, more stable person. I want to enjoy my life without being so bogged down by difficult emotions. |

EXERCISE 3.2 EXAMPLE 3: BUILDING RESERVES THROUGH SOCIAL SUPPORT

Area you selected	Social support
Future goal	2 social events per month, plus at least 3–5 weekly social interactions via text/phone/videocall
Medium-term goal	1 social event per month, reach out to 2–3 people each week to check in
Short-term goal (1 month)	Create list of options for social outings, contact 1–2 people per week
List of weekly tasks to meet short-term goal	- Look through my phone/social media and make a list of people I would like to connect with
- Check local/virtual options to spend time with others
- Text at least 1 person to say hi
Anticipate barriers and problem-solve	- Everybody is so busy it's hard to find time → create a fairly wide list so there is a higher chance of somebody being available; create regularly planned outings so people can plan well in advance
- I feel guilty taking time for myself → commit to focused, distraction-free time with my family before I spend time with my friends
- Going out with others can get expensive → look up free local events; create a budget for socializing so I know what I can afford
Establish supports	- Reach out to childcare to ensure sitters are available if needed
- Talk with partner, family, or friends to see if they can help support my efforts
- Ask friends who are interested to help consider ideas to connect
Identify the larger values	Building a sense of community is important to me. I want others to know that I am there for them in the same way I want them to be there for me.

EXERCISE 3.2 BUILD YOUR RESERVES

Area you selected	
Future goal	
Medium-term goal	
Short-term goal (1 month)	
List of weekly tasks to meet short-term goal	
Anticipate barriers and problem-solve	
Establish supports	
Identify the larger values	

Building your reserves takes many small shifts over a long period of time. Use the plan you have created here to build your momentum over the next few weeks and months. Think about scheduling your goals into your calendar or setting a monthly reminder to check in on your progress. If you get stuck or fall off the pace, just do your best to pick back up when you can. Keep those long-term values in mind, and you will be in good shape.

IN-THE-MOMENT COPING

While you work toward refueling your well-being, it is also important to have a plan for how to cope with the stressful moments that pop up day to day with your teen. There are many situations in which your teen (or you) may struggle to stay calm. A few common examples include a teen pushing back on a limit, annoying their sibling, ignoring a house rule, leaving a mess, making a decision you don't agree with, or lying. Or perhaps you are low on reserves (for reasons that may have nothing to do with your child), and now minor things start to set you off.

While it is understandable that you lose your cool sometimes, doing so is usually not the most useful choice in terms of addressing your teen's behavior. Beyond that, it may not even be the choice you wanted to make. It almost goes without saying, but the more control you have over your emotions, the less likely you are to say or do something you regret, and the more likely you are to make use of effective parenting strategies. With that in mind, it can be helpful to plan for how you are going to respond in moments when you are most likely to boil over. That doesn't mean you can never be angry, or frustrated, or worried around your child. Rather, you want a set of skills to cope with those emotions and then make your own decision about how to parent, instead of having an intense emotion choose for you.

EXERCISE 3.3 COPING IN ADVANCE

In Exercise 3.3, create a plan to cope with stressful moments using the following steps. To help you get started, take a look at the listed examples and sample coping plan below.

1. **Find a grounding mantra or helpful thought**
   It is easy to get caught up in a wave of emotion when you are upset. Strong emotions impact our thoughts, which in turn impact behavior. For example, if you feel anxious about your teen failing school, you may start to think about how they are ruining their future by not studying, and then in turn yell at them for 20 minutes to get their work done. Not necessarily the best choice. The aim of a grounding mantra is to find some sort of phrase that helps bring you back to Earth. It can be serious, lighthearted, or sentimental. The main idea is to have a sentence that you can repeat to yourself over and over in a moment of distress that helps you ride the wave of emotions and make it through to the other side. Your other option is to use a helpful thought, which is usually specifically linked to the situation you are upset about and allows you to find a different perspective. If you can decrease the intensity of your feelings and come up with helpful thoughts, your parenting choices will be more thoughtful and less reactive. Circle any of the examples below that you like, or write in your own ideas in the lines provided.

   a. **"She's only a kid, she's only a kid, she's only a kid."** This mantra resonates for many parents. It is a firm reminder that the person in front of you is the child, and you are the adult. The idea behind this mantra really applies well beyond those early childhood years and is certainly still the case for your teenager. The behaviors and decisions you see in front of you are those of an individual with less wisdom and experience than you have. They are struggling, and their

brain is trying to find a solution to their distress. You are the adult, and you hold the responsibility of the interaction going well. Reminding yourself of this is a good way to knock the wind out of the rage sails that may be building inside of you.

b. **"Only 30 more minutes until they're at school!"** It is perfectly acceptable to remind yourself that a break is coming soon. In fact, knowing that there will be some upcoming relief can make it much easier to get through whatever situation is currently causing you frustration. Needing a break from your teen does not mean you love them any less, so feel free to use this often!

c. **"Preserve."** In this case, "preserve" refers to a desire to preserve the relationship with your teenager. Often, parents respond reactively when they are trying to change their child's behavior and in doing so can slowly chip away at the parent–child bond. The idea of this mantra is to reorient yourself to the longer-term value of prioritizing your connection with your child. You can still set limits and make parenting decisions that feel right to you, but the tone and word choice you use is important too.

d. **A motto or slogan you know**. Sometimes parents like to use a motto from a team, club, or organization they have been involved with. It could be a sports team, a club, a business, a service-based institution, or something else. These mottos likely have nothing to do with parenting or your child, but they are familiar and burned into your head. Sometimes all we need to cool off is to anchor ourselves with a familiar phrase or statement.

e. Other ideas you have for a coping mantra or helpful thought:

_____

_____

_____

2. **Create a list of calming activities**

These can be sensory experiences that pull your attention away from an argument, strategies for taking a break, or tasks that boost your mood. If you're not sure where to start, just think about small moments in the day that make you smile or feel at peace. Make sure to come up with options that are easy and almost always possible. You may feel perfectly calm taking a hike in the forest, but that is not going to be a realistic option at 9:30 p.m. on a Wednesday when your teen refuses to do their homework. A great option that works for many people is to take a few slow, deep breaths. Inhale for 5 seconds, exhale for 7 seconds. Repeat three times. It is a fast way to calm your body down and takes very little effort. Here are a few examples of other activities that could help you feel more regulated:

a. *Sensory*: smell a strong lotion, perfume, or food; put on white noise or calming background music; take a sip of tea; place a cold washcloth on your forehead; take a hot shower; rub your neck or shoulders; taste something strong (suck on a sour candy or bite into a lime)

b. *Space*: take a walk; step into another room; spend a few extra moments in the bathroom; block out extra stimulation by closing your eyes or putting on headphones

c. *Mood boosting*: play your favorite song; stretch; watch a funny video; play with your pet; think of a favorite memory

3. **Make use of old skills**
The next step is to think about what tools you have used to handle stress in the past. When you have had bad workdays, fights with friends, gotten a flat tire—anything. What do you do, in general, to make yourself feel better? Did you have a song that you *loved* in college? One that you and your roomie always put on when one of you was having a bad day? Put it on the next time you are feeling tense. Have you always texted a certain person to vent about relationship drama? Or maybe there is a favorite show you watch whenever work is stressing you out. The problems you face as a parent may look very different than the ones you have faced in your past or in other areas of your life. However, your body's response to stress is similar, and it can be really useful to use the same skill across situations. Consider the following examples: text a close friend for support; give yourself a pep talk; count backward from 10; make yourself your favorite snack from childhood; put on cozy pajamas; look at photos from your favorite vacation spot.

4. **Decide when to use your coping tools**
Here are times that tend to be useful for people:
   a. *When you notice yourself becoming stressed.* Some conflicts come up out of nowhere, like when you walk into your kid's bedroom and discover they definitely did *not* clean up, or you find out they went to a party that you specifically told them not to. When situations like this pop up it is smart to use your in-the-moment coping skills ASAP.
   b. *To prepare for conflict that you know is coming.* There are probably some predictable stress points between you and your teen (such as morning wake-up, homework, chores, ending screen time, etc.). If certain battles happen again and again, it's smart to use your coping plan ahead of time. For example, say your grounding mantra or use a sensory relaxation skill right before you go to wake up your teen. Or, put on that favorite song as you commute home toward the evening chaos. It will help lower any tension starting to creep in.
   c. *Daily resets.* As this chapter has already discussed, there is just lots of stress in daily life. Some parents find it helpful to set a few reminders throughout their day to use their skills, even if you are not expecting anything bad to happen. This may be a lunchtime chime on your phone reminding you to take a deep breath. Maybe you commit to 5 minutes of stretching when you get out of bed in the morning. Whatever it is, the idea is to create small habits in your day to reset your baseline stress so you have a little more buffer to help absorb stress that comes up later on.

5. **Create reminders**
The best coping plan in the world does not help if you do not remember to use it. Come up with an idea of how you are going to remember the skills you want to try. Here are a few ideas:
   a. *Gather coping items and leave them in a visible space.* Write your mantra on a piece of paper, grab your favorite lotion, print a picture that makes you smile, and find a few packets of the tea you love. Throw them in a small box or bag

that sits on the counter in plain view so they're in reach when you start to feel upset.
    b. *Set alarms for the predictable stressors.* Edit the text of the alarm to include a skill or your mantra.
    c. *Use sticky notes.* If most of the family chaos tends to happen in the kitchen or living room, put up a few red sticky notes on the walls. The bright color will catch your eye, and it's a visual cue to remind you of your skills.
    d. *Ask for help.* See if you and your partner can come up with a little signal to give each other when a skill might be helpful. If you do not have a coparent living with you, try to think of a close friend or family member who can check in with you. Let them know that you are working on feeling calmer and want them to ask how it's going every few days. Social accountability can be a great motivator and may give you the boost of support you need.

Now, put it all together and write it down in Exercise 3.3. If you are banking on keeping a mental coping plan in your head, think again. There are way too many pieces to try to keep straight, and as much as people say they have great memories, alarms, planners, and sticky notes exist for a reason. For those parents who really do have a strong mental checklist, the ability to think logically takes a nosedive in moments of stress. Brains go straight into survival mode, which can make it hard to recall your coping list and then pick which tools to use. Take some of that work off your shoulders by keeping your written coping plan handy.

EXERCISE 3.3 EXAMPLE: WRITING YOUR COPING PLAN

Step	Options
Coping mantra	- I've been through worse, I can get through this - I'm the adult, they are the kid - He's acting this way because he feels stressed
Calming activities	- Open a window and take a breath of fresh air - Use my vanilla lotion - Make myself hot cocoa
Skills that have worked before	- Call my sister - Text my parent friends - Put on my favorite playlist - Watch highlights from my favorite team - Sit alone in the bedroom for a few minutes
When I need my skills most	- Sunday nights when the pre-week stress builds up - Tuesday-Thursday mornings when I have to be at work early
Reminders	- Set an alarm on my phone Sundays at 5 p.m. Text to read: He's acting like this because he's stressed about the week - Set alarm T/W/Thu at 6 a.m. Text to read: READ COPING PLAN - Leave the hot cocoa packets on the counter. Put vanilla lotion on the kitchen table where I'll see it

EXERCISE 3.3 WRITING YOUR COPING PLAN

Step	Options
Coping mantra	
Calming activities	
Skills that have worked before	
When I need my skills most	
Reminders	

> **COMMON STUCK POINTS TO IN-THE-MOMENT COPING**
>
> In this box is a list of stumbling blocks that parents often hit when trying to make use of in-the-moment coping. Underneath each common stuck point, you will find tips and considerations that can help address each issue. At the end of the chapter, you will have a chance to make note of any examples that would be helpful for you to keep in mind.
>
> ---
>
> **"This seems too intense or unnecessary."**
> Some parents find this level of strategizing to be too specific, too much work, or unnecessary.
>
> → Do not underestimate how important this is. Unless you can honestly say in your heart of hearts that you have never lost your cool with your teen and only ever make logical choices (instead of emotion-based reactions), do everybody a favor and create a plan.
>
> ---
>
> **"I feel overwhelmed by this."**
> Many parents describe feeling so flooded with emotion or so disconnected from their emotions that it is really hard to know where to start with a coping plan. Each idea feels too little to make a real difference, or too much to plan for.
>
> → If this sounds like you, consider asking a friend, partner, or family member for suggestions on where to start. If you are currently in mental health treatment, talk to your provider about what they think could be helpful for you. These people likely see you differently than you see yourself. They may have good ideas about what skills might be a good fit.
> → Also, keep in mind that the coping plan you come up with now is not a contract signed with blood. You can change it! Write down a few ideas and commit to trying them for two weeks. After two weeks, decide what to keep, what to tweak, and what to swap out. It is great to experiment to see what tools work best for you in heated moments. While it would be nice to have the "perfect" plan in place starting tonight, a workable plan that makes sense over time is way more important.

TRY IT OUT: CAREGIVER COPING

Now that you have completed the Building Reserves and In-the-Moment Coping Plan exercises, it is time to put them into practice. Take a picture of each plan or write it out in a notebook or on your phone. Do your best to follow through on your week one goal and try out your coping plan. Complete Worksheet 3.1 to increase your chances of success.

WORKSHEET 3.1

1. When will you try to use these skills during the week?

2. How will you remember to complete the building reserves goals and use the coping plan?

3. What barriers, including any of the common stuck points listed on previous page, do you think may interfere in using the skills, and how do you plan to troubleshoot them?

4. List three things that will help you complete this task and make sense of this skill. As a reminder, this could include reminders, skill review, social support, accountability measures, or other ideas you would find useful.

    1. _____

    2. _____

    3. _____

4
Making Sense of Behavior

UNDERSTANDING YOUR TEEN'S BEHAVIOR WITH THE CAR TOOL

If you are hoping to change a behavior, you first want to understand why the behavior is happening and what keeps it going over time. You can do so by using the acronym CAR: Context-Action-Result (CAR). *Context* refers to what is happening in your child's life that might be affecting them and making it more likely for the problem behavior to occur. *Action* is your teen's behavior. *Result* refers to the outcome of this behavior. In other words, what was the situation your teen was in, what did they do, and what happened next? When you pay attention to the Context, Action, and Result of problem behaviors, you are likely to find negative patterns and can start to create new, more helpful ones.

START WITH THE CONTEXT

It is easy (and natural) for parents and caregivers to focus on their teen's behavior and what sort of consequences come afterward. Those are important pieces of the puzzle, but they leave out context, which is key. For example, say your teen starts to have a hard time in math. They don't seem to have good notes, they don't have the homework written down, and they never know when the next test is. Their grade starts to drop and you get frustrated; why can't your teen start being more responsible? But perhaps there is something else going on that is playing a role. Maybe their eyesight got worse and they can't read the board. Perhaps there is a bully in that class who is making your teen feel anxious and distracted. Maybe their ADHD symptoms are worsening, and their medication needs to be adjusted. If you only focus on the Action and Result, you miss very valuable information that could help your child.

There are three Context factors to pay attention to:

1. Overall environment around your child
2. In-the-moment stressors
3. Expectations and strategies that caregivers use

This chapter will focus on the first two. The rest of the book provides in-depth guidance on the third.

ENVIRONMENTAL CONTEXT

There are many environmental factors in a person's life that influence mood, skillfulness, and behavior, especially for teens who struggle with mental health. For example, anxiety, mood, or attentional difficulties will impact a teen's ability to manage emotions, control impulses, and problem-solve. That is a hurdle they live with all the time no matter what situation they are in, and it will certainly make it harder for them to act in a skillful way when stressed. There are also the many environmental factors (academic pressure, political unrest, etc.) outlined in Chapter 1 that teens are living with. Rates of mental health diagnoses have skyrocketed in recent years, partly due to these factors that they do not have control over. Other examples of environmental factors would be a child who is bullied at school, going through a transition, or feeling like their siblings get all the attention. These circumstances can raise your teen's baseline level of stress and make it easier for them to lose their cool or make a poor choice.

TAKING STOCK OF THE ENVIRONMENTAL CONTEXT

In Exercise 4.1, you will find a list of common environmental stressors that can influence a teen's behavior. There is an empty row at the end for you to add in other parts of your child's life that aren't already on the list. Read through the list and rate how much you think each stressor impacts your teen on a scale of 1 (plays no role) to 5 (plays a huge role). For anything you have rated a 3 or above, write out a few ways that it seems to influence your child. The first row includes an example.

Making Sense of Behavior   33

EXERCISE 4.1 TAKING STOCK OF ENVIRONMENTAL CONTEXT

_____3_____	**Example: Family stress:** Busy work schedule; not home to give regular help. Fighting w/ brother; teen feels like he never has enough alone time/space
_____	**Family stress** (family arguments, sibling rivalry, lack of support, estranged caregivers)
_____	**Social stress** (peer pressure, fitting in, making new friends, bullying, peer conflict, dating)
_____	**School stress** (pressure, workload, hard teachers, violence in schools)
_____	**Learning difficulties** (learning disorders, developmental or intellectual delays, need for extra supports from school)
_____	**Physical health** (chronic illness, health of close family, school sick days)
_____	**Mental health** (anxiety, depression, ADHD, oppositional behavior, substance use, eating concerns, serious mental illness)
_____	**Big transitions** (moving, new schools, new siblings, loss in the family)
_____	**Developmental shifts** (different responsibilities and expectations, desire for more independence, hormonal/sleep shifts due to puberty)
_____	**Limited access to basic needs** (unstable housing, food insecurity, no/limited health insurance)
_____	**Chronic or systemic hurdles** (systemic racism, poverty, lower access to resources/support, lack of accessible healthcare)
_____	**Global events** (political unrest, climate events, public health crises)
_____	

IN-THE-MOMENT CONTEXT

Now that you have considered your teen's overall environment, it is equally as important to try to find patterns about the *specific* situations that typically lead to unskillful choices. As the caregiver, you want to figure out the who, what, when, where, and why that sets off your child. As a reminder, noticing common triggers will help you create new patterns.

> **COMMON STUCK POINTS THAT IMPACT TEEN BEHAVIOR**
>
> Here is a list of common hurdles that can have a negative impact on teen behavior. Along with each, you will find a clear explanation of how it plays a role in teen mental health and teen behaviors.
>
> ---
>
> **Unstructured tasks**: Most kids struggle with open ended periods of time and do better with some structure, especially those with mental health difficulties. Anxious kids tend to have an easier time when they know what to expect. There is less uncertainty, they have time to prepare for what is coming, and they know they won't be caught by surprise. Kids with depression are often more withdrawn and less motivated to structure themselves. Having an existing structure takes off some of the burden, creates a predictable flow to the day, and sets clear expectations of what they need to be doing. For kids with ADHD, unstructured times can leave their brain looking for stimulation (which they might get by bugging their brother, sneaking out of the house, or scrolling the internet for hours). On the other hand, structure gives their brain something to focus on, making it easy to go about their day without a bunch of problem behaviors popping up.
>
> ---
>
> **Difficult/boring tasks**: All teens have natural strengths and weaknesses, as well as different preferences. Tasks that are more difficult or less enjoyable are going to lead to more problem behaviors. This is true even for adults. For example, when you have a pile of dishes waiting for you, you might grumble or put it off until the morning. Teen are the same, though some have reactions that are bigger, such as bargaining, arguing, crying, yelling, complete refusal, or storming out of the house. Bigger reactions are especially likely to happen if your teen had to stop an activity they love (like screen time) and switch to one they dislike (like homework).
>
> Given that that these jobs are more difficult or strongly disliked, it's not really a big surprise that you see more problematic behavior. This is important to keep in mind when you're having the same fights repeatedly (like fighting over every math assignment). As a parent, this constant battle is really frustrating because it seems like these expected tasks should not be such an issue. But for your kid, that task is *really* unappealing or *really* difficult, and their brain is just trying to find an out.
>
> ---
>
> **Time of day**: Some teens are morning people, while some do better in the evenings. If you know that your child does not fully wake up until 11:00 a.m. on a weekend, do not ask them to finish all of their chores by 11:30 a.m. on Saturday. Nobody will be happy with the result. That does not mean your entire day has to be scheduled

around your teen's sleep schedule, but you can make strategic choices for the tasks you care about most. After all, it is not your child's fault that their internal clock gets entirely shifted during the teenage years.

Mismatched setting: Lots of caregivers notice that their kids tend to do better in some settings than in others. For example, their teen is an angel in school and in public, but falls apart at home (or vice versa). If your teen seems to be more skillful in a certain setting, think about what might be working for them in that situation. If home is better, is it because they have more one-on-one attention, can stretch/snack when they want, or aren't worried about being called on by the teacher? If they do better at school, is that because there's more structure, friend support, or stimulation to keep them occupied? These are all just examples, but if you can identify what is working for your kid, you can think about how you can extend it to other situations. If your child does better at home because they can take breaks whenever they want, you can probably talk to the school about setting up a break system during the day. If your child does better in school because they have their friends there, it may be useful to think about a schedule that allows them to see friends more on the weekdays.

Unmet physical needs: Does your child get hangry when they haven't eaten? Does their anxiety go way up when they are tired? Are they more irritable when they feel too hot? There are a lot of physical needs that impact a person's comfort and ability to function well. Some teens may struggle to be aware of physical discomforts (for example, they don't realize they're getting too warm until they are already sweating) or have not reached the developmental independence necessary to take care of their needs. This can play a major role in how teens act and are often relatively simple fixes.

Parent/caretaker factors: How you behave when you interact with your child is going to influence what happens next in a few different ways. First, as mentioned in Chapter 2, consistency is crucial. You have a lot of stuff going on in your life day to day, and it is natural for your mood and patience to go up and down. This is completely reasonable, but if your own changing bandwidth leads to you respond differently to your child's behavior each time you interact, it gets pretty confusing for a teen's brain. When you can, try asking yourself if your responses are based on your teen and their behavior or your own internal stress.

Parent/caretaker factors also matter because humans tend to mirror each other. So if you walk in the door and immediately raise your voice when you see them sneaking screen time, your teenager is likely to follow suit automatically. Their emotional baseline is going to increase as yours increases. You've probably experienced this in your own life. When somebody starts speaking to you with an attitude, you get on edge. If someone is kind or calm when discussing a concern, you're less likely to raise your hackles. Keep that in mind as you enter situations with your kid. When you're able to stay neutral or calm, there's a better chance that your child will as well. It's not foolproof, and they still might be upset, but at least you didn't accidentally trigger a gut reaction from them that you didn't need to.

Also keep in mind that your behavior can be a positive force in the long run. How you act in moments of calm and in moments of stress are things that your child's brain is naturally going to take in and may copy down the road. If you're somebody who gets angry and then yells and storms off, it is not a huge surprise if your child does the same. And the flip side? If you get mad and then go to make yourself a cup of tea or go for a walk, it will not be a mystery when your teenager picks up the habit. There is not a one-to-one match between parent behavior and teen behavior, and the connection that does exist is not necessarily immediate. Still, the influence you have on your teen gives you a really good opportunity to show them helpful, productive options for coping. When they are older and out of the house, those automatic patterns of behavior will start to show themselves in moments of stress without them having to think too hard.

EXERCISE 4.2 TAKING STOCK OF IN-THE-MOMENT CONTEXT

To complete Exercise 4.2, review the list of stuck points on previous pages and circle any factors that you think impact your child in a meaningful way. Consider how you see this play out. For example, you might circle "unmet physical needs" and make note that anxiety symptoms go way up when sleep is low, while problem-solving is great when your teen is well rested. The list of stuck points is certainly not exhaustive; there are many different things that can play a role in how a teenager behaves. Other common contextual factors are transitions, social settings, new activities and places, crowded or overstimulating events, being told no, and facing rejection. In the lines below, jot down any other triggers you know play a role in your teen's behavior from day to day.

_____

_____

_____

_____

_____

BEING AWARE OF CONTEXT IN ORDER TO SHAPE WHAT COMES NEXT

You have just taken the time to think through what sort of environmental and in-the-moment factors may be impacting how your child acts. There are two ways you are going to use this information: changing what you can, and building empathy for what you can't.

Change What You Can (and Want To)

When you recognize the types of situations that do not work well for your child, you can start to think about changing those situations. If your child does better with structure, can you create more of a routine? If they struggle with transitions, setting two-minute warning chimes might help a teen's brain start to mentally prepare for a change in activity. In other words, are there any shifts you can make that will make it easier for your child to behave appropriately?

Of course, there are limits to how much you can (and should) change for your teen. If they hate math, it does not mean you give them permission to skip their math homework for all time. However, there may be some things you can do to help (especially if mental health symptoms are making math even more difficult). Perhaps your teen needs a tutor, one-on-one time with the teacher, or extra time on math tests. Maybe you have a snack on the desk when they sit down to start the assignment. It could be that their favorite down time activity (e.g., video games, playing with the dog, texting their friends) comes right after math gets done. None of these are a cure-all, but they are steps you can plan for before the math worksheet is on the table, and might make it a little bit easier for your teen to stay calm and appropriate during a difficult task. For specific details on appropriate accommodations, see Chapter 8.

Allow Your Awareness to Increase Your Empathy

There are some factors that you cannot change for your teenager. Take the math homework example: your teen cannot skip homework forever and might hate it no matter what sort of accommodations you offer. That is okay. Discomfort is a part of life. In these moments, it is still important to acknowledge what is making it hard for your kid. Doing so will make it easier for you to empathize with what they're going through and soften your own frustration or anger when teen problem behaviors (e.g., yelling, procrastinating, arguing) pop up.

After repeated battles, many parents feel like their teen is being difficult on purpose or refusing to try hard enough. After all, why can't they just get with the program? Can't they see how much easier things would be if they would just behave? And there are certainly some instances where teenagers *are* trying to be a pain and *are* making a poor choice out of spite. But for many kids who struggle with mental health difficulties, it's just not that simple. No teenager is waking up in the morning thinking:

- *Hmm, what can I do to make my life hard today?*
- *How can I guarantee that my mom absolutely loses it during dinner?*
- *Wow, I am so grateful to have so much trouble focusing on my homework. How about I celebrate by being paralyzed with indecision for the next three hours while my dad gets increasingly annoyed that I'm not done with homework yet.*

Teens who struggle with mental health issues experience symptoms that make typical home, school, and peer interactions so much harder than they are for others. Because of this, they can be easily overwhelmed by environmental and in-the-moment contexts. Most teens with mental health difficulties are truly struggling to find the right skills or enough bandwidth to make the more helpful choices in hard moments. If you as a caregiver can remember this, you will stop seeing the problem behavior as mean, intentional, cruel, lazy, manipulative, or worse. You can approach your teenager with support and validation and start to find a pathway out together.

GET CLEAR ON THE ACTION

The Action portion of the CAR acronym refers to what your teen is doing in the middle of the situation you are looking at. There are a few ways parents can start to view this part of the process in a helpful way.

1. *Be specific.* As mentioned in Chapter 2, it is useful to be crystal clear about your teen's exact behavior. Saying they were rude, misbehaving, all over the place (and so on) is not specific enough. Similarly, when parents say "he just flew off the handle" or "her behavior was a disaster," they are not actually giving much information about the exact problem behaviors that were present, which makes them harder to change. When thinking about the Context-Action-Result tool, remember to clearly label the behavior, almost as if you were looking at stage directions in a play.
    a. Example: *Rude behavior*
        Instead: rolled eyes, cursed, used disrespectful tone
    b. Example: *Flew off the handle*
        Instead: yelled, slammed the door, threw a book on the ground
    c. Example: *Well, that was a disaster!*
        Instead: teen stalled while getting ready, pleaded to stay home, cried, began to hyperventilate as we got into the car
2. *Think about Action in terms of unhelpful versus helpful or unskillful versus skillful.* Try to avoid talking about it as "good" behavior versus "bad" behavior. While this might seem nit-picky, language matters. When you label something as "bad" every day, you and your teen will both start to assign moral judgment to it, which can easily bleed into how you and your teen start to think of your child as a human being. It is not helpful to anybody for a teenager to internalize the idea that they, as a person, are bad at their core.

    In some instances, behavior *may* seem bad from a moral standpoint. However, the threshold for when a behavior becomes "bad" is highly subjective and based on individual and cultural values, as well as *context*. For example, somebody might say that spilling somebody's secret without permission is bad. But what if the secret was that your teen's friend was cheating on their boyfriend and your teen thought the boyfriend should know? What if somebody was being pressured to do things they did not want to do but asked your teen not to tell anybody? What if somebody was thinking about ending their life, but swore your teen to secrecy? Somewhere along that line, the "bad" behavior actually seems like the very right thing to do. Point being, assigning moral judgment is a tricky game because any seemingly "bad" behavior could make complete sense based on the person's values and context. Given this, using that term is rarely worth the risk to your child's self-perception and your overall judgment of them.

3. *Identify the behavior you want to decrease and what you want to replace it.* Many parents and caregivers focus on the behavior they do not want to see: yelling, eye-rolling, procrastinating, and so on. This makes sense. Human brains are inclined to look out for threats so you can respond more quickly to them. The brain is less focused on things that are going well, because why spend mental resources on a situation when there isn't a problem? From a survival standpoint, this makes lots of sense. When it comes to supporting your child, it can keep you stuck for a few reasons.
   a. You see what you want to see. If you are hyperfocused on what your child is doing wrong, you will notice it tenfold. At the same time, if you are not actively watching for the behaviors you want to see from your kids (e.g., speaking to you calmly, taking a break when upset, staying focused on a task), it is easier to miss them when it happens. This unfairly colors your opinion of your teen's behavior and robs them of an opportunity to be acknowledged.
   b. Focusing on the bad makes it harder to reward small steps in the right direction. When thinking about Context-Action-Result, you do not *only* use it to identify negative patterns. You also want it to find helpful patterns so you know what to do more of! Most adults can relate to this. If you had a boss who only ever focuses on your weaknesses, it is very easy to minimize (or even forget) what is going well. Positive habits fall by the wayside because nobody is focusing on them. Knowing the behaviors you want to see will allow you to find the context and results that you want to keep around.
   c. In the midst of a teen's mental health struggles, it is easy to lose sight of how you want your family to function. Often, caregivers are just holding on for dear life, hoping the storm fades quickly. In this sort of mindset, it would take most parents two minutes or less to list 10 problem behaviors they want their teenager to work on. However, would it be as easy to list the behaviors they do want to see instead? Most parents actually feel a little stuck when asked for specifics. They say things like "better behaved" or "less argumentative." Those are great broad concepts, but (as you may remember) specificity is important! It is useful to consider what skillful behaviors are important to help your child build. If your teen has an attitude problem, what do you want to replace it with? Being able to speak respectfully, using skills to manage emotions, or taking a break when annoyed? All are excellent options, and there is no right or wrong option. But you need to pick one, at least to start with. If you have not figured out what your goal is, it is going to be an awfully long road trying to help your child make it to the end.

EXERCISE 4.3 IDENTIFYING ACTIONS AND WHAT YOU WANT TO SEE INSTEAD

Following is a list of common areas parents and caregivers would like their teens to work on with examples of specific problem behaviors and possible replacement behaviors. Circle any problem behaviors your child does, as well as the desired replacement behaviors. Use the empty box provided to write in other behaviors you care about. The goal of this exercise is to get more specific about the behaviors you want to work on so you know what behaviors you can use the CAR acronym for to start to understand better.

General Area	Specific Problem Behaviors	Possible Replacement Behaviors
Attitude/ disrespect	• Eye-rolling • Inappropriate gestures • Appearing ungrateful • Scoffing • Ignoring house rules • Dismissive language • Name calling/cursing • Speaking over parents • Always getting the last word	• Appropriate faces/body language (straight face, open stance) • Positive tone • Expressing thanks • Following house rules • Calling parents by their preferred term (example: Mom, Mother, Ma'am) • Listening when parents speak • Allowing parent the last word
Not listening	• Ignoring when parents speak • Speaking over parents • Failing to follow directions • Repeating problem behaviors after being told not to	• Making eye contact • Allowing others to finish their sentences • Following instructions • Working to stop problem behaviors once asked to stop
Not helping	• Leaving a mess • Refusing to do chores • Needing multiple asks before completing a task • Refusing to help	• Picking up after self • Completing expected chores • Helping without being asked or after the first ask • Offering to help
Outbursts/ dysregulation	• Speaking over people • Hurtful language • Cursing • Yelling/screaming • Kicking/hitting • Throwing objects • Breaking things	• Allowing others to speak • Indoor volume • Clear/respectful communication • Asking for/accepting skills help • Accepting parent decisions calmly • Using coping skills to regulate • Problem-solving • Respecting personal space • Safe hands and feet

General Area	Specific Problem Behaviors	Possible Replacement Behaviors
Procrastination	• Getting distracted by other people/items/activities • Stalling on tasks • Needing multiple reminders to complete a task • Partially completing tasks • Not finishing tasks	• Planning ahead for tasks • Distancing self from distractions • Starting tasks early • Using coping skills to manage stressful tasks • Setting alarms to stay on task • Completing tasks after the first ask • Completing tasks fully
Low motivation	• Not making plans • Waiting to be asked • Completing tasks part-way • Refusal to try new things	• Brainstorming ideas • Making plans • Taking initiative to plan outings • Fully completing tasks • Willingness to try something new
Irritability	• Complaining • Focusing on the bad • Easily set off • Snapping • Hurtful words • Defiance • Staying upset longer	• Showing acceptance • Calm/appropriate language • Take a break when upset • Respectful tone/language • Willingness to listen • Returning to emotional baseline quickly
Low independence	• Lacking self-care • Needing support to complete academic/household tasks • Not gathering information on interests/future plans • Needing prompts to do things • Relying on others to get things done/problem-solve	• Taking care of self • Completing tasks on own or with minimal support • Looking into information on interests/future plans • Taking steps to initiate interests/future plans • Asking for input while making own plans/decisions
Too rigid	• Refusal to try new things • Wanting things a specific way • Intensely frustrated by change • Inflexible routines/behaviors	• Willingness to try new things • Accepting changes • In control of emotions when something changes • Flexible around routines/behaviors

Continued

Continued

General Area	Specific Problem Behaviors	Possible Replacement Behaviors
Risky behaviors	• Making quick decisions • Not asking for help • Sneaking out • Speeding • Talking to online strangers • Drug/alcohol use • Unsafe sex • Sending/looking at explicit material via text/social media	• Thinking through decisions • Asking for help • Safe driving (following speed limit and traffic laws) • Keeping personal info private • Following house rules about going out, drug/alcohol use, sex • Not sharing/looking at explicit material via text or social media
Shutting down	• Dismissing attempts to talk • Opting not to share thoughts/feelings • Opting not to participate in family activities • Withdrawing to own space	• Willing to hear others out • Willing to share about thoughts/feelings • Participating in family activities • Being present in family spaces

With a good perspective on the behaviors you do and do not want to see, you will have an easier time making full use of CAR.

REVIEWING THE RESULT

The last section of the CAR acronym is about pinpointing the results of your teen's behavior. In other words, what is the outcome of their actions? It is important to pay attention to this because it will help explain why certain behaviors may be repeating when others do not. There are two types of results: reinforcement and punishment. Reinforcement is any outcome that is, in some way, positive to your teenager. The outcome *reinforces* (aka rewards) the behavior and will increase the chances of that behavior happening again. On the flip side, negative consequences are typically called punishment. Most people use punishment to refer to things like detention or being grounded. When talking about behavior change, punishment is broader than that. It refers to anything that is *punishing* (aka unpleasant), to your teenager. Those could be traditional "punishments" like being grounded, but it can include anything that just feels bad in some way. For example, feeling embarrassed, being rejected, or losing a favorite piece of clothing are all punishing experiences. Behaviors that are followed by punishment are less likely to occur again because your teen's brain does not want to relive that same discomfort.

When using Context-Action-Result, you will look for what outcomes might be reinforcing or punishing. One very important thing to note is that there are many rewarding and punishing parts of your teen's life that have nothing to do with you as a parent. These come from peers, teachers, coaches, school systems, jobs, and even their own body. Four important categories include internal or sensory outcomes, external outcomes, social outcomes, and parental outcomes. In Box 4.1 are a few examples of common types of reinforcement and punishment within each category.

Box 4.1

Outcome Type	Action	Result (type of outcome)
Internal/sensory outcomes: stem from within the individual	Touch a hot stove	Feel pain (punishment)
	Eat a cookie	Taste sweetness (reinforcement)
	Bug sibling until they react	Rush of adrenaline/stimulation (reinforcement)
	Raise hand in class and give wrong answer	Feel flush and anxious (punishment)
External outcomes: real-world consequences	Work hard on an essay	Teacher gives good grade (reinforcement)
	Wake up late	Miss the bus you needed (punishment)
	Stop showing up to basketball practice	Drop from varsity to the JV team (punishment)
	Remember to clock in for work	Get paid full amount (reinforcement)
Social outcomes: feedback from friends, peers, authority figures, or other people	Tell a joke in class	Classmates laugh (reinforcement)
	Give the teacher attitude	Get scolded (punishment)
	Tell a friend's secret	Friend is mad (punishment)
	Always offer support	Get thanked by friends (reinforcement)
Parental outcomes: good and bad consequences that parents are responsible for doling out	Lie about a bad test score	Get grounded (punishment)
	Give Mom a compliment	Mom smiles back (reinforcement)
	Very responsible about walking the dog	Allowed to stay out later (reinforcement)
	Refuse to turn off screen when asked	Phone gets taken away (punishment)

One particularly important type of consequence is worth noting: emotion. Emotions can be hugely reinforcing or punishing. The rush of joy and acceptance a teenager gets when they make their friends laugh is intoxicating. The happy butterflies on a first date can make a teen smile for days. At the same time, the anxiety they feel trying a new activity, despair that arises when they are lonely, or frustration they feel when they cannot get the right answer is very, very punishing. As a caregiver, it is important to acknowledge the full weight of these emotions and how they impact your teenager's behavior. Especially in the current environment in which kids are faced with both many positive opportunities and looming worries—emotions are key.

In general, as the parent or caregiver, you want to be aware of the many different reinforcements and punishments that your teenager is experiencing. Even if you cannot control their internal state, protect them from the world, or demand that all peers be nice to them;

understanding the role of these factors will give you a clearer picture of why your child is acting the way they are. The good news is that you do have a say in how *you* respond to your teen's actions, and there are a few common reinforcers that parents can make use of.

1. *Attention*: Human beings are very tuned in to other people. Without even being aware of it, individuals are constantly seeking feedback from others to inform their next move. While your teenager might pretend that they don't care about what you think, your attention still matters to them. Parent attention is not the only type of attention that matters; friends, teachers, coaches, all matter, too. But still, your attention is meaningful. Chapter 5 is dedicated to this, so for the time being assume that all attention (even when you raise your voice or lecture them) is at least somewhat reinforcing.
2. *Praise*: As a more specific form of attention, praise feels really nice. Most people like to be acknowledged or thanked for their efforts, and this is true for teens as well. They may not give you the satisfaction of knowing how much your praise means, and some might feel a little bit uncomfortable with it at first, but it is highly reinforcing over time.
3. *Tangible rewards*: Teenagers like *things*: a new phone, new apps for that phone, gift cards, games, takeout, tickets, shoes, spending money, and so on. Of course, not every family can afford to spend money on tangible rewards to shift their teen's behavior, and others might not want to. That is okay! Just know that it is one of the tools in the toolbox.
4. *Freedom*: A big reinforcer for many teenagers is independence. Developmentally, this is the stage when individuals start to control their own lives more. Granting more independence can be an extremely powerful way to reinforce skillful behavior. Examples include extending curfew, granting more freedom with money or clothing, asking for less information about their plans, allowing activities you were on the fence about, or increasing freedom to get places on their own.
5. *Limiting nonpreferred tasks and situations*: Parents and caregivers can reward kids by limiting the things they don't like, such as lessening chores as a reward for progress in other areas. Others may shift expectations in certain circumstances (e.g., a teen may usually need to watch their brother on Saturdays, but are told they can pause that during a busy semester working on college applications). Parents can limit how often teens have to join the family movie night, attend community events, or show up to large family events.

On the opposite end of the spectrum, you want to think about common parent-enforced punishment for behaviors.

1. *Removing attention*: If attention is rewarding, the opposite of that is *ignoring*. Removing your attention from inappropriate behaviors can play a major role in decreasing those behaviors. Chapter 5 is dedicated to this topic.
2. *Removing preferred items*: Losing access to the things teens like is a clear punishment, whether it be phones, video games, the WiFi password, the really nice new bag you bought them, or their favorite snacks that you lovingly stocked. These are all items you let them use, and you can remove or limit them as appropriate.

3. *Removing privileges*: Freedom is rewarding, and losing that freedom is punishing. Moving curfew earlier, saying no to outings with friends, limiting WhatsApp access, or organizing schedules without teen input are all potential negative outcomes.
4. *Giving warnings or reminders*: Most teens do not like to feel nagged. Repeated reminders or check-ins can be a natural consequence for repeated unskillful behavior. For example, you might call them after they forget to text when they get to their friend's house, or check in on homework progress for a week after they fail a few assignments.
5. *Increasing chores or nonpreferred tasks*: This is quite self-explanatory, but no teens are looking for an extra serving of chore duty. There are likely many household tasks you could use help with, and extra chores can serve as reasonable punishment.
6. *Apologies and repairs*: Teens can do some really problematic things. Sometimes this causes emotional pain for others or physical damage to property. It is an appropriate punishment to have a teen repair the harm they cause. Examples include verbal or written apologies, paying to repair broken items, being responsible for the cleanup of a mess they made, taking over a sibling's task to make up for prior mean behavior.

MAKING SENSE OF THE RESULTS

With these reinforcement and punishment options in mind, it is time to consider how they could link to your teen's behavior. To do this, think about the Results like a math equation. Add up how much a behavior is reinforced and how much is it punished. If a behavior is more reinforced than it is punished, that behavior will probably happen again. If the behavior is more punished than it is reinforced, it's less likely to happen again. Importantly, your teens are not necessarily aware of this math equation. Instead, their brain is rapidly taking notes on what feels good and bad, often without the teenager even realizing it. Here are two examples.

Situation 1: Teenager with anxiety and a learning disorder who gets nervous about tests. The morning of a test, this student makes jokes in class as the teacher is giving instructions. The Context here includes a history of anxiety and learning disorder and that it's test day. The Action here is making jokes in class. If this was a math equation, how would the Results add up?

Results	Reward	Punishment
Classmates all laugh (feels really good)	+20	
Teacher scolds teen (feels embarrassing)		−15
Teacher is distracted and delays the test for a few minutes (feels big relief)	+20	
Test got started late so teen only has 30 minutes to work on it instead of 35 minutes (feels a little relief)	+5	
Couldn't finish last question because of the shorter time		−10
Teacher emails parents, who take away phone for the afternoon		−20
The next day somebody brings up the joke and laughs again	+5	
Total Reward/Punishment =	+55	−45
Overall Total =	+10	

Understanding the results: This behavior was punished in a number of ways, and it was rewarded in others. Overall, the behavior was *more* reinforcing than it was punishing. This teen's brain has learned that interrupting a math test with jokes works out fairly well. So the next time this person is in the same situation, what are they going to do? *Make a bunch more jokes.*

Situation 2: A teenager with anxiety and ADHD has been bored after school. Parents convince them to try out for soccer, but they have not played since elementary school. The teen is extremely anxious about embarrassing themselves and is on edge when they show up to tryouts. Some of the Context we have is anxiety and difficulty with attention or hyperactivity, as well as a new activity. The Action here is trying a new activity. What are the Results?

Outcome	Reward	Punishment
Intense anxiety all day		−30
A few kids on the field say hi (feels welcoming)	+15	
Some of the older players are grouped together chatting and laughing, but do not acknowledge teen (feels excluded)		−5
Coach starts introductions and it's hard for teen to focus (feels like a struggle)		−10
Teen messes up later in practice and has a very hard time controlling frustration (yells at self out loud, and then feels embarrassed)		−25
Coach praises teen for good effort	+10	
Total Reward/Punishment =	+20	−70
Overall Total:		45

Understanding the results: In this situation, trying a new activity was difficult for this teenager. The emotional toll of nerves, frustration, and embarrassment added up. Though there were some positives, they paled in comparison to the negative. In the future, it will be really hard for this teenager to work up the nerve to try a new activity again without some additional help.

In both examples, you can see lots of different outcomes impact a teen's overall understanding of their behavior and their future actions. The amount of reinforcement or punishment a teen gets is based on *their* experience of the outcome, not what the parents think it should be. For example, a parent could say "Everybody messes up. Making a mistake at soccer tryouts shouldn't feel that bad." That's a fair perspective, but it does not mean your teen can suddenly adopt the same mindset. Parents experience emotions differently than kids, especially when mental health is involved. As you work through CAR for your own teen, estimate how much you think these factors impact *them*, not how much they would impact you.

RESHAPING THE RESULTS

With the Results math equation in mind, recognize that in order to change behavior, the overall total of reinforcement and punishment also has to change. For specific details of how to do this see Chapter 9, which covers reward and punishment in greater detail. For now, consider the following general approach. When looking at the Results, it is easy for parents to focus on how they can increase punishment to stop problem behaviors. This is understandable. Often, the gut reaction is to heap on punishment to make it clear that a problem behavior is *not okay*. Plus, teenage problem behavior can cause strong anger, anxiety, and frustration for parents, who in turn respond with more reactive consequences. For lots of reasons you'll read about later, increasing punishment to stop inappropriate behavior is almost never going to be the first option.

Instead, you want to focus on increasing more skillful behaviors by making them more reinforcing and much less punishing. Parents can consider ways to reinforce their teen each time they make a skillful choice, and decrease any of the aversive side effects that might come with it. For example, if your child does not like going to the big family dinner because they get overwhelmed by all of the questions directed at them by their aunts and uncles, you could agree that your teen can a) be on their phone after the first hour of the dinner, and b) sit far away from the aunts and uncles so they are out of the line of fire. Then when your teen shows up, they are rewarded with phone time and the sense of discomfort is minimized.

In the instances when you do want to focus on stopping a specific problem behavior, you will try to decrease how reinforcing the behavior is and increase more punishing outcomes. If the grumbling and negotiating starts up before leaving for the family dinner, you might a) state the expectation for them to attend and then stop engaging in the negotiation, or b) inform them that WiFi will be shut off if they choose to stay home. In other words, you turn down the reward by minimizing attention and turn up punishment by taking away the internet access.

PUTTING TOGETHER CONTEXT-ACTION-RESULT

Having worked through each part of the Context-Action-Result tool, it is time to put it all together. In the following table you can see how the different sections come together. Use this to adjust the way you think about your teenager's actions, and it will give you a roadmap for how to plot a new course. At the end of the chapter, you will find a blank Context-Action-Result template. Use it to fill in the factors that are most relevant for your teenager.

CONTEXT	ACTION		RESULT	
The context that is impacting your teen: Decide what can be changed, and build empathy for the things that cannot.	Teen's specific behaviors: If you would like behavior to change, be clear about what would replace it.		What happens after your teen's behavior: Notice what outcomes are reinforcing and what are punishing, and how the sum total informs what your teen does the next time they are in the same situation.	
Environmental • Family stress • Social stress • Learning difficulties/mental health difficulties • Physical health • Life transitions • Access to basic needs • Chronic/systemic barriers • Global events • Others	<u>Current Behavior</u>	<u>Preferred Replacement Behavior</u>	**Reinforcement** • Attention • Praise • Tangible rewards • Freedom • Limited nonpreferred tasks/situations	**Punishment** • Ignoring • Loss of preferred items • Removal of privileges • Warnings/reminders • Repairs
In-the-Moment • Structured vs. unstructured tasks • Type of task (hard/nonpreferred) • Time of day • Home vs. school vs. public settings • Parent–caretaker factors • Physical needs • Others				
Strategies • Positive Attention • Validation • Schedule/routine • Reward planning				

Making Sense of Behavior   49

EXERCISE 4.4 TEST YOUR KNOWLEDGE OF THE CONTEXT-ACTION-RESULT TOOL

While reading the story below about a teen who is struggling, keep the CAR acronym in your mind. Circle text that notes a contextual factor that may be impacting this teen's behavior. Use a square outline to mark the Actions you identify, and underline the Results you notice.

Situation: Jordan is a 16-year-old junior living with his mom. His older sister recently went off to college. Jordan has struggled since transitioning back to school in person after the remote learning that took place during COVID. He feels awkward around classmates. Recently, he has been saying he does not want to go to school. When his mom asks what is wrong, Jordan says he has constant worry about difficult coursework and upcoming college applications. His anxiety seems to be spiraling, and his pediatrician thought he might meet criteria for an anxiety disorder. This week, Jordan has been refusing to get out of bed, staying under his covers when his mom tries to wake him, often sitting on his bed to rub his back. When Jordan stays hidden, his mom begins to remind him of how important each day of class is and how stressful it will be to miss it. Jordan gets more and more upset, eventually yelling at his mom to leave. Worried about arriving to work late, Jordan's mom eventually gives up and storms out of the room. As she is walking out the door for work, she tells Jordan that she expects him to get to school or he is going to be in trouble. Jordan decides to stay home. After a few more hours of sleep, he watches TV and scrolls on his phone for the rest of the day. When his mom gets home, she is exhausted and too tired to fight Jordan. She tells him that they'll talk about it in the morning, but that he better be up for school the next day.

Exercise 4.4 ANSWER KEY Test Your Knowledge of the Context-Action-Result Model

As a reminder, the circles show context factors that might be impacting Jordan's general mood and baseline stress. Squares shows his actions. Underlined text shows the results of his behavior.

Jordan is a 16-year-old junior living with his mom. His older sister recently went off to college. Jordan has struggled since transitioning back to school in person after the remote learning that took place during COVID. He feels awkward around classmates. Recently, he has been saying he does not want to go to school. When his mom asks what is wrong, Jordan says he has constant worry about difficult coursework and upcoming college applications. His anxiety seems to be spiraling, and his pediatrician thought he might meet criteria for an anxiety disorder. This week, Jordan has been refusing to get out of bed, staying under his covers when his mom tries to wake him, often sitting on his bed to rub his back. When Jordan stays hidden, his mom begins to remind him of how important each day of class is and how stressful it will be to miss it. Jordan gets more and more upset, eventually yelling at his mom to leave. Worried about arriving to work late, Jordan's mom eventually gives up and storms out of the room. As she is walking out the door for work, she tells Jordan that she expects him to get to school or he is going to be in trouble. Jordan decides to stay home. After a few more hours of sleep, he watches TV and scrolls on his phone for the rest of the day. When his mom gets home, she is exhausted and too tired to fight with Jordan. She tells him that they'll talk about it in the morning, but that he better be up for school the next day.

What you hopefully notice from this example is that there are many contextual factors adding to Jordan's current mood and behavior. In the moment, his actions include lots of avoidance (e.g., staying in bed, pushing his mom to leave). The results in this case are mostly rewarding. Though Mom expresses frustration, he spends the day sleeping and using screens, and gets out of a big lecture or punishment at the end of the day because his mom is too exhausted.

TEST YOUR CAR SKILLS . . . LATER

In most of the chapters of this book, this is where you would find another exercise labeled Test Your Skills. In this case, you would be asked to work on the following:

1. Which contextual factors you would want to change (and how), and which you would want to build empathy for
2. What replacement actions you would want to see from Jordan
3. How you would change the results to try to decrease the unskillful behavior and increase the skillful behavior

While you might be able to do some of this already, the rest of the book will give you most of the strategies you need to complete this task. Since you do not yet have all the skills you need, this Test Your Skills task will come at the very end of the book when you can try putting all of the information you have learned together.

TRY IT OUT: CAR

Even though you do not have all of the tools you will eventually make use of, you can still put the CAR acronym into practice at home. This exercise is two parts: deciding what context to address and mapping out Context-Action-Result patterns in your own home over the next week.

EXERCISE 4.5 DECIDE HOW TO APPROACH THE CONTEXT

In Exercises 4.1 and 4.2 you identified the environmental and in-the-moment factors that influence your teen before they even act. In this next exercise, start by writing down everything you previously marked as significant. Then, indicate with a check mark if you would like to try to change that barrier in some way, or simply focus on empathizing with your teen's situation. The goal is not to clear away every obstacle your child has faced. As you likely know, overcoming adversity can encourage growth and empowerment in many people. Still, for the contextual factors that are making it much harder for your teen to be skillful *and* seem reasonable for you to shift, this is an opportunity to start brainstorming possible pathways forward. To do this, write down a few ways you could try to address it. For the situations you do not want to change or cannot change, write a sentence that will help you empathize with your teen's experience. There is no need to solve everything in one sitting or find the perfect resolution. Feel free to come back to this exercise every so often as you get new ideas, and take your time trying out one thing at a time. See Example 4.5 for ideas.

EXERCISE 4.5 EXAMPLE: PLAN HOW TO APPROACH CONTEXT

Context	Please put a ✓ in the column you would like to focus on:		Possible pathways out or empathizing statement
	Try to change	Build empathy	
Family stress Siblings fighting all the time	✓		• Create plan for each kid to have alone time • Get headphones to help teen tune out the noise
School stress Pressure, workload		✓	It must be really stressful to hear everybody talking about how important this next year is.
Mental health Anxiety/ADHD	✓		• Ask school counselor for more support • Ask pediatrician for referral to therapist/psychiatrist covered by insurance or low fee
Puberty Mood swings		✓	It's not my kid's fault that hormones are all over the place as a teenager.
Chronic or systemic hurdles Low income, less access to things in our town		✓	These hardships are difficult for me as an adult to face; it wouldn't surprise me if it added a weight to my teen's shoulders, too.
Global events So much scary news	✓		• Limit how much the news is on • Talk about joining the fight on important causes, youth-focused groups/virtual volunteering • Give info on what people are already working on
Type of task Really hates math		✓	I also get more annoyed when I have to do jobs I hate.
Parent factors Hard time sticking to house rules when I'm tired	✓		• Pick one rule to be consistent about and commit to it for a month. Let everything else go for now.
Physical needs Always does worse when hungry	✓		• Stock pantry with bananas and granola bars so easy snacks are always there.

EXERCISE 4.5 PLAN HOW TO APPROACH CONTEXT

Context	Please put a ✓ in the column you would like to focus on:		Possible pathways out or empathizing statement
	Try to change	Build empathy	

TRACKING CAR AT HOME

Worksheet 4.1 is your opportunity to track the Context-Action-Result patterns in your home. Start by picking one or two behaviors that your teen is struggling with, as well as the replacement behavior you would like to see. For the next week, pay attention to when those behaviors occur and fill in the chart that follows. Be as specific as possible. The goal here is to become more aware of how the context and results influence your child's actions. Once you see the patterns, you can use the skills in this book to help you reshape them. In the examples, you can see how the current pattern may not be reinforcing the behavior the parent actually wants to see.

WORKSHEET 4.1

Problematic Action(s):

_____

_____

_____

Replacement Actions you would like to see:

_____

_____

_____

CONTEXT The context impacting your teen.	ACTION Teen's specific behaviors	RESULT What happens after your teen's behavior.	
		Reinforcement	Punishment
Example 1: School alarm goes off, teen had late night studying, has least favorite class 1st period	Hits snooze until I come to wake him up	I get lunch packed, drive him to school	Lecture him the whole car ride
Example 2: School alarm goes off, least favorite class 1st period	Get out of bed on time	Gets favorite breakfast	At breakfast I remind him of the chores he has when he gets home, has to take the bus (takes forever)

5

Selective Attention

Using Attention to Shape Behavior

WHAT IS SELECTIVE ATTENTION?

Chapter 4 introduced the idea that attention is reinforcing and rewarding. As social creatures, humans are constantly going to seek connection and look toward other people for feedback. Selective attention, when caregivers *select* when to give attention, is a skill that uses this idea to help encourage more appropriate choices. This happens by purposefully creating more opportunities for teens to get attention throughout the day, giving attention to skillful behaviors, and removing attention from unskillful behaviors. In other words, you are filling their attention cup, rewarding your teen with attention for being skillful, and ensuring that you do not accidentally reward unwanted behavior by focusing on it.

WHY SELECTIVE ATTENTION MATTERS

Selective attention is a hugely important skill because it sets the stage for a warm, positive relationship and lowers how often teens and caregivers feel badly about their interactions. This can help create a sense of long-term connection and reduce problem behaviors. Prioritizing selective attention can be a major shift for families who are used to focusing on inappropriate behavior, losing sight of what is going well. One common trap that caregivers fall into is assuming that "bad attention" is punishing. Parents believe that raising their voice, using a sharp tone, or repeatedly saying "no" to a teen will be *so* negative that the problem behavior will stop. This may work for some teens, but it is often not the case. This "negative" attention may not be 100% rewarding, but as long as you are engaged with your teenager, they are getting feedback (social reinforcer), stimulation (internal reinforcer), and a chance to get their way (parental reinforcer).

In fact, many people learn from a very young age that inappropriate behavior is a really good way to get attention quickly. Think back to when your teen was a toddler. There may have been times where they were playing quietly by themselves with no issues. You finally had 10 minutes of peace, so perhaps you sat down to rest or took care of some tasks around the house. Parents have limited time, so it would have made sense to shift your attention toward other things if your kids were doing fine. That's all well and good, but it is not directly rewarding for your child. Now consider times when things were not going so well. Perhaps your then-toddler hit their sibling, threw something on the ground, or started to scream. You likely came running into the room to see what was wrong. Again, this makes sense because the brain is programmed to pay attention to potential threats. Unfortunately, what happens in this sort of pattern is that a child very quickly learns that misbehaving is a quick way to get attention from their caregivers. Fast forward to the teenage years and the same sort of pattern plays out. Teens who negotiate, argue, have outbursts, or get into fights are much more likely to pull you into an interaction than the teen who simply does what they are told. For that matter, the cycle extends well into adulthood. When people keep to themselves or problem-solve without a fuss, they are rarely the first person to get their needs addressed. On the contrary, the people who make a scene or push back are much more likely to be the focus of other people's attention. That is not to say that big, giant displays of emotion do not come with some negative consequences. All it means is that being bigger, louder, or acting in unexpected ways is a fast way to get attention from others, and attention is extremely powerful.

It is important to point out, once again, that this pull for attention is not always an intentional decision on a teen's part. They are not usually plotting the best strategy to bring their parent or caregiver back into the room. Instead, over time, their brains simply pick up on the following pattern: sitting quietly does not get a reaction, but crying (or screaming, pushing, fighting, etc.) does. As the saying goes, "the squeaky wheel gets the grease."

USING SELECTIVE ATTENTION WITH YOUR TEEN

As caregivers, this reliance on attention is actually good news because you have some control over how much you respond to different behaviors. There are a few ways you are going to use selective attention to encourage more appropriate behavior:

1. *Replace negative interactions with neutral or positive ones*: When there is a problem behavior present, try hitting pause on your initial urge to focus on the bad and instead respond in a neutral or positive way.
2. *Build in attention that is not attached to behavior*: Increase the amount or quality of attention you give to your teen in general so their overall need for attention is met and they are less likely to act out as a means of getting on your radar.
3. *Give positive attention for skillful behavior*: Increase the positive interactions you have around your child's skillful behavior so you reward the behavior you want to see more of.
4. *Active ignoring*: Remove attention from the inappropriate behavior you do not want to accidentally reward.

LOWER THE NEGATIVE INTERACTION COUNT BY GOING NEUTRAL

To start shifting overall dynamics in your household, start by decreasing how many of the interactions are negative and increasing the number that are neutral. Try aiming for a 1:2 or 1:3 ratio, with one negative interaction for every two to three positive ones. For parents who have teens who are struggling, it can be easy for most conversations to focus on the bad. In fact, there often seems to be an endless list of concerns to talk through or a steady drip of problem behaviors you find yourself reacting to. For example, imagine that it is a Sunday afternoon during the school year. Your teen has been out with friends, and you know that there are chores to be done, homework to be finished, and a backpack to be packed. When your kid strolls in the front door, you have a few things going through your mind. First, you are getting pretty worried that your teen is not going to complete everything they need to. Second, you're probably a little annoyed that they have been out with friends rather than taking care of what needs to be done. Third, you know you have about 60 seconds before your teen retreats to their room and are out of contact until dinner. So you jump on the chance to voice your expectations and worries:

> *Hey, I noticed that the garbage hasn't been taken out yet. And have you finished your history essay? Once that's done, don't forget to put it in your bag along with everything else lying around the living room. I do not want to have to remind you 5 times tomorrow morning.*

You likely know how this conversation ends. Your teen will probably scoff, roll their eyes, or push back against your comments. You will feel annoyed and frustrated with your child's disrespect and lack of ownership, and your kid will wonder why they bothered coming back home in the first place. The entire thread of conversation almost guarantees a negative outcome.

One way to shift this encounter is to make good use of your caregiver coping skills. This makes it more likely for you to stay calm and collected so you do not end up in a battle. After doing that, you can try to replace your negative tone or word choices with ones that are neutral. Another option is to minimize the focus on problem behaviors and instead respond to behaviors or situations that are completely unrelated to them. Keep in mind that you don't have to push yourself to be overly cheerful or positive. Your only goal is to have an even, calm presence. Using the example from above, when your teen walks through the door, try a few low-key comments or gestures. You can say hi, look up from your phone as you wave, or maybe comment on their outfit or the drink they grab from the fridge:

> *Oh I see you're wearing the new hoodie you got last week.*
> or
> *Good to know you're drinking the milk. I'll make sure to grab more when I'm at the store.*

These are all pretty bland comments. They probably won't get much of a response out of your teen, and (on their own) won't create a major change in your relationship. Still, they serve a few important purposes.

First, neutral interactions can fill the attention cup. When you wave, say hi, notice an outfit or a choice, you are making it clear that you're paying attention. Your teen is not going to jump for joy (and may even cringe or grumble under their breath), but the attention still registers in their brain. With each neutral interaction you have, you fill the attention cup just a little bit more and decrease the need for your teen to act out to pull your focus. Keep in mind that this will be most helpful once you start to add in lots of little neutral moments through the day.

Second, neutral interactions can give caregivers and teens a break from constant fighting. While parent–teen conflict is normal for many families, it is still hard to deal with. Frequent, high-stress moments can result in families expecting the worst out of every interaction. Teenagers assume their parents will always be unhelpful, judgmental, harsh, or unfair. Parents will enter conversations predicting their kids will be dismissive, disrespectful, ungrateful, or argumentative. That's a hard mindset to live with because neither side is feeling love or support and it is draining to constantly fight. Further, when you assume the worst is coming, you tend to ignore anything that happens to go well. So, conversations that could have been okay turn into a battle because nobody will give the other person the benefit of the doubt.

Neutral interactions can start to break down this cycle by intentionally setting up non-conflict moments throughout the day. Neutral actions aren't necessarily good, and they may even feel a little bit weird at first, but they are explicitly *not bad*. There is no judgment. There is no criticism. There is no reminding your teen of that task they really hate to do. Neutral interactions are just little moments between a parent and a child that are designed to be "fine" instead of awful. If you can add in enough neutral interactions over time, you can chip away at the belief that every conversation is going to be terrible.

PUSH YOURSELF TO FIND THE POSITIVE AND ENGAGE MEANINGFULLY

A second option you have to shift the household dynamic is to replace negative interactions with ones that are intentionally positive (not just neutral). In these situations, the parent is actively working to increase the parent–child bond or create joy or meaning. In addition to the base-level attention you give during neutral interactions, you will add extra signs of engagement, support, and interest. This might include a squeeze on the shoulder as you walk by, saying a few positive words, or giving evidence of your care and consideration:

> *I hope it was really nice to see your friends.*
> *It's such a beautiful day, I'm really glad you got to go out for a little.*
> *Looking forward to hearing about your day if you have time.*

If you have a teenager who is talkative, you can focus on validating their experiences (see Chapter 6 on validation) or reflecting what they say. Reflecting is literally just summarizing or repeating back your teen's words without changing their meaning or offering a new perspective. To help understand the difference, take the following example when the parent doesn't use reflection versus when they do.

Parent not using reflection:

TEEN: The park was okay, but some of the kids just seemed so annoying.

PARENT: I'm sure they were just there to enjoy the day like everybody else.

TEEN: Yeah, they were just being dumb. They took up all the picnic tables so we couldn't sit!

PARENT: Well, I certainly hope you didn't cause any trouble.

TEEN: It just seems so obvious that they could have left space for other people.

PARENT: It sounds like you're being awfully harsh. I'm sure they weren't trying to bother anybody; try not being so negative all the time.

Parent using reflection:

TEEN: The park was okay, but some of the kids just seemed so annoying.

PARENT: Glad to hear the park was okay, except for the kids who seemed annoying.

TEEN: Yeah, they were just being dumb. They took up all the picnic tables so we couldn't sit!

PARENT: Ah, got it. It's frustrating they didn't leave any open tables.

TEEN: It just seems so obvious that they could have left space for other people.

PARENT: Right, you feel like they should have known better and been able to clear up some of the space.

As you can see, the tone in the first version of the conversation is quite different than the second. In the second, reflecting is just repeating what the teen is telling you without trying to change anything. You are simply demonstrating your full attention. What you will likely notice is that the more you reflect, the more your teen will be willing to share over time. If they are not worried about your judgment or you trying to get them to see things *your* way, it is a much lower threshold to tell you things.

Your current relationship with your child will impact whether you choose to focus on neutral interactions, positive interactions, or both. Families with higher conflict may need to start with neutral comments. After all, if you are regularly iced out by your teen and they hate being touched, then a hug or a squeeze is probably not going to help at this moment in time. Start by replacing negative interactions with neutral ones and move up from there. On the flip side, if you and your teen have a good relationship, a mix of neutral and positive interactions will help fill their attention cup and keep your bond strong.

EXERCISE 5.1 TEST YOUR KNOWLEDGE OF RESPONSES

Read through the sample statements that follow and practice identifying which responses are negative, neutral, or positive.

Selective Attention

Response Type	Statement
	Do you have to chew so loudly?
	I like that shirt you picked out.
	I see you went with the red jacket today.
	I'm heading to the drug store later, let me know if you need anything.
	I'm getting so sick of telling you to pick up after yourself.
	Why do you have to ruin the activity for everybody else?
	I overheard you studying algebra before. I've heard this unit is tricky.
	This looks like such an interesting project you're working on!
	I love when you come out with us.
	You're setting a bad example for your siblings.
	It seems like the new video game you're playing has a ton of levels.
	It's so nice that you got a little time to relax.
	If you're going to act so poorly, you're definitely not getting a later curfew.
	You have the best sense of style.
	I put your new sweater on the sofa.
	I can't believe I raised such a disrespectful child.
	I'm always amazed at how many plans you're able to keep up with.
	You know, your cousin *never* acts like this.
	I'd love to go for a walk with you if you're interested.

Exercise 5.1 ANSWER KEY Test Your Knowledge of Responses

Response Type	Statement
Negative	Do you have to chew so loudly?
Positive	I like that shirt you picked out.
Neutral	I see you went with the red jacket today.
Neutral	I'm heading to the drug store later, let me know if you need anything.
Negative	I'm getting so sick of telling you to pick up after yourself.
Negative	Why do you have to ruin the activity for everybody else?
Neutral	I overheard you studying algebra before. I've heard this unit is tricky.
Positive	This looks like such an interesting project you're working on!
Positive	I love when you come out with us.
Negative	You're setting a bad example for your siblings.
Neutral	It seems like the new video game you're playing has a ton of levels.
Positive	It's so nice that you got a little time to relax.
Negative	If you're going to act so poorly, you're definitely not getting a later curfew.
Positive	You have the best sense of style.
Neutral	I put your new sweater on the sofa.
Negative	I can't believe I raised such a disrespectful child.
Positive	I'm always amazed at how many plans you're able to keep up with.
Negative	You know, your cousin *never* acts like this.
Positive	I'd love to go for a walk with you if you're interested.

EXERCISE 5.2 TEST YOUR SKILL IN REPLACING NEGATIVE RESPONSES

On the next page is a list of all the statements from Exercise 5.1 that were negative. In Exercise 5.2, try replacing the comments with ones that are neutral or positive. Keep in mind that some of the behaviors mentioned in the comments are ones you would probably want to eventually address. That is fine, and the other chapters in this book will cover skills you can use to do that effectively. The goal of this exercise is to practice replacing negative commentary. As a reminder, doing so can help you focus on building the relationship you want with your child, while minimizing any attention they're giving directly to inappropriate behavior. Of course, there are many ways to rewrite these sentences. The answer key will outline a few different options.

Original Statement	Rewrite
Do you have to chew so loudly?	
I'm getting so sick of telling you to pick up after yourself.	
Why do you have to ruin the activity for everybody else?	
You're setting a bad example for your siblings.	
If you're going to act so poorly, you're definitely not going to get that late curfew you want.	
I can't believe I raised such a disrespectful child.	
You know, your cousin *never* acts like this.	

Exercise 5.2 ANSWER KEY Test Your Skill in Shifting Negative Responses

Original Statement	Rewrite
Do you have to chew so loudly?	I'm glad this isn't too spicy for you. I was worried I put in too much pepper.
I'm getting so sick of telling you to pick up after yourself.	There's a bin on the floor you can throw your stuff into.
Why do you have to ruin the activity for everybody else?	I know it wasn't your first choice to come, but I am still glad you're here.
You're setting a bad example for your siblings.	Your siblings look up to you so much.
If you're going to act so poorly, you're definitely not going to get that late curfew you want.	I can see this isn't your favorite activity.
I can't believe I raised such a disrespectful child.	There is a lot going on in the house right now.
You know, your cousin *never* acts like this.	Seems like there is a lot on your mind tonight.

Common Stuck Points to Neutral and Positive Interactions

Here I have listed hurdles that parents often experience when trying to shift away from negative interactions. Underneath each common stuck point, you will find tips and considerations that can help address each barrier. At the end of the chapter, you will have a chance to make note of any examples that would be helpful for you to keep in mind.

My own emotions.
Caregivers' own worry, annoyance, or frustration can easily lead to a negative remark or look. This is especially true when it comes to situations with your children, because the stakes feel so high.

→ Return to your caregiver coping skills for help managing your emotions in tough moments.

There is a sense of urgency to address problems *now*.
Many parents can feel time flying past them, and the speed seems to increase as kids get older. The sensation that time with your teen is fleeting can be uneasy. And given how often teens are in and out of the house on any given day, it's hard to know when there will be a good time for a talk. Because of this, parents can easily become overanxious and overeager during interactions with their teens, making it much more likely to go poorly.

→ For multiple reasons, when it comes to parent–teen tug-of-war battles over problem behaviors, you should consider dropping the rope and just letting some of the issues slide, at least temporarily. Usually you have somewhat more time to work through them than you think you do, and being planful rather than reactive can make those conversations go better. Additionally, for the purposes of selective attention, the aim is to limit or rework these conversations so there are fewer interactions (i.e., less attention) focused on unskillful behaviors and negative spirals. If you comment on the negative behavior every time it happens, it only amps up the reward for that behavior!

→ For readers wondering how exactly you are supposed to get your child to do things without reminding them, see the Context-Action-Result tool and Chapter 9 on reward plans. These will help you consider what situations lead to the most productive reminders and conversations, what sort of tools could replace any nagging you find yourself doing, and what rewards can encourage your child to complete tasks without as much direct nudging from you. You are not barred from ever giving your child a push, but the main idea is to be selective and strategic so you can decrease the interactions that are likely to turn negative.

> **I have a difficult time with reflection.**
> Sometimes conversations that could be neutral go south because parents struggle with reflection. Rather than simply reflecting back what a teen has said, parents hear what kids say and respond in ways that aim to solve a problem, provide a different point of view, or get the teen to change their behavior. For example:
>
> > TEEN: *The park was okay, but some of the kids just seemed so annoying.*
> >
> > PARENT [PROBLEM-SOLVING :] *Well, did you think about how you could find other areas to be away from them?*
> >
> > Or
> >
> > PARENT [DIFFERENT POINT OF VIEW :] *Oh come on sweetheart, they were probably just out having a nice time! Not everybody is annoying just because they don't cater to your every wish.*
> >
> > Or
> >
> > PARENT [ENCOURAGING DIFFERENT BEHAVIOR :] *Did you even try to introduce yourself? I think you would be a lot happier if you just tried being friendlier.*
>
> → All of these responses are understandable, but they send the message that you do not trust that your teen was able to handle the situation. Beyond that, they certainly do not prioritize the goal of strengthening your connection to your child. Cue your teen retreating to the bedroom and refusing to share more details with you.

BUILD IN ATTENTION

As noted previously, one part of selective attention involves increasing how much attention your teen gets during the day. When you give attention that is not related to any particular behavior (good or bad), you fill the attention cup and decrease their need to seek attention in problematic ways. To do this, you can use a conflict-free zone or one-on-one time.

CONFLICT-FREE ZONE

As the name suggests, a conflict-free zone is a specific time of the day where you intentionally reduce fighting by committing to a calm, low-intensity space. Think through your family's schedule and pick roughly 15 to 20 minutes when you and your teen are in the same general place in your home. Examples include the 20 minutes in the afternoon when your kids are grabbing a snack, the dinner table, or perhaps the 15 minutes before bed. The aim is to create moments of the day where you and your teen can count on neutral or positive interactions that are not linked to any specific behavior your teen is doing. It's a chance for everybody to come into a shared space without having to be on high alert for the next fight that's about to happen.

During conflict-free zone, you will still work to swap out negative responses for ones that are neutral or positive. Another good rule of thumb is to purposely avoid any hot-button topics. Things like homework, chores, house rules, and upcoming family events are all important, but are not to be raised during the conflict-free zone. It is your choice whether you tell your kids that a specific part of the day is a conflict-free zone. Some kids are eager to have reassurance that if they emerge for dinner (or your other specified time) they will not be faced with criticism or reminders about unpleasant topics. Others will not necessarily care. You know your child best and can decide what seems appropriate.

Another important factor of a conflict-free zone is that you are responsible for following the guidelines, but your teen is not. In a perfect world they will also steer clear of any hot-button topics (like extending curfew or borrowing more money), but it is not an expectation. If your teen pushes buttons, do your best to let them know you will talk about it later and stay calm (see Chapter 3 on caregiver coping). It can be very helpful to let them know a specific time when they are free to bring it up again. That way they understand you are not fully shutting the conversation down, which makes it more likely for them to accept the pause. This is especially important for teens with ADHD or anxiety, who may be so eager to talk that they struggle to let it go.

Conflict-free zone works particularly well for teens and parents who are on rocky footing. If your communication is strained, fights are frequent, and your teen is not very interested in being around you, a conflict-free zone is an excellent place to start.

ONE-ON-ONE TIME

For caregivers with teens who are more willing to spend time together, a good set up is one-on-one time where you and your teen do an activity together. One-on-one time is based on a treatment called Parent Child Interaction Therapy (PCIT), which promotes a strong relationship and appropriate behavior by allowing parents to practice responding to their child in play situations. PCIT is geared toward younger children, but many of the same ideas can be useful for teenagers with just a few changes. Like conflict-free zone, you want to aim for a short portion of your day (5–10 minutes) when you and your teen are actively engaged in an activity together while using the same guidelines as above. One-on-one time is a great chance to practice praising skillful choices and positive characteristics that you notice (more details follow). One-on-one time is a bit shorter than conflict-free zone because your teen is getting a more concentrated dose of positive attention. It is typically helpful for parents to tell their teens about one-on-one time. Make it a standard event for everybody to plan around. It often becomes a very meaningful time of the day, and you are more likely to stick with it if you know your teen is expecting it.

> **COMMON STUCK POINTS OF BUILDING IN ATTENTION**
>
> In this box is a list of obstacles that parents often experience when trying to build in attention. Underneath each common stuck point, you will find tips and considerations that can help address each barrier. At the end of the chapter, you will have a chance to make note of any examples that would be helpful for you to keep in mind.

It's hard to remember or plan for.
With so much going on each day, it can be tricky to remember conflict-free zone or one-on-one time.

- → As with anything else you plan in your life, it can be helpful to set an alarm or create a calendar alert. You can also pair it with an activity that already happens every day, like having breakfast or driving to school. If it is possible to do it at the same time each day, it will become easier to remember over time. For families who really cannot find a daily chunk of time, aim for every other day or three times a week. While this is a skill you will get more out of the more you put in, any time is better than no time.

It's hard to bite my tongue when I see inappropriate behavior!
Just because you are on your best behavior during conflict-free zone or one-on-one time, does not mean your teen is! That can make it really tempting to chime in with a reminder, redirect, or criticism.

- → When your teen says or does something annoying or frustrating, ignore it (see the section on active ignoring later in this chapter). If they become aggressive or break a house rule, you can use whatever consequence you typically would or calmly end one-on-one time and try again tomorrow.

I find myself asking lots of questions.
Adults often use questions to try to connect with teens. Unfortunately, questions can accidentally imply criticism, especially for teens who are anxious or depressed. Questions also tend to steer the conversation to things the adult cares about, instead of what the teen wants to talk about.

- → You may be genuinely curious when you ask your teen why they chose a particular scene to draw, cookie to bake, or videogame to play. But your teen may take that question to mean you do not like their choice. Swap out your question for a statement. Instead of, "You went with the chocolate chip cookies?" try "You went with the chocolate chip cookies!" The change of punctuation (and intonation) can make a big difference in how your comment is received.
- → The other good option is to replace questions by leaving some quiet space or reflecting what your teen is telling you. In either case, your teen will be more likely to start sharing what is on their mind. And if they do not want to talk at all, that's okay too! It's nice for your teen to know they can connect with you and not have to have a whole conversation.

It's impossible to find an activity we both like for one-on-one time.
Families spend a lot of time trying to compromise on an activity that both the teen and parents enjoy. That seems reasonable for a full day outing or a vacation, but a 5- to 10-minute interaction is not the time to worry about finding the perfect shared experience.

→ Let your teen take the lead. Think of this as an easy way for your teen to get a little bit more of a say in their day while sharing something they think is meaningful with you. It is quite powerful to have a parent show interest in something simply because their teen cares about it. That does not mean you have to allow activities that go against family rules or values (like extra screen time, trips to buy food outside of the family budget or lifestyle, or activities that tend to get out of control). But aside from these types of exceptions, try to let your teen decide what you do. Who cares if you have to watch that stupid viral video for the tenth time or play a board game you find boring? If doing so means your teen gets to feel your support, and you have a few moments of peace and connection, this is a fairly low cost and high reward sacrifice for you to make.

I can see one-on-one time dragging on.
For some families, one-on-one time is so nice that teens ask for more and more time. Parents often feel pulled to turn 5 minutes into 15, 20, or even 30. That quickly becomes unrealistic to do on a regular basis, and families stop offering one-on-one time all together.

→ Commit to the shorter amount of time. If you happen to have extra time on any given day, that is fine, but it is not the expectation. Do not burn out by overdoing it.

PUMP UP THE (LABELED) PRAISE

In addition to increasing your neutral and positive interactions, labeled praise is one of the core skills caregivers can use within selective attention. Labeled praise is exactly what it sounds like: you are labeling behaviors or characteristics that you appreciate or see value in. This is different than unlabeled praise, which refers to general positive statements that do not include anything specific. Examples of unlabeled praise include things like "good job," "neat," "awesome," "cool," or even "I love so much about you!" Unlabeled praise is lovely. It can lead to a nice, positive interaction. Parents do not have to feel pressured to constantly identify each and every thing thing they love about their child.

That said, unlabeled praise does not give your teen much (if any) information about what behavior or characteristic you are so happy about. Since they have no idea what they did well, they have no way of knowing what to do more of. This applies to adults at work too. If your boss tells you that you're "doing a good job" during your end of year review that is great, but it does not exactly tell you what (if anything) is helping you stand out or get to the next step of your career. Just like it is helpful for you to know your specific strengths at work, labeled praise becomes really important when you are trying to help your child improve in specific areas.

You can label praise lots of things, including specific behaviors or choices, things that your teen has created, ways they see or process information, or characteristics that they seem to embody. Here are a few examples:

- *I really appreciate you texting me when you got to your friend's house.*
- *Thank you so much for listening the first time I asked.*
- *Awesome job getting up and ready for school on time this morning.*
- *That is such a cool piece of art you made.*
- *It's really quite special how well you are able to read other people. You have a real ability to know how people are feeling, no matter what situation you are in.*
- *I love how willing you are to support other people who need extra help.*
- *I'm so amazed at how independent you're becoming.*

Labeled praise is useful for a few reasons. As mentioned above, it tells your teen exactly what they are doing well and what they can continue to do to get positive feedback. It also creates a road map that your child can follow in the future. Each time you use labeled praise for the behavior, you are placing another brick in the pathway. The next time your teen's brain is eager for a dose of attention or feedback, they have a whole series of bricks pointing them in the right direction. Any parent who has ever had a good performance review at work knows that positive feedback helps keep you on track.

On the flip side, parents who have had job reviews also know how demoralizing it is to only get criticism without being acknowledged for the positives. This applies to teenagers as well. It is important and motivating for teens to know that their parents are noticing appropriate steps in the right direction. All too often, teenagers are making a genuine effort to improve in certain ways but find that those efforts go unnoticed. This often occurs because they are making some progress while struggling in other areas at the same time. When this happens, parents tend to focus on the parts that are falling behind. Teens feel like there's no point in trying because nobody seems to notice, and their efforts will never be enough. This is especially likely to play out for teens with mental health difficulties because they are more likely to doubt their own abilities, and the effort they need to overcome symptoms can be highly punishing.

Labeled praise is also useful in that it is a really strong dose of focused attention. Everyone can tell when someone is really paying attention instead of phoning it in. Imagine chatting with your teen on the way home for their soccer game. You know there's a major difference between when you give a vague compliment like "Wow, that was really great, honey" versus when you look them in the eye and describe each of their amazing contributions in detail: "Oh my gosh, you worked SO hard till the very end! I could see that the one striker was really trying to outpace you, but you did such a great job of staying with them. That last steal of yours was amazing!" That's the kind of comment and enthusiasm that will stick with your teenager long after the day has passed.

LABELED PRAISE IS FOREVER

When you notice appropriate behavior and remember to praise in real time, you are giving your teen immediate feedback that clearly links their skillful behavior to a rewarding outcome. That is great. But one of the other nice things about labeled praise is that you can use it whenever you remember to, even if the moment has passed. Maybe over the weekend your teenager really did a good job of keeping their distance from their moody older brother and was super flexible when it came to the schedule. Perhaps you didn't think much of it at the time, but come Monday morning you reflect on how skillful they were. Monday afternoon when they come home from school, you can absolutely circle back to their behavior from over the weekend:

> *By the way, I noticed what an awesome job you did giving your brother extra space this weekend. I really appreciate your willingness to just go with the flow.*

Labeled praise after the fact can be very meaningful because it shows that you were *so* impressed that you're still thinking about the behavior a few hours or days later. Remember this, and make sure you do not pass over opportunities to label praise just because you didn't use it right away.

PRAISE THE EXPECTED

For caregivers of teens with mental health difficulties, praise can be hard. Sometimes there is so much difficult behavior happening in the household that is tricky to spot behaviors that seem worthy of praise. And sure, it would be easier to praise behavior that was really above and beyond, like your teen cleaning the whole house or making you breakfast in bed. But it is harder to praise behavior that you, or society as a whole, expects from all teens by default, like getting homework done. If you feel like you can never find any behavior worthy of praise, make a list of behaviors that you think most kids should be doing. This might include accepting parental decisions, getting to school on time, answering questions in class, asking for help, or even getting through the day without aggression. Then review the CAR acronym from Chapter 4. Remember all the different contextual factors, including symptoms, that impact your child and make it difficult for them to function. It is likely difficult for them to do things like accept your decisions calmly or ask for help without considerable effort. When you keep that in mind, it starts to feel much more reasonable to praise those behaviors.

AVOID FALSE APPRECIATION

Note, you should not praise behaviors or traits that are truly not present. Imagine your child is in the middle of a yelling, screaming rampage that is the worst you've ever seen. It is not helpful to say, "Thank you so much for trying to be skillful" when they are clearly *not* trying to be skillful. It will not feel genuine. Your kid will know that you are lying, and it will undermine the faith they have in everything else you say. You can, however, praise behavior that is a step in the right direction, even if it isn't perfect. So when your kid is having the yelling, screaming rampage but you notice they are trying to take a deep breath or manage to calm themselves down a little more quickly than normal, it is totally appropriate to say, "Hey, thank you so much for trying to calm yourself down." Paying attention to the steps they are taking to improve is meaningful; just don't make up stuff that isn't there.

USE PRAISE TO KEEP YOUR TEEN ON TRACK

One of the best uses of labeled praise is to keep an interaction positive when you can tell it is about to take a nosedive. This works when you notice your teen is starting to become a little agitated but is still showing some appropriate behavior. Many times, parents ignore what's going well and end up commenting only when their kid crosses the line. For example, you and your teen are in a back-and-forth negotiation and at some point they finally snap and yell at you. You say, "I cannot believe we are doing this again. You are not allowed to speak to me that way." As soon as that happens, this conversation falls into the negative interaction category, and you've accidentally given attention for behavior you didn't want to see.

An alternative option is to sneak in some labeled praise before your kid hits their breaking point. As you are negotiating back and forth, your overly persistent teen may at least be listening to what you have to say before jumping in. That is your opportunity to label praise: "I appreciate that you're able let me finish my thoughts so we're not talking over each other." Not only did you just show recognition for what your teen is doing well (see page 71 for benefits), but you have also primed their brain to stay on track by drawing attention to appropriate behavior. It's almost like a little thought bubble popping up in your teen's head saying, "Oh, that's right, I'm letting my parent finish their sentences right now!" This is most effective when your teen is still relatively calm. If they are inches away from their boiling point, this sort of praise may backfire and lead to your kid doing the exact opposite of what you want just to prove a point. Use your judgment, but do not be afraid to try it out a few times!

TAILOR PRAISE TO FIT YOUR TEEN

As with anything else, praise is not a one-size-fits-all skill. Teenagers have different styles and preferences, and families have different patterns that they have fallen into. Some teenagers are really uncomfortable with praise when they first hear it. Here are a few common reasons why this might be the case (circle any that you think might be true of your household):

- A teen is used to getting more criticism than positive feedback.
- The family as a whole does not often express appreciation or recognition.
- The teen or caregiver struggles to talk openly about emotions or express their love or support verbally.
- A teen might have such a low self-image that praise is difficult to believe.
- Higher anxiety teenagers may find praise scary because they think it sets up higher expectations for their behavior next time.

In these instances, teens often respond to praise by ignoring it, dismissing it as "no big deal," or even asking their parents why they are being so weird. Do not let this initial reaction throw you off course. While it might feel odd at first, this is likely about the discomfort that comes up when people change their habits. It takes some getting used to! At the same time, it is okay to be mindful of your word choice and tone so the praise lands a little better. This may mean swapping out a bright, cheerful tone for one that is more reserved and serious. Your words can be brief and to the point, instead of overflowing and flowery. And you may even express your appreciation via text or sticky note on the bedroom door.

If you make all of these adjustments and are still getting major pushback after a few weeks, it may be time to do some additional exploring. You can try to ask your teen if there is anything in particular they do not like about praise. If they know and are willing to tell you, you can talk with them about their feelings or try to shift how you praise to meet your teen where they are at. If they do not know ("I don't know, I just don't like it!") or do not feel comfortable telling you, think about whether any of the stuck points below might be impacting your delivery or use of praise.

COMMON STUCK POINTS OF LABELED PRAISE

In this box is a list of hurdles that parents often encounter when trying to use labeled praise. Underneath each common stuck point, you will find tips and considerations that can help address each barrier. At the end of the chapter, you will have a chance to make note of any examples that would be helpful for you to keep in mind.

My own emotions during difficult times.
It is hard to point out positives when you are anxious that your teen is going to fail out of high school, angry that they provoked their sibling for no reason, or numb from all of the chaos happening around you.

→ If this sounds familiar, review Chapter 3 to help you stay emotionally balanced and make better use of this skill.

Praise is not something I ever got or does not align with my background.
Many caregivers note that they struggle with praise because it is not something they grew up with or is actively minimized in their culture. This is a very common experience, and you as the parent are allowed to make choices about which skills align with your own parental style and values.

→ If you find yourself hesitating to praise for either of these reasons, Chapter 6 explores these factors in much greater detail. Feel free to skip ahead to that section to consider whether praise is in line with your long-term goals for yourself and your teenager.
→ In the meantime, know that lots of research shows praise and positive attention to be very useful in improving relationships and shaping better behavior. Even for behaviors that people "should" do, acknowledgment is important. Consider your life as a parent. A core part of your job is to help make sure your teen's basic needs are met. Even though having food in the house is "expected" for a parent, it is awfully nice when your teenager says

thank you for stocking the snacks they like or getting dinner on the table. Will you boycott if you don't get thanked? Probably not. Does it make you feel a whole lot better about how much energy and effort you put in? Absolutely. Kids are the same.

I notice that my praise is often followed by a corrective comment or redirection. For example, "You are so kind when you want to be. Too bad you can't treat your brother that way." Or "You're GREAT at math, so why don't you sit down and take care of it now."

→ Teens are smart, and they will notice if praise just becomes a means to an end. If you accidentally fall into this pattern, work to give praise separate from any additional comments or instructions.

My praise feels forced.
It can be easy for praise to sound fake. This can partly be addressed by tone, but a more serious issue pops up when parents are attempting to praise something good while internally focusing on the bad. For example, you find it ridiculous to praise your kid for putting away their laundry, but you're trying to follow the book's suggestions, so you grit your teeth and say "thank you for cleaning up" anyways. Your effort is appreciated, but your kid may see through to your angst.

→ If you notice this happening, go back to the CAR acronym and review all of the factors your child has to contend with. Then really consider what behaviors on their part you *do* appreciate. You don't have to praise for putting away the laundry, but maybe you can show genuine appreciation for their willingness to take the initiative some days, or their ability to be considerate of your preferences.

My teen is convinced that I only praise them because I have to as their parent.
This comes up all the time, especially when teens are depressed or have low self-esteem. Teenagers do not believe the positive things their parents tell them because they think their parents HAVE to love them, and therefore cannot be truthful.

→ If this is happening in your household, an honest conversation can be helpful and appropriate. You can acknowledge that yes, as a parent, you may be somewhat biased to some of your child's strengths and will adore and love them no matter what. That does not mean you are blind to their faults, and perhaps may be even more aware of them than other people because you want so badly for their lives to go well. Also, praise is useful for everybody, not just teens, and it is something you like to use in general. In other words, "you're not that special, kid." Praise is good for everybody, and you're not to STOP praising them just because they think you're giving them special treatment.

EXERCISE 5.3 TEST YOUR KNOWLEDGE OF LABELED PRAISE

Read through the sample statements that follow. Next to each, note whether the comment sounds like Labeled Praise, Unlabeled Praise, or Not Praise. Check your responses with the answer key that follows.

Selective Attention

Statement	Labeled Praise, Unlabeled Praise, Not Praise
You're doing a great job sitting quietly through the service.	
I love you SO much!	
Thank you for listening. If only you did that *every* time . . .	
Your friends are so nice.	
You are so good at building things!	
I appreciate it that you keep me posted when your plans change.	
[at teen's event] Nice job!	
It's too bad you aren't doing as well this semester as you did last semester. You used to be so good at getting your homework done.	
[teen shares food] Thank you!	
I know you want more responsibility, but can't you just take no for an answer? You wouldn't be in this mess if you had listened.	
It's so great that you're so organized.	
[reads over teen's essay] Nice . . . nice . . . good.	
Do you really need to show me that video *again*?	
Every single time you bake you leave the kitchen a total mess.	
You have an awfully long list of colleges you're thinking about.	
I can see how hard you're trying this year and it means a lot.	
[teen turns on playlist] I like this song.	

Exercise 5.3 ANSWER KEY Test Your Knowledge of Labeled Praise

Statement	Labeled Praise, Unlabeled Praise, Not Praise
You're doing a great job sitting quietly through the service.	Labeled Praise
I love you SO much!	Unlabeled Praise
Thank you for listening. If only you did that *every* time . . .	Not Praise
Your friends are so nice.	Not Praise
You are so good at building things!	Labeled Praise
I appreciate it that you keep me posted when your plans change.	Labeled Praise
[at teen's event] Nice job!	Unlabeled Praise
It's too bad you aren't doing as well this semester as you did last semester. You used to be so good at getting your homework done.	Not Praise
[teen shares food] Thank you!	Unlabeled Praise
I know you want more responsibility, but why can't you take no for an answer? You wouldn't be in this mess if you had listened.	Not Praise
It's so great that you're so organized.	Labeled Praise
[reads over teen's essay] Nice . . . nice . . . good.	Unlabeled Praise
Do you really need to show me that video *again*?	Not Praise
Every single time you bake you leave the kitchen a total mess.	Not Praise
I can see how hard you're trying this year and it means a lot.	Labeled Praise
You are such a considerate person.	Labeled Praise

TESTING YOUR SKILL WITH LABELED PRAISE

In Exercise 5.4 is a list of all the statements from Exercise 5.3 that were examples of Unlabeled Praise or Not Praise. In this next exercise, try rewriting the comments as labeled praise. Keep in mind that in your real-life interactions, not *all* praise has to be labeled. Further, some of the behaviors mentioned in the comments are ones you would want to eventually address. That is fine, and the other chapters in this book will cover skills you can use to do that. The goal of this exercise is just to have you practice labeled praise. Of course, there are many ways to rewrite these sentences. The answer key will outline a few different options.

EXERCISE 5.4 TESTING YOUR SKILL WITH LABELED PRAISE

Statement	Labeled Praise Version
I love you SO much!	
Thank you for listening the first time I asked. If only you did that *every* time . . .	
Your friends are so nice.	
[at teen's event] Nice job!	
It's too bad you aren't doing as well this semester as you did last semester. You used to be so good at getting your homework done.	
[teen shares food] Thank you!	
I know you want more responsibility, but why can't you just take no for an answer? You wouldn't be in this mess if you had just listened.	
[reads over teen's essay] Nice . . . nice . . . good.	
Do you really need to show me that video *again*?	
Every single time you bake you leave the kitchen a total mess.	

Exercise 5.4 ANSWER KEY Testing Your Skill with Labeled Praise

Statement	Labeled Praise Version
I love you SO much!	You are so creative and I love that so much.
Thank you for listening the first time I asked. If only you did that *every* time	Thank you for listening the first time I asked!
Your friends are so nice.	Your friends are so nice and it is such a great reflection of what a good kid you are.
[at teen's performance] Nice job!	You played your solo so beautifully!
It's too bad you aren't doing as well this semester as you did last semester. You used to be so good at getting your homework done.	I have seen how organized and focused you can be with homework.
[teen shares food] Thank you!	Thank you for sharing!
I know you want to do your own thing, but why can't you just take no for an answer? You wouldn't be in this mess if you had just listened.	I admire how much you want to try things out on your own.
[reads over teen's essay] Nice . . . nice . . . good.	This is really well organized . . . I can tell you put a lot of time and effort into this.
Do you really need to show me that video *again*?	It's very sweet that you want to share this.
Every single time you bake you leave the kitchen a total mess.	What a nice idea to keep yourself busy this afternoon.

SUMMING UP POSITIVE ATTENTION AND LABELED PRAISE

You should now have a good sense of what positive attention and labeled praise look like, and different ways to build them into the thread of your household. These tools will almost always be your first line of defense when new problem behaviors emerge. For all the reasons outlined previously, these strategies are instrumental in preserving your relationship with your child, building their self-esteem, and making it more likely for them to follow through on appropriate, skillful choices. Once you finish this chapter and read through the rest of the book, you can return to this section as often as you need to refresh your skills. It is common for caregivers to let praise and attention fall by the wayside as they start to work on other skills. However, you should really increase your positive attention when you try out other skills, not decrease it. The warmth and support your teen gets from positive attention and praise creates the solid foundation on which the other strategies can work. Without it, the other strategies in this book may lead to short-term change with a long-term negative impact on your relationship.

ACTIVE IGNORING

If positive attention is one side of the coin, active ignoring is the other. Active ignoring is when you purposefully turn your focus away from problem behaviors as if you have no clue they are happening. Because attention is reinforcing, you want to remove that reward from behaviors that you do not want to see. When you actively ignore, you will remove both verbal (talking, negotiating, yelling, joking, laughing, scoffing, grunting, sighing, etc.) and nonverbal responses (eye contact, smiling or frowning, crossed arms, an eyebrow raise, shaking your head, looking out the corner of your eyes, making a face). This can be somewhat confusing to parents, who feel like if they repeatedly say no or provide just the right explanation, a teenager will finally get the point and change their ways. Unfortunately, this doesn't usually work. As long as you are responding to them, there is a chance the teen will get what they want, and it is worth their time to continue the behavior. With active ignoring, you are acting like a brick wall—the kid can keep going, but will get absolutely nothing back and eventually stop trying.

Active ignoring is an appropriate strategy to use for behaviors that are minor, attention-seeking, or attention-maintained. Attention-seeking behaviors are ones that your teen does to get some sort of response out of you. Attention-maintained behaviors are ones that might be happening for other reasons but end up being rewarded by your attention. Take cursing, for example. Many teens curse because they a) are upset and frustrated; b) hear it from friends, media, or adults; and c) are not skillful enough to communicate in more appropriate ways. In moments of stress, a person's brain tends to slip into patterns they have seen over and over again and do not require much effort. The first few times your teenager curses, it may purely be about the fact that they are upset and frustrated, and this is a default way to express it. However, many parents end up responding to the cursing. They gasp, yell back, or lecture. When this happens, parents have accidentally given attention to the cursing behavior. The teen's brain now knows, "Hey, cursing is a pretty good way to get your parents' attention. The next time you feel like getting under their skin, go ahead and throw in a few curse words!" Oops. Parents accidentally rewarded cursing, so even though it may have started because the teen was upset, there is now an added bonus of parental attention.

In some cases, you may find that ignoring does not entirely solve the problem because the teen is rewarded in other ways, like when friends think they are hilarious or teachers take the bait and get into a control battle. In these instances, parents may choose to pair active ignoring on their end with an added reward for using appropriate language or punishment for hearing about inappropriate language (see Chapter 9 on consequence options).

It can be helpful to think about whether a behavior is purely attention-seeking versus attention-maintained. Attention-seeking behavior will most likely go away completely when you use active ignoring. Attention-maintained behaviors will decrease and become less intense when you use active ignoring. However, they may not go away 100% because they are happening, in part, to serve some other purpose (like expressing anger). To fully eliminate those behaviors, you may have to use active ignoring plus some of the other strategies in this book (like praising calm communication, providing rewards for appropriate language, or punishment for inappropriate language). Active ignoring does not work immediately, and behavior often gets worse in the short term before it gets better. If you plan for this (see tips on next page on managing an "extinction burst"), you will be in good shape to make use of this highly effective tool.

As noted before, active ignoring is useful for minor behaviors, such as nagging, negotiating, name calling, insulting, eye-rolling, scoffing, stomping away, or tossing a pillow or piece of paper. All of these are problematic but are relatively small in the grand scheme of teen mental health difficulties. Caregivers should *not* use active ignoring for behaviors that are unsafe for the teen or others. When safety is in question, parents should do what is needed to keep everyone involved out of harm's way. If you are concerned about the safety of your child or others in the home, speak to your teen's pediatrician or a mental health provider.

Every parent has a threshold for behaviors that they can and can't ignore. For example, some caregivers might be fine ignoring a teen who throws a pillow in their direction out of anger. Other caregivers might find that to be unsafe because the zipper could hit somebody in the eye or break something in the apartment. You get to decide what you count as unsafe. Just keep in mind that many behaviors (like throwing a pillow) occur to get a response out of parents, so responding to them may make them get worse over time until you pair your responses with a strong consequence (see Chapter 9).

Active ignoring will not work for behaviors that have nothing to do with your attention. When your teen doesn't clear their dishes from the table, it's possible they get a little pleasure out of your annoyance, but mostly they just don't feel like moving. When they won't get off their video game, it's because they're having fun (and not just to make you mad). You can certainly ignore it, but it's unlikely to change those behaviors in any real way. That said, there are many behaviors that happen once you insist on them clearing the table or turning off the game that *are* about your attention: whining, complaining, negotiating . . . all ignorable. There is absolutely no need to get into a back and forth about behavior that is purely designed to express their discontent and get a response out of you.

Common Stuck Points of Active Ignoring

The barriers to active ignoring are almost universal. Read through the list of obstacles parents experience when trying to use active ignoring. Underneath each common stuck point, you will find tips and considerations that can help address each barrier. At the end of the chapter, you can make note of any examples that would be helpful for you to keep in mind.

I can't keep ignoring the problem behavior when it gets worse.
The term "extinction burst" refers to behavior that gets worse before it gets better, and it commonly happens when you are trying to get rid of a behavior. You should expect this to happen when you start to ignore your teen's attention-seeking or attention-maintained behaviors. A good example of this is when a teen wants extra screen time and complains until they get it. It is likely that over the last several years, they have learned that if they whine long enough or yell loudly enough, their parents will give in and agree to the extra screen time. "Great," their brain learns, "I have this awesome strategy to get what I want!" Maybe at some point the parents have had enough, and they decide to ignore the teenage temper tantrum, choosing to pretend not to notice when their teen starts to nag and beg. That teen's brain is confused. "Huh," it thinks, "That's weird. This usually really works for me. Maybe I didn't scream loud enough! Maybe my pitch wasn't high enough! Let's try that and see what happens!" In other words, that teen is not going to abandon a perfectly good strategy just because it didn't happen to work this time, leading the complaining to jump from a level 6 to a level 8. When this happens, the parents think active ignoring did not work, and they give up. Or maybe once the teen's volume jumps from a level 6 to a level 8, the parents simply cannot take it and hand over the iPad. Unfortunately, they accidentally just taught the teen to go straight to level 8 next time. That is obviously not the goal, so you want to be prepared!

→ While an extinction burst may make you feel like active ignoring isn't working, just the opposite is true: an increase in the problem behavior proves how much it is linked to your attention, so it is more about getting over the hurdle than anything else. If the parents continue to ignore the burst each time the teen asks for more screen time, eventually the teen's brain will pick up on the fact that it is no longer an effective strategy and there is no point in continuing to yell about it. This is often a really trying period for parents, but keep in mind that these patterns have often taken weeks, months and sometimes even years to develop. It should not take years to undo them, but it certainly takes more than one or two trials of ignoring before a new behavior kicks in. In the meantime, make use of parent coping skills to try to keep your cool (see Chapter 3 on caregiver coping).

→ The other tip is to start by practicing active ignoring with mildly annoying behaviors instead of ones that make your blood boil. That way, when the extinction burst happens and the behavior starts to get a little bit worse, you'll still be able to stick to that ignoring and ride it out until it goes away.

As you get better at active ignoring, you can start using it for the behaviors that really get under your skin.

I take my teen's reactions personally.
Beyond extinction bursts, active ignoring can be difficult because some teenagers become extremely upset when their parents remove attention. They may follow you around the house, insist you don't love them, or ask why you keep ignoring them. They may complain that you never listen and don't care if they get better. This can be truly gut wrenching to listen to.

→   There are a few things to remember in these moments. First, your teen is responding that intensely because they care so deeply about your attention. Second, you are very literally not abandoning them and *of course* you love them. While it may be tempting to respond to these claims and list all the ways you adore and support them—do your best to resist. Your teen is safe, loved, and supported. You are simply unwilling to interact with them when they are behaving inappropriately or unskillfully. That is okay. In fact, it is more than okay—it is important! Teens are absolutely allowed to have big emotional responses, but they also need to learn how to manage those emotions in ways that do not hurt other people or get in the way of their lives. Active ignoring is a valuable lesson in that. Once your teen has calmed down, you can return attention and address any concerns they raised. Also remember, with all the positive attention and labeled praise, there are many opportunities for you to show them your love and appreciation throughout the day, so they should have tons of evidence of this outside of their outbursts.

I feel like I'm abandoning my distressed child.
Some teenager behaviors are very off-putting, like yelling, interrupting, or making demands. Others are more heartbreaking. Teenagers who cry, ask for extra help, or seek reassurance repeatedly are clearly distraught and more obviously looking for support. Many parents find these behaviors extremely exhausting to live with but feel bad if they do not respond.

→   While seeking *some* support is appropriate, anxious kids often overrely on parents to be the calming, fix-it presence and never have the chance to learn those skills themselves. For this reason, active ignoring is still an appropriate option. If you are worried about your teen feeling unsupported by you, you can let them know what the plan is ahead of time:

   I am here for you, but I think my reassurance may actually be making things worse because you never get to see what you can manage on your own! I am team you, and not team anxiety. So from now on, I will answer your questions only once.

Then, when the moment comes and they begin to seek reassurance or a solution, you can answer them one time (just like you said you would). If they continue to ask (which they likely will), you can either completely ignore, or give them one reminder:

I do not think my answers are helping, so I am going to stop responding. I'm happy to keep talking if you want to talk about something else.

At this point, ignoring must kick in. If one reminder turns into four, you are still giving lots of attention to the unhelpful behavior and it will get worse and worse over time.

I worry I'm sending the wrong message.
Some parents really struggle with the idea of active ignoring because they worry that by saying nothing, it looks like they're okay with the behavior. This is especially common for problem behaviors like cursing and disrespectful language.

→ Keep in mind that teens are saying or doing those things because they are upset and do not have better skills *or* because they know the behavior is not okay and want to make you mad. If the teens simply lack more skillful behavior, your best bet would be to reward a more skillful choice rather than commenting on the cursing each time it happens (see Chapter 9). If the teen knows the behavior isn't okay, commenting on it will only make them feel like they've won! Emotionally, it is completely reasonable for parents to feel conflicted about whether or not to say anything about problem behaviors. Practically, it is usually not in your favor to do so (at least not in the moment). If commenting was going to work, the problem behaviors would be gone by now.

→ If you feel like you must address a problem behavior, just do so at a different time. Your teachable moment will land better later in the day or the next morning, without risking the in-the-moment satisfaction your teen gets by getting a reaction from you.

Ignoring makes me feel like I have lost control of the situation.
Parents are sometimes concerned that if they walk away, the teen will think they are in control.

→ Teens can think that all they want, but it does not make it true. In most families with teenagers, parents provide everything for their kids. They have power in almost every way that really matters. In moments of conflict, if your teen's behavior is so frustrating that you are sucked into a debate: How much control are you really holding onto at that point? Active ignoring is truly such a power move. You are so in control of your emotions, so in charge of the situation, you can rise above the angst and move on with your day. No more tug-o-war. *Just drop the rope.*

TEST YOUR KNOWLEDGE OF ACTIVE IGNORING

In Exercise 5.5 is a list of teen behaviors that commonly happen during difficult moments. Next to each, put a check or an ✗ to indicate if ignoring would be an appropriate strategy to try to reduce the behavior over time. If not, include why it would not be appropriate. As a reminder, active ignoring is effective for minor attention-seeking or attention-maintained behaviors. It is not appropriate to use for unsafe behaviors or behaviors that are not related to your attention.

EXERCISE 5.5 TEST YOUR KNOWLEDGE OF ACTIVE IGNORING

Behavior	✓ or ✗ (unsafe/not about attention)
Eye-rolling	
Negotiating	
Staying out too late	
Turning the music too loud	
Hitting a sibling hard	
Cursing	
Complaining	
Repeatedly tapping your foot under the table	
Interrupting	
Leaving dirty laundry on the floor	
Sulking	
Threatening to hurt themself	
Sneaking money from your wallet	
Grabbing a sharp object in anger	
Mean language	
Slamming the door	
Eating your leftovers	
Throwing a book on the floor	
Throwing a book at you	
Taking the car keys without asking	

Exercise 5.5 ANSWER KEY Test Your Knowledge of Active Ignoring

Behavior	✓ or ✗ (unsafe/not about attention)
Eye-rolling	✓
Negotiating	✓
Staying out too late	✗ (not about attention)
Turning the music too loud	✗ (not about attention)
Hitting a sibling hard	✗ (unsafe)
Cursing	✓
Complaining	✓
Repeatedly tapping your foot under the table	✓
Interrupting	✓
Leaving dirty laundry on the floor	✗ (not about attention)
Sulking	✓
Threatening to hurt themself	✗ (unsafe)
Sneaking money from your wallet	✗ (not about attention)
Grabbing a sharp object in anger	✗ (unsafe)
Mean language	✓
Slamming the door	✓
Eating your leftovers	✗ (not about attention)
Throwing a book on the floor	✓
Throwing a book at you	✗ (unsafe)
Taking the car keys without asking	✗ (not about attention)

PRACTICE YOUR SKILLS OF ACTIVE IGNORING IN THE REAL WORLD

In other chapters of this book, a Test Your Skills exercise includes reworking unskillful caregiver responses into ones that are more skillful. But in active ignoring, the most skillful response is zero response, so there is nothing to rewrite or rephrase as a form of practice. Instead, try practicing active ignoring in your own life with people who are not your teenager. You can have a partner or friend pretend to be your teenager talking to you. Try to catch yourself before responding to some sort of inappropriate behavior or comment. Practice actively ignoring that annoying coworker or nosy neighbor. If there is nobody to practice with (or on), watch a TV show or movie with teenagers. Make a mental note of each time there is a behavior that could be ignored. Envision what ignoring looks like for you. What are you doing with your hands and face? What tasks are you turning your attention toward? All of this helps to build that active ignoring muscle and gives you a chance to see what the skill looks and feels like for you.

THE EBB AND FLOW OF ATTENTION AND IGNORING

When you first start to practice selective attention, it is often a good idea to practice one piece at a time. Spend a week or two working on neutral responses, then one-on-one time or conflict-free zone, then add in labeled praise, and eventually move onto active ignoring. Each skill has its own roadblocks and can take time to master. Once you begin to get comfortable with each part of selective attention, you will start to add them together. This is where the magic really happens. As your positive attention and active ignoring become more automatic, you will be able to flip your attention switch off and on, off and on, when it makes sense. This is very useful, since teenagers are often doing some appropriate and inappropriate things at the same exact time. In these moments, you are going to turn the attention away from inappropriate behavior and focus entirely on the things that they are doing well. Imagine you have asked your teenager to put their shoes in their bedroom. They roll their eyes and complain about how annoying you are while carrying their shoes into the bedroom. What do you do?

Option 1: Raise your voice and remind them that they do not speak to their parent that way in this household!
Option 2: Tell them that if that's how they are going to act, they can start cleaning up the rest of the living room until they learn to control their attitude.
Option 3: Say nothing and go back to reading your book.
Option 4: Praise them for putting their things away and ignore everything else.

While the urge to go with option one and two might be strong, they are unlikely to lead to the result that you want. The second you respond to your teen's attitude, they're going to drop their shoes, whip their head around, and continue the fight: "UGH! THIS IS EXACTLY WHAT I MEAN! YOU ARE SO CONTROLLING!" Not only are you both about to say some things you might regret later, but you got in the way of your own goal! Shoes are on the floor (not in the bedroom), and the chances of them being put away are dropping with each word being said.

Option three isn't bad here. If you simply move on with your night without giving any attention to the attitude, those sorts of statements will probably go down over time. But

Selective Attention

number four is the real winner. You will do a lot for both your relationship with your child and their willingness to follow directions if you calmly respond that you appreciate them putting their things away, especially when they had other stuff they wanted to be doing. Let go of everything else, and you avoid a fight you did not really want to have anyways. If your teen is really mad, you'll still probably get a grunt or an eye-roll (both ignorable). But the labeled praise will still have an effect, and you haven't done anything to chip away at your relationship with your teenager. Over the course of any interaction you have with your teen, you can use your attention mindfully. You may briefly shut it down if they start to act up, negotiate, or complain, and reengage once they've moved on. It will be such a weight off your shoulders when you give yourself permission to let some of these (very normal) teen behaviors go and focus on what is going well.

EXERCISE 5.6 TEST YOUR KNOWLEDGE BY PUTTING IT ALL TOGETHER

In Exercise 5.6 is a sample scene of a teenager and parent interacting in the morning. In this example, the parent has a mix of helpful and unhelpful responses. Put a check next to each parent response that is skillful and an ✗ where the parent response misses the mark somehow. Then, see if you can label the skill or identify the general stuck point.

As a reminder, here are some of the skills to watch out for: neutral or positive response, conflict-free zone, one-on-one time, labeled praise, active ignoring.

And here are some of the stuck points to watch out for: negative comments, hot-button topics, difficulty reflecting, missed opportunity for time together, missed opportunity to praise, attending to inappropriate behavior.

✓ or ✗	Statement	Skill/Stuck Point
	Parent (P): Bus is leaving in 15 minutes. You gotta move more quickly packing up your stuff so you don't miss it.	
	13-year-old (13): I'm going as fast as I can.	
	P: Doesn't look like it to me. I see a lot of time spent checking your phone.	
	13: [rolls eyes] What, are you spying on me now?	
	P: I'm not spying you, I'm literally standing right next to you. How could I not see you on your phone?	
	13: Whatever.	
	P: I have a few extra minutes, so if there's time we can talk about plans for your birthday.	
	13: I reeeally want to go out to dinner with my friends.	
	P: I think that's a great idea! Good thinking.	
	13: So I really want to— [gets interrupted]	
	P: Wait! Finish packing! You always get so distracted.	
	13: Ugh, you brought it up! [finishes packing] Okay I'm done! Can we talk about the dinner plan now?	
	P: Yes, but first I want you to know that I really think you should have your little sister come.	
	13: What!? No! It's my birthday with my friends. I don't want her there! She is always bugging me.	

Selective Attention

✓ or ✗	Statement	Skill/Stuck Point
	P: Well you know she just wants to hang out with you so badly! It's really not that bad, it's kind of sweet when you think about it.	
	13: It's not sweet, it's annoying. I don't want her there.	
	P: Okay fine, she doesn't have to come. But I think you're being a little mean.	
	13: I'm being mean!? You always take her side! You're SO annoying. Ugh.	
	P: Okay miss, I think that's enough.	
	13: Fine, I don't want to talk about it anyways. I have to go.	
	P: On your way out the door, don't forget to grab the garbage and put it out.	
	13: FINE! [stomps away with garbage and backpack]	
	P: No need for all the attitude!	

Exercise 5.6 ANSWER KEY Test Your Knowledge by Putting It All Together

✓ or ✗	Statement	Skill/Stuck Point
✗	Parent (P): Bus is leaving in 15 minutes. You gotta move more quickly packing up your stuff so you don't miss it.	Missed opportunity for praise
	13-year-old (13): I'm going as fast as I can.	
✗	P: Doesn't look like it to me. I see a lot of time spent checking your phone.	Negative comments
	13: [rolls eyes] What, are you spying on me now?	
✗	P: I'm not spying on you, I'm literally standing right next to you. How could I not see you on your phone?	Attending to inappropriate behavior; negative comments
	13: Whatever.	
✓	P: I have a few extra minutes, so if there's time we can talk about plans for your birthday.	Neutral response, one-on-one time
	13: I reeeally want to go out to dinner with my friends.	
✓	P: I think that's a great idea! Good thinking.	Labeled praise
	13: So I really want to— [gets interrupted]	
✗	P: Wait! Finish packing! You always get so distracted.	Negative comments
✓	13: Ugh, you brought it up! [finishes packing] Okay I'm done! Can we talk about the dinner plan now?	Active ignoring
✗	P: Yes, but first I want you to know that I really think you should have your little sister come.	Hot-button topics

Selective Attention

✓ or ✗	Statement	Skill/Stuck Point
	13: What!? No! It's my birthday with my friends. I don't want her there! She is always bugging me.	
✗	P: Well you know she just wants to hang out with you so badly! It's really not that bad, it's kind of sweet when you think about it.	Difficulty reflecting
	13: It's not sweet, it's annoying. I don't want her there.	
✗	P: Okay fine, she doesn't have to come. But I think you're being a little mean.	Difficulty reflecting; negative comments
	13: I'm being mean!? You always take her side! You're SO annoying. Ugh.	
✗	P: Okay miss, I think that's enough.	Attending to inappropriate behavior
	13: Fine, I don't want to talk about it anyways. I have to go.	
✓	P: On your way out the door, don't forget to grab the garbage and put it out.	Neutral response. *Could have opted to say nothing to avoid a hot-button topic, but if this was an expected task for the teen this prompt was a very neutral reminder.
	13: FINE! [stomps away with garbage and backpack]	
✗	P: No need for all the attitude!	Missed opportunity to label praise; attending to inappropriate behavior

TEST YOUR SKILLS BY PUTTING IT ALL TOGETHER

In Exercise 5.7 is the same script you just saw. All of the stuck points have been boldfaced. Your job in this exercise is to decide what skill you would want to use instead and rewrite the parent's responses based on that. In real life, it is very likely that a parent using skills throughout this interaction would lead to entirely different (i.e., better) reactions from the teenager than the ones in the script. For the sake of you getting practice, this example will assume that the teen was going to react the same no matter what, so their responses are all the same as in the previous example. It's okay if your responses do not make perfect sense with the next part of the script. Keep in mind there are many ways to be skillful during conflict and there is no one "right" response, but you can see examples in the answer key on the next page. As a reminder, skills include: neutral or positive response; conflict-free zone; one-on-one time; labeled praise; active ignoring.

Selective Attention

EXERCISE 5.7: TEST YOUR SKILLS BY PUTTING IT ALL TOGETHER

Script	Rewrite (Skill you want to use) Statement
Parent (P): Bus is leaving in 15 minutes. You gotta move more quickly packing up your stuff so you don't miss it.	
13-year-old (13): I'm going as fast as I can.	
P: Doesn't look like it to me. I see a lot of time spent checking your phone.	
13: [rolls eyes]	
P: You know I can see that?	
13: Whatever.	
P: I have a few extra minutes today, so if there's time we can talk about plans for your birthday.	
13: I reeeally want to go out to dinner with my friends.	
P: I think that's a great idea! Good thinking.	
13: So I really want to— [gets interrupted]	
P: Wait! Finish packing! You always get so distracted.	

Continued

Continued

Script	Rewrite (Skill you want to use) Statement
13: Ugh, you brought it up! [finishes packing] Okay I'm done! Can we talk about the dinner plan now?	
P: Yes, but first I want you to know that I really think you should have your little sister come.	
13: What!? No! It's my birthday with my friends. I don't want her there! She is always bugging me.	
P: Well you know she just wants to hang out with you so badly! It's really not that bad, it's kind of sweet when you think about it.	
13: It's not sweet, it's annoying. I don't want her there.	
P: Okay fine, she doesn't have to come. But I think you're being a little mean.	
13: You always take her side! You're SO annoying. Ugh.	
P: Okay miss, I think that's enough.	
13: I don't want to talk about it anyways. I have to go.	
P: On your way out the door, don't forget to grab the garbage and put it out.	
13: Fine! [stomps away with garbage and backpack]	
P: No need for all the attitude!	

Exercise 5.7 ANSWER KEY Test Your Skills by Putting It All Together

Statement	Skill/Stuck Point
Parent (P): Bus is leaving in 15 minutes. You gotta move more quickly packing up your stuff so you don't miss it.	[labeled praise] Great job getting started on the packing. Bus is going to leave in about 15 minutes.
13-year-old (13): I'm going as fast as I can.	
P: Doesn't look like it to me. I see a lot of time spent checking your phone.	[labeled praise] I appreciate you trying to move quickly!
13: [rolls eyes]	
P: You know I can see that?	[actively ignore eye-roll; neutral comment] It looks beautiful out, so at least the walk to the bus will be nice.
13: Whatever.	
P: I have a few extra minutes today, so if there's time we can talk about plans for your birthday.	
13: I reeeally want to go out to dinner with my friends.	
P: I think that's a great idea! Good thinking.	
13: So I really want to— [gets interrupted]	
P: Wait! Finish packing! You always get so distracted.	[neutral comment] I shouldn't have distracted you! I don't want to make you late. Finish up, and then we can chat.
13: Ugh, you brought it up! [finishes packing] Okay I'm done! Can we talk about the dinner plan now?	

Statement	Skill/Stuck Point
P: Yes, but first I want you to know that I really think you should have your little sister come.	[neutral comment] Yes! I want to hear about who you want to invite. *If I know sister is a hot-button topic I would not bring it up at this time. If I didn't know, I might say: I heard your sister talking about how excited she is for your birthday!
13: What!? No! It's my birthday with my friends. I don't want her there! She is always bugging me.	
P: Well you know she just wants to hang out with you so badly! It's really not that bad, it's kind of sweet when you think about it.	[reflecting] Ah, I get it. It seems like she's kind of a pain right now. I'm sure she thinks she's being sweet, but it obviously isn't how you see it.
13: It's not sweet, it's annoying. I don't want her there.	
P: Okay fine, she doesn't have to come. But I think you're being a little mean.	[labeled praise] I appreciate you being honest with me. I'll think a little bit about the options.
13: You always take her side! You're SO annoying. Ugh.	
P: Okay miss, I think that's enough.	[actively ignore; neutral comment] So who is at the top of your list?
13: I don't want to talk about it anyways. I have to go.	
P: On your way out the door, don't forget to grab the garbage and put it out.	[labeled praise] No problem sweetheart, thanks for telling me calmly. On your way out the door, don't forget to grab the garbage and put it out.
13: FINE! [stomps away with garbage and backpack]	
P: No need for all the attitude!	[labeled praise] Thank you for taking care of that, it's a really big help.

DO NOT UNDERESTIMATE THE POWER OF SELECTIVE ATTENTION

Selective attention is one of the most difficult skills for caregivers to master. It can also feel a little underwhelming. You might be asking yourself, "Am I really just supposed to sit here pretending not to hear my kid complain?" Because of this, many parents and caregivers give selective attention a brief try before moving past it in favor of other skills. Word to the wise: do not abandon selective attention. Not only is it effective on its own, but it has staying power well beyond many parenting tools and is the foundation for almost all other conflict and behavior management strategies out there. There are countless cases of families whose teens start improving, only to face a back slide. Upon closer look, it turns out the parents had either been cutting out one-on-one time and forgetting to label praise, and/or starting to attend more and more to those attention-seeking or attention-maintained behaviors. It is okay if it does not come naturally to you or takes more practice than you thought. Like any skill that has ever been worth learning, this takes practice and effort to master and maintain. This is a skill worth taking the time on.

TRY IT OUT: SELECTIVE ATTENTION

It is time to put all of the skills discussed in this chapter into practice in your own life. Below is a plan to help you decide which skills to begin with over the next few weeks. As you now know, there are so many parts to selective attention, so it is okay to start small and add on over time. Complete the exercise in Worksheet 5.1 to increase the likelihood of following through successfully this week. Next week, review your answers and decide if you want to keep them the same, or challenge yourself a bit more. Slowly build your skill over time.

WORKSHEET 5.1

1. Do you want to try neutral responses, positive responses, or both?

   _____

   Pick a time of day when you will try to practice neutral or positive responses.

   _____

2. Do you want to try conflict-free zone, one-on-one time, or save this for later?

   _____

   If you want to try it, pick a time of day when it might work best.

   _____

3. Do you want to try labeled praise this week or save it for later?

   _____

   If you want to try it this week, what 1–2 behaviors do you want to try to label praise?

   _____

4. Do you want to try active ignoring this week or save it for later?

   _____

   What 1–2 behaviors do you want to try to actively ignore this week?

   _____

5. How will you remember to practice (alarms, sticky notes, plan with partner, etc.)?

   _____

6. What barriers, including any of the common stuck points listed earlier in the chapter, do you think may interfere in using the skills, and how do you plan to troubleshoot them?

   _____

   _____

7. List three things that will help you complete this task and make sense of this skill. This could include reminders, skill review, social support, accountability measures, or other ideas you would find useful.

   1. _____

      _____

   2. _____

      _____

   3. _____

      _____

6

Validation

Helping Your Child Feel Heard

WHAT IS VALIDATION?

In simple terms, validation is used to express that a person's experience or perspective makes sense and/or is worthwhile. It is both one of the most powerful and most underutilized skills in parenting. Not only can it strengthen relationships, but it can help teens stay regulated, generate trust, and understand their emotions and behaviors without judgment. To help demonstrate what validation looks like, here are a number of examples:

- *It is important to me to understand your point of view—let me make sure I get this right . . .*
- *I can understand why you feel annoyed right now.*
- *It makes sense to me that you thought your friend was mad at you because they didn't answer your text for a few days.*
- *I can see how, from your perspective, I wasn't being fair because I usually warn you before changing our plans and I didn't this time.*
- *No wonder you're anxious—lots of people get nervous before tests.*
- *I think many kids in your shoes would also hate your teacher right now.*
- *I imagine you're having a hard time telling me what's on your mind because you're not sure how I am going to respond.*
- *I know you're upset with yourself. We can work on that, though I'm sure it's hard to stay calm and collected with so many stressful things happening at once.*
- *No wonder you got so down on yourself after the interview. After how hard it has been to find the right job, I'm sure it was easy for your thoughts to go to a bad place.*

You will notice that in all of these sample statements, regardless of the specific situation or phrasing, the key element is an acknowledgment of somebody's experience. In many instances, the simple act of actively listening or reflecting back what your child has said is validating. As a parent or caregiver, you can do immense good by being present and engaged with your teen, because doing so sends the message that their perspective matters and is worth your time. Often, validation is also aided by an awareness of how your child's experience makes sense within their specific context. As outlined in Chapter 4, this could mean the details of the current situation or past events; factors within your child's day; the broader home, school, and work environment; relevant health or mental health symptoms; or cultural or global factors.

WHAT VALIDATION IS NOT

It is important to understand that validation is not praise. It's not just saying thank you or showing your child appreciation. As great as praise is, validation is a skill focused more on recognizing where somebody is coming from rather than giving them credit. Validation is also not the same as agreeing with or condoning a teen's response. You'll notice that none of the examples on the previous page include phrases such as "you're right," or "I think this response was the best one to have," or "go ahead and keep reacting the way you are over and over again." Instead, validation simply tries to put words to how your teen's brain led them to react the way they did.

WHY VALIDATION MATTERS

For reasons described later in this chapter, many caregivers move too quickly past validation or skip it altogether, and in doing so miss a crucial opportunity to connect with their teenager while de-escalating distress. Validation is important for a number of reasons. First, it helps kids see that their emotions, wants, and needs are being heard. Most adults can relate to how valuable this is. After all, there are few things more frustrating or disheartening than explaining your experience to somebody close to you and feeling like the other person *just doesn't get it*. Feeling misunderstood or unheard can, in turn, push a teen further into fight or flight mode. This drives up the emotional or behavioral intensity as their brain desperately tries to find a way to get their parent to understand. Remember, kids with anxiety, depression, ADHD, and other mental health concerns already struggle with emotion regulation, so it is particularly important to use skills that help them stay calm.

This brings up a second benefit of validation: it can decrease emotional or behavioral outbursts and increase willingness to problem-solve. To be clear, validation is not going to eliminate every battle. However, when it is used effectively to help teens feel understood, it will often result in a decreased sense of urgency to show distress, meaning that emotions and behaviors can remain more stable. Further, if a teenager feels like their parent *gets it*, they will be more likely to listen to any suggestions the parent comes up with. As most parents can attest to, interacting with a child who is calm and receptive to input leads to more meaningful, productive conversations than interactions with a child who is escalated or closed off.

Validation is also a useful tool to help teens understand their layers of emotion without shame. Using validation, a parent might say, "I can see by your clenched fist that you might be angry, or anxious, or both. That would make sense since you're being asked to try this new thing and you really don't want to." In doing so, a parent connects a physical response (e.g., clenched fist) to an emotion (anger or anxiety), which can help youths notice patterns and put words to their behaviors and feelings. Over time, labeling patterns in this nonjudgmental way can undercut negativity that some people link to their emotions. By simply stating facts and acknowledging a teen's perspective, we send the message that their feelings are okay—not inherently good or bad, just signals in their brains and bodies that give them information. Decreasing shame can be hugely protective when it comes to minimizing anxiety and mood symptoms. It also helps the parent–child relationship remain strong because kids are not feeling as judged or criticized by their parents for reacting the way their brains are telling them to.

This highlights a final, important benefit of validation. Validation helps to preserve and strengthen the parent–child bond. Having a parent understand an experience, recognize emotions, label patterns, acknowledge distress, and relay all of this in a neutral and understanding manner goes a long way toward increasing the sense of trust and support between a child and their parent. Kids who receive this type of warm, empathic response, rather than criticism or punishment, are more comfortable sharing information with their parents. This can increase connection and honesty, which allows parents to maintain a meaningful role in kids' lives through all the twists and turns of growing up. Having complete honesty from kids can sometimes be scary. After all, there are many conversations that are difficult for parents to navigate and many choices that are hard to watch play out. However, most parents say this fear pales in comparison to the worry of their children *not* being open. The more validation a parent can infuse into a relationship, the more likely they will be able to help shape and support their child well past the teenage years.

In many cases, for the reasons listed above, validation will provide enough support that your teen can regulate themselves and resolve their concerns on their own. However, it is worth noting that validation is not a magic cure for all problems. In those instances, validation is a starting point (albeit a very important one) and you may need to use other tools like de-escalation or consequences to help your teen make skillful choices. Needing these other tools should not serve as a reason for you to abandon validation or rush through it. On the contrary: providing a heavy dose of validation (meaning starting with *at least* three to five validating statements) will still increase your chances of being able to work with a regulated child who is receptive and able to follow through on next steps.

Common Stuck Points of Validation

Listed here are common hurdles that parents encounter when trying to use validation. Underneath each common stuck point, you will find tips and considerations that can help address each barrier. At the end of the chapter, you will have a chance to make note of any examples that would be helpful for you to keep in mind.

I am not sure how my child is feeling.
Some teens keep things to themselves or show few signs of distress. When this happens, parents are often unsure of what they are supposed to be validating.

→ It is okay to guess what your teenager is experiencing based on what you know about them, their situation, or their behaviors and expressions. You might say something like:
  - *I can imagine you might . . .*
  - *Somebody else in your shoes could feel . . .*
  - *Based on your expression you seem to be . . .*

Then give your child a chance to correct you. If you got it wrong, you can thank them for clarifying. The more you practice and the more feedback you get from your child, the more likely you will be able to pick up on any subtle clues they are giving.

My own emotions.
When teens are distressed, parents often are as well. You may find yourself anxious about your child's choices, angry with their reaction, or distressed watching them struggle. Regardless of the reason, strong feelings on the part of the parent can result in emotion-based responses rather than validation.

→ There is no magic fix for this. Parents are susceptible to emotion-based thinking and behavior as much as any other human is. In fact, parents may be more susceptible to it. Not only are you probably sleep deprived and pulled in a hundred directions, but the love you have for your child is so immense and overpowering that it can quickly amplify any emotional reaction you may be having. This is an instance in which it is helpful for parents to make use of their own coping skills (see Chapter 3) to try to stay emotionally grounded. Not only can it help you respond more appropriately, but it will serve as an important model to your kids about how to be skillful in stressful moments.

I try to show them I understand by telling them about my own experience.
Parents and caregivers often try to normalize their teen's distress by sharing ways in which they can relate. This is great in theory, but in many instances, directing the conversation onto yourself can leave them feeling like you care more about your own experience than theirs.

→ Remember the aim: the goal of validation is to help your child feel heard and increase connection. Try to find a response that will do both things. If only acknowledging their perspective (without sharing how you can relate) feels too impersonal—that is fine! Feel free to provide a brief statement about how you have experienced something similar before. If you notice that your desire to connect is starting to overshadow your attempts to acknowledge your teen's own experience, cut it short. If you do decide to share about yourself, do not be surprised if your child says something along the lines of, "Okay, but it was different for you," or "See, you think you get it, but you just don't understand." They might be right. After all, things really are different for individuals across generations. But even if they are wrong, the point of this skill is to see a situation through your teen's eyes, *not* to make them see how you dealt with the same thing. Be willing to drop this and return your focus to how they are responding.

I think I have a better idea of what is going on than they do.
During a meltdown or argument, it is very tempting to cut through all of the back and forth and spell out what you think is really going on, whether or not it matches what your child is telling you. The hope is that by boiling the situation down to its (seemingly obvious) root, everybody can move on more quickly. For example, countless parents have told their teenager that "This is not that big of a deal, you're just exhausted from staying up too late." Or something along the lines of, "There isn't anything to worry about, it just feels like a big deal because you haven't done it before."

→ To be fair, parents are right a lot of the time. You have the advantage of a fully developed brain and years of experience. The kid in front of you IS probably overtired, and the teenage meltdown is more likely first-time jitters than a real chance of something really going wrong. However, even if you are right, your teen still feels angry, sad, or frustrated. Dismissing that perspective completely ignores the fact that they are experiencing a really uncomfortable emotion. Repeatedly overriding their perspective, even with the noble goal of making them see logic or calming them down is likely lowering their trust in you or increasing shame. A teen can only hear "You're not X, you're Y," so many times before it takes a toll. Eventually, they either start to think their emotional radar is off or that there is something deeply wrong with them for having reactions their parents say they shouldn't.

Jumping to action items or problem-solving too soon.
Whether you are eager to minimize your child's distress or are just hoping to prevent a battle, many parents skip validation and hop right to encouraging action or offering solutions. This is well-intentioned, but can result in your child feeling unheard and unwilling to take your ideas seriously.

→ It can be so hard to sit by and watch your teen spiral out when there is a seemingly easy solution staring them in the face. Signs that you might be falling into this trap include:
  - Saying "but" in your validating statement. Doing this shifts your phrase away from validation and toward solutions, which your child may not be ready for.
    Example: *I know you're really anxious **but** it probably won't be so bad if you breathe.*
  - Rushing your child to act early within the conversation.
    Example: *I see this is hard. Just try to get through it quickly!*
  - Laying out options you think are best.
    Example: *Well, why don't you go ahead and call your friend for help. Or maybe I can just email your teacher so we can get the answer for you right away!*

→ Do yourself a favor and try to be patient. Starting with validation increases the chance of a positive resolution because:
  - Having taken the time to make sure you know where your teen is coming from, your advice is more likely to be helpful.
  - Your child will trust that you understand their perspective and will therefore be more likely to hear you out.
  - It is possible your child will be able to generate solutions on their own, which will increase their buy in and create a sense of empowerment.

Both you and your child will likely be calmer and more regulated, making it easier to actually follow through on recommendations.

I don't want it to seem like I am agreeing with my child.
Parents worry that acknowledging a child's perspective is the same thing as agreeing with it. This can be worrisome for parents who want to minimize a child's anxious or negative thoughts, escalated behaviors, or choices they believe are inappropriate.

→ Good news: as outlined above, validation is not the same as agreement or permission! It is just acknowledging somebody else's perspective. If you are still worried about it, it is okay to include a small caveat such as, "I do not see it this way, but I can understand how you might . . ." or "I have a different perspective, though I recognize you are feeling . . ." If you get sighs or eye-rolling, be prepared to practice validation without these phrases.

My parents *never* would have said something like this.
Many caregivers express this sentiment, and often what they are really concerned about is that validation is either "too soft" or goes against cultural, generational, or parenting values.

→ The first point to remember is that validation does not impact any limits that you set. Because it is not agreement or permission, you can still hold a boundary or deliver a consequence while you validate a teenager's perspective. For example, "It makes sense you're angry because you *love* watching that show. It is still time to turn off the TV."
→ Next, ask yourself whether you agree with how your caregiver responded to you, or if it is just what you are used to. It is very easy to adopt a parenting style simply because you witnessed it growing up. That is not necessarily bad, but it is worth determining if your current responses are based on your genuine preference versus a habit you picked up.
→ Then, consider differences between then and now. You may be a different person than the one who raised you, just as your child is likely to be different than you are. There may also be differences in the environment in which you

> were raised as compared to the one your child is in now. These changes may warrant a different approach than the one you grew up with.
> → If you have taken all of this into account and still worry the act of validation itself is problematic, then consider your long-term values. Is your value to have a strong relationship with your child, to help them thrive, to maintain a strict hierarchy at home, to mirror family structure and style that is typical in your community, or something else?
>
> All of these are reasonable values to hold, and you as the parent get to decide which one is most important to you. Once you have prioritized, ask yourself if using validation could help or hurt that value, and if the outcome is worthwhile even if it means a different value may take a backseat. For example, let's say your teen is confident and healthy and does not typically struggle with mental health issues. You have a fairly good relationship at baseline, and it is very important to you to maintain a strict household hierarchy. In this case, it seems like your child and your relationship are both totally fine. You do not necessarily need the extra boost and connection that validation provides. So you may choose to skip validation because you prefer to maintain a strict hierarchy at home and you believe validation blurs the lines too much. That is okay.
>
> On the other hand, perhaps your child has anxiety or you struggle to get along. If your top priority is to help them feel secure in their emotions or strengthen your relationship, then validation becomes more important. This can be difficult if it means going against your standard practice or weathering judgmental looks from the grandparents. Keeping that long-term value in mind can help increase the motivation to stick with this skill.

TEST YOUR KNOWLEDGE OF VALIDATION

Read through the sample statements in Exercise 6.1. Put a check next to each example of validation, and an ✗ where the parental response misses the mark somehow. Keep in mind that examples of nonvalidating responses could include criticism or negative talk, or could simply be ones that ignore, minimize, or dismiss what the child is conveying.

EXERCISE 6.1 TEST YOUR KNOWLEDGE OF VALIDATION

✓ or ✗	Statement
	It makes sense that you're worried because a lot is up in the air right now!
	I know it's hard to wake up, but you have to get ready for school.
	I hate trying to talk to you when you're acting this way.
	I hate that you're stressed, but once you get the work done you'll feel better.
	I can tell that you're so angry that I turned off the TV.
	I get it. [checks phone] You're really upset.
	There's no need to be this anxious, it's going to work out okay!
	You're just hungry.
	I can see why you would be so upset right now since it didn't turn out the way you wanted it to.
	I don't even want to hear it. I told you that you would be upset if you didn't keep track of your things, and I was right.
	It's common for people with low mood to have really negative thoughts, so it makes a lot of sense that your brain went there.
	You have no right to be mad at me. You broke the rules, not me.
	Thank you so much for helping today, I really appreciate it.
	[notices teen looks annoyed] Did I remember to tell you that I'm making your favorite dinner tonight?
	Please don't say you're going to quit soccer. I know it's hard to motivate yourself right now, but I'm really worried you're going to feel worse later.
	Wow, you must feel so stuck right now if you thought your only option was to hide this for so long. That must have been really difficult.
	I know exactly what you're going through. The exact same thing happened to me when I was younger. I was so worried about getting into college that I just worked all the time and never enjoyed myself. But don't worry, I ended up getting into a great place and probably didn't need to stress myself out so much.
	You're telling me you feel lonely right now. How about I call your friends and invite them for dinner? Or maybe you could go to the park and you can find some people to hang out with?
	Do not say that-you are *not* stupid. Why would that thought even cross your mind?
	You are so scared things are going to turn out badly again. For somebody who has had such awful experiences before, that feeling makes perfect sense.

Exercise 6.1 ANSWER KEY Test Your Knowledge of Validation

✓ or ✗	Statement
✓	It makes sense that you're worried because a lot is up in the air right now!
✗	I know it's hard to wake up, but you have to get ready for school.
✗	I hate trying to talk to you when you're acting this way.
✗	I hate that you're stressed, but once you get the work done you'll feel better.
✓	I can tell that you're so angry that I turned off the TV.
✗	I get it. [checks phone] You're really upset.
✗	There's no need to be this anxious, it's going to work out okay!
✗	You're just hungry.
✓	I can see why you would be so upset right now since it didn't turn out the way you wanted it to.
✗	I don't even want to hear it. I told you that you would be upset if you didn't keep track of your things, and I was right.
✓	It's common for people with low mood to have really negative thoughts, so it makes a lot of sense that your brain went there.
✗	You have no right to be mad at me. You broke the rules, not me.
✗	Thank you so much for helping today, I really appreciate it.
✗	[notices teen looks annoyed] Did I remember to tell you that I'm making your favorite dinner tonight?
✗	Please don't say you're going to quit soccer. I know it's hard to motivate yourself right now, but I'm really worried you're going to feel worse later.
✓	Wow, you must feel so stuck right now if you thought your only option was to hide this for so long. That must have been really difficult.
✗	I know exactly what you're going through. The exact same thing happened to me when I was younger. I was so worried about getting into college that I just worked all the time and never enjoyed myself. But don't worry, I ended up getting into a great place and probably didn't need to stress myself out so much.
✗	You're telling me you feel lonely right now. How about I call your friends and invite them for dinner? Or maybe you could go to the park and you can find some people to hang out with?
✗	Do not say that-you are *not* stupid. Why would that thought even cross your mind?
✓	You are so scared things are going to turn out badly again. For somebody who has had such awful experiences before, that feeling makes perfect sense.

TEST YOUR SKILLS: VALIDATION

In Exercise 6.2 is a list of all the statements from Exercise 6.1 that were not good examples of validation. Identify what stuck point occurred or where the parent went wrong. As discussed earlier, possible stuck points include uncertainty about the child's feelings, parent emotions, parent turning the conversation to themselves, parent "knowing better" than the child, jumping to action items or solutions, concern about agreeing with the child, concern validation is "too soft" or does not align with values.

In some instances, there may not have been a "stuck point," but rather some other strategy the parent used (like praise or distraction) that did not validate the child. Once you have identified this, rewrite the statement to focus exclusively on validation.

EXERCISE 6.2 TEST YOUR SKILLS: VALIDATION

Original Statement	What Went Wrong	Rewrite
I know it's hard to wake up, but you have to get ready for school.		
I hate trying to talk to you when you're acting this way.		
I hate that you're stressed, but once you get the work done you'll feel better.		
I get it. [checks phone] You're really upset.		
There's no need to be this anxious, it's going to work out okay!		
You're just hungry.		
I don't even want to hear it. I told you that you would be upset if you didn't keep track of your things, and I was right.		
You have no right to be mad at me. You broke the rules, not me.		
Thank you so much for helping today, I really appreciate it.		
[notices teen looks annoyed] Did I remember to tell you that I'm making your favorite dinner tonight?		

Original Statement	What Went Wrong	Rewrite
Please don't say you're going to quit soccer. I know it's hard to motivate yourself right now, but I'm really worried you're going to feel worse later.		
I know what you're going through. The same thing happened to me when I was younger. I was so worried about getting into college that I worked all of the time and never enjoyed myself. But don't worry, I ended up fine and probably didn't need to stress myself out so much.		
You're telling me you feel lonely right now. How about I call your friends and invite them for dinner? Or maybe you could go to the park and you can find some people to hang out with?		
Do not say that: you are *not* stupid! Why would that thought even cross your mind?		

Exercise 6.2 ANSWER KEY Test Your Skills: Validation

Original Statement	What Went Wrong	Rewrite
I know it's hard to wake up, but you have to get ready for school.	Jumped to action items	I know it's hard to wake up, you had to stay up so late studying.
I hate trying to talk to you when you're acting this way.	Parent emotions (anger/annoyance)	It is probably hard to speak with me calmly because you're so upset right now.
I hate that you're stressed, but once you get the work done you'll feel better.	Jumped to problem-solving	Having this much work must feel overwhelming and stressful.
I get it. [checks phone] You're really upset.	Checked phone, sent child the message that it wasn't important	I get it. You're really upset. [keep eye contact]
There's no need to be this anxious, it's going to work out okay!	Parent "knowing better"	I think things will probably work out okay, but of course you're anxious if you think they'll go badly.
You're just hungry.	Parent "knowing better"	You're saying you feel so frustrated right now.
I don't even want to hear it. I told you that you would be upset if you didn't keep track of your things, and I was right.	Parent emotion or concern validation is "too soft"	Having your phone is so important to you and it must feel awful that you misplaced it.
You have no right to be mad at me. You broke the rules, not me.	Parent emotion or concern validation is "too soft"	I am not changing the rules, but I understand why you are mad about the limit I am setting.
Thank you so much for helping today, I really appreciate it.	This is praise instead of validation	N/A

Original Statement	What Went Wrong	Rewrite
[notices teen looks annoyed] Did I remember to tell you that I'm making your favorite dinner tonight?	This is distraction instead of validation	*Hmm, it looks like you're annoyed right now. Is that because of what your brother said, or is there something else?*
Please don't say you're going to quit soccer. I know it's hard to motivate yourself right now, but I'm really worried you're going to feel worse later.	Parent emotion	*You feel so down and unmotivated it seems impossible to keep doing soccer even though you used to love it.*
I know what you're going through. The same thing happened to me when I was younger. I was so worried about getting into college that I worked all of the time and never enjoyed myself. But don't worry, I ended up fine and probably didn't need to stress myself out so much.	Parent turning the conversation to themselves	*I remember feeling anxious about this when I was your age, but I bet it feels even harder now given how competitive your school is.*
You're telling me you feel lonely right now. How about I call your friends and invite them for dinner? Or maybe you could go to the park and you can find some people to hang out with?	Jumped to problem-solving	*You're telling me you feel lonely right now, which makes sense because you have been so isolated lately.*
Do not say that: you are *not* stupid! Why would that thought even cross your mind?	Parent worried about agreeing	*I think you are really smart, but it must be easy to talk down to yourself if you always feel like you're missing things in class.*

TEST YOUR SKILLS BY STAYING THE COURSE WITH VALIDATION

It is one thing to validate your teen once during a conversation, but it is another thing to stay the course and make use of validation again and again. Exercise 6.3 is designed to help you practice how to prioritize validation during a conversation no matter what your child says using a sample conversation between a parent and a teenager. In this exercise, the parent's response is boldfaced and your job is to rewrite any sentence that is not fully validating. Do your best to validate the teen's statement no matter what they say. There are many possible ways to validate, but you can see examples in the answer key. If this conversation was happening in real life and parents were making use of validation throughout, teenagers would likely regulate and respond more productively as the conversation progressed. However, for the sake of the exercise, the child's response will always continue to be escalated so you get extra practice.

EXERCISE 6.3 TEST YOUR SKILLS BY STAYING THE COURSE WITH VALIDATION

Script	Your Rewrite
14-year-old (14): I just can't do anything right. I failed my test, none of my friends want to hang out with me, and I messed everything up at practice today.	
Parent (P): Whoa, whoa, whoa. Where is this coming from? You're amazing—why would you say that?	
14: Because it's true! I ruin everything I do.	
P: That is *not* true. You didn't fail your test—you got a C, and I'm sure whatever happened with your friends and at practice was no big deal.	
14: Dad, a C is *horrible*. And you have no clue. You always tell me stuff is fine, but what would you know. It's not like you're there.	
P: Okay, where is this coming from? Are you just fighting with your girlfriend again? Is that why you're so negative right now?	
14: See what I mean?! This has nothing to do with my girlfriend. You're not even listening to me.	
P: Okay, okay. I just feel like this is out of nowhere. You're a good student and friend and athlete. I'm sure things aren't as bad as they seem.	
14: Sure, Dad. Whatever you say.	
P: Yeah, just take a deep breath. Everything is fine. If there are any real problems we can sort them out.	
14: Don't worry about it. I'll deal with it myself.	

Exercise 6.3 ANSWER KEY Staying the Course with a Teen

Script	Rewrite
14-year-old (14): I just can't do anything right. I failed my test, none of my friends want to hang out with me, and I messed everything up at practice today.	
Parent (P): Whoa, whoa, whoa. Where is this coming from? You're amazing—why would you say that?	Wow—I am not sure where this is coming from but it sounds like it was a miserable day and you're feeling really down.
14: Because it's true! I ruin everything I do.	
P: That is *not* true. You didn't fail your test—you got a C, and I'm sure whatever happened with your friends and at practice was no big deal.	I am not sure if that is really the case, but if you feel like you failed, and your friends are mad, and practice was terrible, I can see why your brain went there.
14: Dad, a C is *horrible*. And you have no clue. You always tell me stuff is fine, but what would you know. It's not like you're there.	
P: Okay, where is this coming from? Did you just stay up too late last night and now you're really tired? Is that why you're so negative right now?	It must be really hard to feel like I'm not getting it. I bet it's even worse since I know you had to stay up late to study and you're probably exhausted.
14: See what I mean?! This has nothing to do with staying up late. You're not even listening to me.	
P: Okay, okay. I just feel like this is out of nowhere. You're a good student and friend and athlete. I'm sure things aren't as bad as they seem.	Fair enough—I thought being tired may have been adding stress, but I hear what you're saying. It seems like everything is overwhelming and you're not sure I can be helpful.

Script	Rewrite
14: Sure, Dad. Whatever you say.	
P: Yeah, just take a deep breath. Everything is fine. If there are any real problems we can sort them out.	Yeah, you seem pretty annoyed, which makes sense since I keep misunderstanding.
14: Don't worry about it. I'll deal with it myself.	
P: Well, okay, but I'm happy to give you some suggestions if you want.	I get that you want to figure it out solo because it seems like I can't be helpful. I would really like to sit here and keep listening so I can understand better and be there for you.

In reading though the answer key for Exercise 6.3, you may have noticed that the entire tone of the interaction seems to shift. This is the case even though the teen's responses are exactly the same as the first script. Of course, the hope is that the teen's responses will shift (and that would likely be the case in real life). Still, there may be times when a teenager is just too upset to respond reasonably in the moment, and the parent can still lead with care and concern.

SPECIAL CONSIDERATIONS: USING VALIDATION WHEN A CHILD SEEKS REASSURANCE

One question that parents ask is whether there is such a thing as too much validation. The general answer is no: if your teenager is responsive to validation and/or is becoming more regulated, you can continue with validation for as long as it is helpful and aids connection. The one main exception to this is when you have a child who seeks reassurance excessively. This is typical for people who have high anxiety or obsessive compulsive disorder, and often involves asking parents the same questions over and over in order to help soothe worries or doubt. For example, a teenager may repeatedly ask if a parent is mad at them, whether they will do okay on their upcoming project, or if their friend really likes them. While brief reassurance seeking is appropriate in some situations, it becomes inappropriate when questions continue regardless of parent response and/or when the teen's distress becomes more intense. In these cases, continually validating the anxiety often does nothing to resolve it and may even keep the cycle going.

If this sounds familiar, it can be helpful to provide one to three validating statements and then stop. If your teen has OCD and reassurance seeking is a compulsion, you can respond less than that (or not at all), but you will likely want to let your teen know the plan ahead of time. If your child's distress remains high and reassurance seeking questions continue after the initial validation, you can validate this *one* more time, inform the child you will no longer be responding, and let them know how they can move forward with you. For example, "I hear how anxious you are. My answers don't seem helpful at this point so I'm going to stop. I know this will be upsetting. I'm happy to keep talking if we can change topics." Know that while your teen may become very distressed at first when you stop providing that reassurance, doing so encourages their brains to start finding alternative options to soothe their anxiety.

TRY IT OUT: VALIDATION

Now that you have completed each validation exercise, it is time to put this skill into practice in your real life. Start by practicing this skill with a partner, family member, or close friend. Tell them you are trying to practice and spend the time trying different options to see what feels comfortable for you and validating for them. Once you have done this, try validation with your child. As always, complete Worksheet 6.1 to increase the likelihood of following through on this task successfully, and write down your attempts at validation below.

WORKSHEET 6.1

1. When will you try to use this skill during the week?
   _____
   _____

2. How will you remember to practice this skill?
   _____
   _____

3. What barriers, including any of the common stuck points listed earlier in this chapter, do you think may interfere in using the skills, and how do you plan to troubleshoot them?
   _____
   _____

4. List three things that will help you complete this task and make sense of this skill. As a reminder, this could include reminders, skill review, social support, accountability measures, or other ideas you would find useful.

   1. _____
      _____

   2. _____
      _____

   3. _____
      _____

7

Building Meaningful Routines

WHAT ARE MEANINGFUL ROUTINES?

Meaningful routines include consistent schedules and expectations within the household that involve activities that bring a sense of joy or engagement for teenagers. While some families are quite strict about things like sleep, chores, and mealtimes, that is not the case for many people. This is particularly true during the teenage years when activities change by the day or season, and every person in the family seems to be moving in different directions.

Unfortunately, this can lead to a few different problems. First, there is a higher chance that things get missed. When everybody is operating on their own schedule, it is easy to forget that the car needs to be filled with gas, the dog needs to be walked, or somebody needs help studying. Cue the last-minute panic or running late as everybody scrambles. A lack of routine can also feed into higher conflict. While you as the parent may have a rough idea in mind about what your teen is supposed to spend their time on, your teen may be thinking something entirely different. Sure, they're responsible for bringing down their laundry—but they thought you only meant once every three weeks, right? *Of course* they were going to take out the trash; they were just going to do it in the morning! Because there is gray area in household expectations and timing, it is easy for both sides to feel annoyed.

Another concern is that some mental health symptoms can get worse without a meaningful routine. A lack of clarity can heighten anxiety for kids who do better knowing expectations and being able to plan ahead. Inattention and hyperactivity can pop up when there is not a clear structure. For kids with mood difficulties, it is very easy to slip into further withdrawal or passivity when there is not a specific schedule to follow. That is not to say that a lack of routine creates these mental health symptoms, more that it can feed into them.

Given this, it can be very useful to put a meaningful routine in place. If you are somebody who relies on your planner or calendar, some of this chapter will probably be familiar to you. If you typically prefer to go with the flow, these strategies may take some getting used to. Though it involves some up-front effort, meaningful routines can save you time on the backend, lower the emotional intensity in the household, and help manage some mental health symptoms. There are three main parts to cover:

1. Creating daily routines
2. Adding in household expectations
3. Making time for meaningful activities

In looking at these three areas of focus, you may already have a sense of which ones will be most important for your teenager. While creating a daily routine is generally useful, it may not be entirely necessary for every single teenager. Some kids are naturally good with time management or love their independence. If they are following their own internal clock and getting everything done, there is no need to complicate the situation. Similarly, if there are rarely miscommunications or frustrations about chores, family activities, or household goals, you may not need to do a thorough review of household expectations. And if you notice that your teen has lots of different activities they enjoy and find meaningful, you do not have to revamp their extra-curricular calendar. It can still be useful to read through the sections for useful tips, but this is one chapter in which you can pick and choose the domains that fit your particular teen's needs.

CREATING DAILY ROUTINES

There is a fairly basic process you can use to build a routine that works for your family. Rather than trying to create a schedule that works from morning until night, it is usually helpful to break it down into sections with a morning routine, afternoon routine, and evening routine. You could change these categories depending on what works best for your own family. Then pick one area you want to start with and follow the steps below. Once you have the outline clear, write out the schedule for all to see. Pro tip: put it in a plastic sleeve so it does not get crumpled or covered in stains.

1. *Ask your teen to create a to-do list for the routine.* This is a useful place to start because it gives your teenager a chance to add the items that they feel are important. It is also a way to help you gauge how on top of it your teen really is. If it seems like they're forgetting lots of things they need to do, it may be a sign that they need a little bit more support and structure. If they remember most of the items, it's possible they're ready to do most of this on their own without as much help from you.
2. *Add in items that were missed.* After your teen has started the to-do list, you have a chance to add anything they forgot. This is a good opportunity to introduce any new tasks that were not previously part of the household expectations.
3. *Decide how much support you will give.* In many cases, is it very appropriate for parents to help their teens as they move through their day. Unfortunately, help can sometimes get extended to the point where parents feel resentful, or where teens feel micromanaged. Get concrete about what everybody's role is and how you are willing to help. You can do this by delegating tasks and deciding if you will give reminders.
    a. In terms of tasks, get specific. In the morning routine, who is making the breakfast and who's responsible for clearing the plate? If your child is taking medication, are they doing that on their own or are you giving it to them? Are they responsible for making their lunch, or will you? This is a good place to ask for your teen's input on what they find helpful.
    b. Depending on how independent your teenager is, you may or may not need to give reminders for them to complete certain tasks. If they struggle with executive functioning tasks, like planning ahead and organizing themselves, they might need prompts. Decide how many reminders you are willing to give. There is no magic number, but it can be helpful to think of how many reminders you are currently giving and cut that number by 20%. So if you currently give 10 reminders, aim for eight. Once they seem to be doing well with the eight reminders you can lower the number again. This creates a pathway for more independence without completely pulling away support.

4. *Set clear time estimates.* Once you have your to-do list and have divided up the tasks, write out the timeline so that everybody knows about how long that phase of the day should take. It's typically helpful to work backward. Decide when everything needs to be finished and use that as your end point. Then estimate how long each task takes.
   a. This is another good place for you to get a sense of how aware your teenager is by asking for their guesses first. Over the course of the week, compare their guesses to how long it actually takes them to finish their tasks. For teens who struggle with time management, it can be a useful exercise to build awareness.
   b. Include transition time. Many parents forget how many minutes are lost to teens moving from one room to the next or getting sidetracked. Once you have added this up, you can figure out when that phase of the day needs to start.
5. *Decide on a reward for completing the routine tasks.* This last step focuses on reinforcing your teenager for appropriately completing the to-do list on time, and with the agreed upon number of reminders. The reward you choose will depend on your teenager and their individual strengths or weaknesses. A teenager who likes to be independent and usually manages their own schedule might not need a big reward for completing their daily tasks—perhaps just labeled praise or a show of appreciation.

More significant rewards may be necessary for teenagers who struggle to get through their daily routines. Some kids with anxiety might end up delayed because they procrastinate or are trying to avoid part of their day. Teens with depression might feel overwhelmed or unmotivated, leading them to bow out of things they are supposed to do. Adolescents with attentional difficulties might lose focus, get thrown off by disorganization, or struggle with time management. Thinking about the CAR acronym, you might be able to see how context and results make task completion very difficult for teens with these symptoms. In those cases, setting up clear expectations (like you are doing right now) can be a very helpful contextual change. Adding a reward for meeting the expectations helps to increase the overall reinforcement, making it more likely to happen again and again.

If possible, make the reward an enjoyable activity that your teenager has access to once the routine is done. This works because it is logical and sustainable. For example, if your teenager is ready for school early, they have time to read or play with the dog. If they complete homework by 9:15, they have some time for screens or something social before their 11 p.m. curfew. In other words, they moved through their tasks quickly enough to allow for more fun. Unlike tangible rewards, many activity-based rewards are cheap, making it easier for parents to keep up with over time.

Logical, activity-based rewards are not always possible, and may not be motivating for your teenager. In those cases, take a look at Chapter 9 for other ways to reinforce skillful behavior. You might make use of tangible rewards (like a smoothie on the way to school if your teen got to bed on time the night before) or some sort of point system that they can use to earn bigger rewards.

Whatever reward system you go with, be consistent. This is what gives routines some teeth and helps motivate your teen to take more initiative. They only get the reward if they complete the tasks on time *and* did not need extra reminders from you to do so. If they were late or needed extra prompting, there is no reward. Over time, this will encourage them to move more quickly and take more responsibility for getting the tasks done. If you give the reward without them meeting the requirements, or forget to give the reward when they did, progress won't stick.

ADDING IN HOUSEHOLD EXPECTATIONS

Many parents find they have constant battles around asking teenagers to take care of basic tasks, like hygiene or helping around the house. As you work to create your routine, it is useful to add in any household expectations that involve tasks your teenager is supposed to be doing. This could be related to chores, helpful behavior at home, schoolwork, or activities. This will not include expectations around attitude, relationships, or values. For example, things like using appropriate language, being kind, or focusing on education may all be important in your household but are *not* specific tasks your child could tick off on a checklist. However, to-do list items like making the bed or reading can be folded into the routine. The advantage of this is that it allows you to help make these behaviors more of a habit, and they are reinforced with the same reward you were already going to be using. This means less work for you because you do not have to find a separate reward for each task.

CONSIDERING EXPECTATIONS FOR YOUR TEEN

In Exercise 7.1 is a list of expectations that parents commonly have for their teenagers. Put a check next to any expectations that you would like to be a regular part of your teen's routine. You might not include everything you check off; this is just a chance to brainstorm what sort of tasks you would like to loop into the routine beyond "wake up on time . . . get dressed . . . eat breakfast." This list is not exhaustive, and there is space at the bottom to add in other tasks that are important to you. Note that every parent and household is different, and you only need to circle the behaviors that truly matter to you and align with your family values. Once you have made your way through the list, you can pick one or two to start with that your teen has some potential to work on now, and then expand from there.

EXERCISE 7.1 CONSIDERING EXPECTATIONS FOR YOUR TEEN

_____ Make the bed	_____ Empty backpack/lunch bag	_____ Take out the trash
_____ Clean up after self	_____ Make or help to make meals	_____ Tidy common areas
_____ Shower	_____ Set the table/clear the table	_____ Take care of the family pet (feed, walk, etc.)
_____ Dental care (cleaning braces, retainers, etc.)	_____ Wash dishes	_____ Sweep/vacuum
_____ Clean the bathroom	_____ Empty or clear dishwasher	_____ Clean windows
_____ Change sheets	_____ Wipe down table/counters	_____ Mow the lawn
_____ Put laundry in the hamper/do laundry/put away laundry	_____ Put away groceries	_____ Wash the car

Once you have selected the tasks that are important to you, consider what is reasonable to include on your teen's routine based on their current context. If they have lots of free time, they can probably take on a bit more responsibility. If they are in a stressful stretch at school with tons of homework, you can opt to keep the expectations limited. If their symptoms are improving (or flaring) you can shift expectations up or down. Whatever you decide, be very clear about what the expectation means. Countless families have gotten into major fights over what making the bed really includes. If you have certain chores that do not need to happen every day, note that on your routine checklist. There might be other parts of the routine that you want to include as a reminder to your teenager, but you don't want to link it to a reward. For example, you might like it if they shower, but are not going to withhold a preferred activity if they choose not to. In that case, underline, star, or bold each of the tasks that must happen to get the reward. The unmarked items will still serve as a reminder, but everybody will know they are not hard and fast.

COMMON STUCK POINTS OF CREATING DAILY ROUTINES AND HOUSEHOLD EXPECTATIONS

Listed here are common obstacles that parents encounter when creating or sticking to a daily routine and household expectations. Underneath each common stuck point, you will find tips and considerations that can help address each barrier. At the end of the chapter, you will have a chance to make note of any examples that would be helpful for you to keep in mind.

We've tried routines in the past and they never stick.
Most families have tried some version of a routine at some time or other. It often goes well for the first week or two, and then it falls off. Truthfully, behavior change is hard and sticking to a more structured routine can be a lot of work. Fortunately, there are a handful of ways to make it a bit easier to maintain.

→ First, make sure your routine is realistic! Routines often fall apart because they have so many tasks jammed in that everybody feels overwhelmed. While it may be tempting to include every self-care task, a few chores, and day-to-day prep in the routine, cut down the routine to the essentials (at least to start) and it will not feel quite so daunting to keep up with. If it does not seem like it is possible to cut anything from the list, look through the tasks and rank order how important they are. Keep the top handful. If you still cannot bring yourself to completely eliminate options, consider an alternating schedule. Some tasks may have to happen every other night instead of daily, so you might end up with a Monday/Wednesday/Friday/Sunday list and a Tuesday/Thursday/Saturday list.

→ Use visual aids. It doesn't have to be fancy, but make a chart with the daily routine. If you have access to a computer and printer, type it up and print many extra copies. Make the font large and easy to read. Then put a copy in every major room in the household so your teen doesn't have to run back to the fridge to check each step.

→ Set one alarm to check the routine before it starts and another to review it at the end of the day. If you do not even remember to pay attention to the routine, change your morning alarm text to "Check routine!" Then, set a second alarm near the end of the day to quickly review it. Most families fall off the routine because the parents stop checking in on it, so teens lose motivation to keep following it. If *you* consistently go through it and give the appropriate rewards, you will see much more consistent use of routines over time.

My teenager doesn't want to help create the routine.
Some teenagers find routines to be boring or a tool their parents are using to micromanage their lives. When this happens, they may try to boycott the routine entirely.

→ You can start by validating your teen's lack of interest in the routine. If that still doesn't lead to anything productive, you can let them know that the routine will get made with their input or not, and this is their opportunity to have a say if they want it. If they still decline, you have free rein to create whatever routine you want. That includes the tasks, division of labor, number of reminders, timeline, and rewards. As you follow through on the rewards (or refrain from giving them when your teen does not get on board), it is very likely your teen will realize that it is in their interest to work with you. While it may be tempting to say "too late!"–this is a good opportunity for you to welcome their input.

My teen's sense of important tasks/timeline/need for help is way off base.
This happens all the time, especially for teens who have ADHD or anxiety. Teens are convinced a certain part of the day will take them 30 minutes when it is easily 45–60. Or they insist they don't need any help or reminders but constantly forget to take care of stuff. Parents are often tempted to insist on more realistic plans from the start.

→ If you demand a specific routine from the start, your teen may think you're being controlling. Instead, use this as an opportunity to show your teen that you are on their team, willing to listen to their input, and believe in their abilities. If they think they can get through their afternoon homework routine with no reminders—great! Best case scenario, they are very motivated and actually do it. Worst case scenario, they weren't quite skillful enough and will have a valuable learning experience when they do not get the desired reward.

→ If this makes you nervous, remember that routines are not written in blood; they can be changed after a week or two if they were not working out! So while it's tempting to take control and insist on scheduling the routine your way from the start, do your absolute best to resist that urge. If you hold off on making changes until after your teen has tried it their way first, the shifts appear much more supportive and less controlling. Also remember Chapter 5 on selective attention; this is not the place for shame or blame. Instead, highlight what your teen did well and neutrally adjust the plan. For example:

Instead of: *I knew you weren't going to be able to keep up with everything. Now you're two weeks behind on homework because you were too stubborn to listen to me!*
Try: *I love that you were motivated to try getting stuff done on your own. It looks like that was tricky for the last two weeks, so the next two weeks I'm going to give two reminders. We'll check in after two weeks and can always make shifts if we need to!*

→ The idea of changing routines is also important to remember as your teen's context, development, and/or symptoms change. Periods of greater stress may require fewer tasks or more support. As they get older or have periods of relative calm, your teen might need less oversight. You can scale the system up and down as you need to, but try to stick with a system for at least a week (preferably two) before adjusting. That gives the plan enough time to start working and decreases rash, reactive changes in stressful moments.

It is really hard for *me* to stick with the routine.
Everybody works differently, and you may not be a person who is drawn to structure. If your child seems to be doing just fine with more flexibility, there is no need to put together a strict routine. However, if you know your child does better with clear plans, then it is worth trying.

→ The first recommendation is to try to figure out where routines go wrong for you. Do they feel overwhelming? Is it hard to check every night? Does it make you anxious or annoyed? Perhaps you yourself struggle with attentional difficulties and organization is not your strong suit. If you can "diagnose" the pitfall, you have a better chance of finding a pathway forward.
→ For parents who find routines overwhelming, try limiting the routine to the absolute essentials. Sure, your teen may end up skipping a few tasks you would like to see them do, but a shorter routine is more useful than one you can't keep up with.
→ If you forget to check on the routine, try using alarms or putting a copy someplace you absolutely cannot miss (like above the handle of the front door or on the bathroom mirror).
→ For parents who feel anxious or annoyed about the routines, go back to your long-term values. How does this routine serve you and your family?

Remembering the overall purpose can help people overcome the emotional hurdles that pop up.
→ For any caregivers with their own difficulties planning, organizing, and staying on top of tasks, think about the skills you are trying to get your kids to learn. Think of using planners, visual aids, and building habits. None of those will make following a routine easy, but you can learn new skills for yourself and teach your teenager at the same time.

Our schedule is so crazy it's hard to have a set routine.
Whether a parent's work schedule is constantly changing, or a teen's after-school activities switch from day-to-day, many families have a hard time coming up with a consistent schedule. There are three main workarounds to this.

→ The first option is to create a routine for each day of the week. Print them all and rotate them every day. This takes a lot of up-front work, but can completely get rid of the mental calculations you are having to figure out every single day. If you go this route, just know you'll probably need to remake the routine at the start of each school semester and summer since activities typically change.
→ The second option is to create two versions of the routine, one that is the full list and one that is shortened. The full list will include every task you want completed and is the list that will be used when you and your child actually have enough time to get through it. The shortened version will include only the essentials and will be used on days where somebody has to leave early or arrive late. Instead of having a specific start and end time, focus on a total amount of time that each phase of the routine should take. In other words, the full routine may have an evening phase that starts at 8:00 p.m. and ends at 10:45. The shortened routine may just have the requirement to complete all tasks within 60 minutes.
→ A final option can be to set up a 20-minute weekly family meeting where you review the standard routine and make any adjustments as needed. Perhaps there is a dentist appointment or a cancelled practice that you need to account for. Or maybe your teen has an upcoming event they need to shop for in the coming days. Spending a few minutes to get organized as a group is a good general practice even when your schedule is fairly consistent, but it is especially helpful if your day-to-day changes a lot.

I have a hard time being okay with my teenager needing to be told or rewarded for doing stuff around the house.
Many caregivers express this, believing that teens should be contributing members of the family. This is a totally understandable point of view. However, if your teenager was going to start helping around the house out of the goodness of their

Building Meaningful Routines

heart, they probably would have by now. If they haven't, there are a few things to keep in mind.

→ It is very possible that your teen does not see how the tasks in the routine are tied to larger values (like being helpful or considerate). While you might assume that the link between behavior at home and larger values is obvious, it may not be to your child. For example: to you, tidying up common areas may be a sign that each person in the home respects everybody else's space. To your teenager, tidying up has nothing to do with how much they respect other people. In fact, they don't really mind the mess, so it would not necessarily occur to them that stray items could possibly mean that much to you. You may be skeptical that your teen could be so oblivious, but many adolescents have a hyperfocus on their own internal experience and are not automatically great at perspective taking. If there is any chance this could be the case in your household, have a conversation with your teenager about the value of their help and why certain household chores truly matter to you in a big picture way. For example:

a. **Instead of:** *I don't understand why it is so hard to clean up your stuff!*
Try: *I am a calmer person when my space is neat. By picking up after yourself, you help make the house feel welcoming and relaxing to me.*
b. **Instead of:** *Why am I fighting with you to put your laundry in the basket?*
Try: *By throwing your clothes in the hamper you free up space in my head and my schedule to take care of other really important things, like making dinner. Each two-minute task you take care of is a huge help to me.*

You can try this type of communication before putting specific rewards in place. It is possible that creating a better understanding will help get your teenager on board with the household expectations.

→ If that does not work, it is possible that your teenager can see how their behavior links to larger values but does not find them internally motivating enough to impact their choices. This could happen because they do not prioritize the same values you do, or because there are other types of reinforcement or punishment at play here. Consider these two examples. You may really value thoughtfulness. Your teen probably isn't against being thoughtful, but it may not be their top priority. Maybe they care more about being smart, or athletic, or a good friend. While you spend your day doing lots of thoughtful things for your family, they spend their afternoons studying, or practicing, or socializing. The other scenario is that you and your teen do have the same values, but something gets in the way of acting on them. Maybe their worries, low mood, or disorganization interfere with their desire to take thoughtful action.

> In either of these instances, you want to return to the CAR model to see if you can switch up any contextual factors or results. While there might be multiple things you can change, two useful options are making use of reminders and rewards. They do not have to be intense or complicated, but your teen really may need extra support and scaffolding to shift these behaviors. Try not to worry too much about how this will impact your teenager in the long term. Most people will build habits and shift values as they grow up, and your model will be an important guide for them in this respect.

MAKING TIME FOR MEANINGFUL ACTIVITIES

Beyond the day-to-day to-do lists, chores, and household expectations, it is important to build time for meaningful activities. This idea stems from a treatment that is backed by research called Behavioral Activation, which was initially developed to help people with depression. The idea is that when mood drops, people tend to withdraw from the world around them. While this can sometimes be protective by saving them energy and effort, there are fewer and fewer opportunities to experience joy or meaning. Over time, this can make mood worse, and it becomes more difficult to reverse the downward spiral. To combat this, people are asked to find activities across a variety of categories that promote fun, connection, and/or engagement. While this is particularly important for teens with low mood, it is a good general strategy to keep in mind for all teenagers. There are five different categories of activities to think about when aiming to boost mood and meaning. They are:

1. *Fun*: This category is about pure enjoyment. What does your teen do that boosts their mood or creates a spark of joy in them?
2. *Social*: How can your teenager connect with other people?
3. *Physical*: What are options to help your teen move or feel grounded in their body?
4. *Mastery*: This domain is about creating a sense of accomplishment. It focuses on activities that allow teenagers to build a skill or make progress toward a goal.
5. *Service*: The idea is to find ways to give back to others. It is a nice opportunity to shift focus away from the self and toward others, can foster a sense of self-worth, and may lead to positive interactions.

It is typically helpful to have a mix of activities across the different categories. Often, teens are doing a lot of fun ones (or a lot of social, or a lot of physical), but are not so well balanced. And while some of these categories naturally overlap, and it is okay to have more interest in one category than the rest, building a range of interests is useful. Not only does it offer opportunities for new experiences and perspectives, but it is also protective. Say your teen is heavily into their sport. Depending on the sport, this may add in a bit of the social element if they hang out with teammates, and some of the mastery element as they get better and better. But what happens when your teenager gets injured and is out for a few weeks? Or they go off to college or their first job and are no longer playing their sport? These situations can leave teens with a huge void, often leading to a worse mood or heightened anxiety.

To help avoid these outcomes, parents can help their teens start to get creative about the types of activities they spend time on. To do this, you will work through the following steps, which are similar to creating your general routine:

1. *Ask your teen to create a list of activities that fit into each category*: This should include any options they are already doing or things they would like to do. Perhaps they love to bake, play soccer, and go to the movies with friends. Great—those can all get added to the list. Maybe they have always wanted to volunteer at an animal shelter but it hasn't happened yet. That's okay; put it on the list.
2. *Add in ideas of your own*: After your teen has started their list, you can make suggestions about other things to add to the list. This should not turn into a battle. Even if you're convinced that your teen would *love* theater, do not add it if they are 100% opposed. The only exception to this is if you have a teenager who will not create a list or only has one or two ideas for each. You can let them know that variety is important, so you'll be adding some options if they are not able to think of ideas.
3. *Decide how much support you will give*: If your teenager is already doing a variety of different activities across the different categories, they probably do not need much help with this skill. However, most teenagers will need at least some support. This is particularly true for teens with ADHD or depression, who may struggle with the legwork and follow-through. Sometimes this support is practical: Can you help research animal shelters to volunteer at, fill out paperwork for the volleyball league, or chip in for music lessons? Support may be emotional: Does your teen need encouragement to try a new activity, or a cheerleader to help them when they feel bummed about slow progress? Support may also be tangible. Teens can be resistant to trying new activities, and some activities on this list may need to be tied to rewards while your kid gets started. You can loop the different categories into the daily or weekly routine, or make use of other reward strategies from Chapter 9. As with routines, you can scale this support based on your child's general needs and abilities.
4. *Set concrete plans*: Starting and keeping up with activities can be hard. To make it more likely to happen, make some behaviors a matter of habit. Maybe the whole family calls relatives on Sundays (social), or there is a daily walk home from school (physical), or everybody helps to make dinner once a week (mastery). For activities that do not fit so easily into the course of the day, consider scheduling them into the family calendar so you can plan around them. One important tip is to make sure you place equal value on the activities your teen enjoys compared to the ones you want them to enjoy. The fact that your child has fun making "silly" social media videos with their friend is as important as the sense of accomplishment they could feel learning to make their own dinner. If you only push the activities you find valuable, you are likely to lose buy-in from your teen and the relationship will take a hit.

IDENTIFYING MEANINGFUL ACTIVITIES

In Exercise 7.2 is a list of activities that cover the five areas: fun, social, physical, mastery, and service. Check off any items that your teen is already doing, and put a star next to activities they might have an interest in. This is just a chance to see where your teen is already spending a lot of their time, and begin to brainstorm other ways to add enjoyment and meaning to their lives. This list is not exhaustive, and you can think of other ideas that might work for your teen.

EXERCISE 7.2 IDENTIFYING MEANINGFUL ACTIVITIES

Social	Fun	Physical	Mastery	Service
___ Video call	___ TV/movies	___ Walk/run	___ Practice a language	___ Volunteer
___ Text or message	___ Play a game	___ Yoga/stretch	___ Learn a recipe or type of cooking	___ School/club leadership
___ See a movie or get food as a group	___ Outing (beach trip, amusement park, mini golf)	___ Throw a ball or frisbee	___ Try a new hobby (dance, woodworking, indoor garden)	___ Join advocacy groups
___ See a friend	___ Play video games	___ Play a sport	___ Creative outlets (music, drawing, origami)	___ Park clean-ups
___ Go on a date	___ Listen to music	___ Dance party	___ Learn a life skill (investing, car care, sewing)	___ Donate to favorite charity
___ Join a community or youth group	___ Bake	___ Jump rope	___ Build on your current strengths (studying, athletics, kindness, etc.)	___ Read about causes you care about
___ Join a school club	___ See a concert	___ Play with a pet	___ Find a job	___ Help friends/family

TIPS FOR CREATING ROUTINES AND MEANINGFUL ACTIVITIES

There are a handful of tips that will help routines and meaningful activities work for your family. The first is to start small. Whether it is the number of tasks on the list, or the amount of time your teen is supposed to spend doing them; aim to begin with a fairly low number. This chapter doesn't help anybody if you and your teen are left feeling overwhelmed. You can always add more in once everybody adjusts to the new normal. If you are not sure when to adjust, use the 20% rule. Assume that your teenager will not do everything on their list about 20% of the time simply because nobody is perfect, and sometimes things get missed. If they are missing way more than 20%, they may need more support or more time to build up their skills. Once they are consistently only missing that 20%, you can add more in.

The next thing to remember is that routines are changeable. As noted above, writing down a to-do list does not mean you have to stick with it forever. Plan to review it every two to four weeks to make sure it's still working for your family. If there was a chore on the list that has become regular habit, you can stop giving rewards for it or swap it out for another one. If your teen tried volunteering at a park clean up and actually had a really miserable time, find a new service activity! This is how you can add flexibility into your overall structure in a way that meets the needs of your child.

Treat routines and activities like an experiment. You might not be exactly sure what the best set up is for your household. Besides the actual tasks, you can change things like the number of reminders, how specific you are about the daily timeline, or how often you check to make sure the routine is completed. Use the first few weeks or months to play around and see what feels best. Maybe you love structure and had the routine scheduled in 30-minute increments. A few weeks in you might find that is totally too much for your teenager with depression. No problem, you can change it. Even if there are hiccups along the way, you are teaching your teenager important information about how to use and adjust tools in their own lives.

The final tip is to beware of the procrastination trap. No, not your teen's habit of putting homework off till Sunday night. The procrastination trap refers to caregivers who keep waiting for the perfect moment to introduce the new routine, expectations, or activities, and never actually get around to doing it. Common reasons are that "the schedule is just so crazy this week," or "we have people in town so our normal routine doesn't make sense," or "I wanted to type it up and make it look really nice before introducing it." There are 100 reasons why parents put off routines. They are reasonable, but they do not serve you or your teenager. There is no perfect time to introduce change, and there is no ideal font or design to help your teen fall in love with their new chores. Do yourself a favor and set a date in your calendar right now to introduce this tool to your teen. Commit to following through no matter what shape your to-do list looks like or what else popped up unexpectedly. Getting started is often the biggest hurdle to this skill, and any adjustments you need can happen down the road.

TESTING YOUR KNOWLEDGE OF MEANINGFUL ROUTINES AND ACTIVITIES

You now have a strategy in place to tackle three parts of your teen's routine: daily tasks, household expectations, and meaningful activities. That is a lot of different things to keep in mind! To help you test your knowledge, look through the example routines in Exercise

7.3. Next to each part of the routine, take note of any skills or stuck points that you notice along the way. There may be some skills or stuck points that you notice apply to the entire routine, so there is room below the schedule to write a few notes about this. As a reminder, here are some skillful choices to look out for: specific information (clear details of what the task includes, who is responsible for what task, what types of support are in place, clear start or end time); expectations are developmentally appropriate and realistic; rewards are used; there is a mix of meaningful activities.

And here are some stuck points to look out for: information that is vague or unclear (broad descriptions, unclear supports, no start or end times); expectations that are too hard or not realistic; lack of rewards; lacking meaningful activities.

EXERCISE 7.3 TESTING YOUR KNOWLEDGE OF MEANINGFUL ROUTINES AND ACTIVITIES

Task: *Morning Routine*	Skill Used or Stuck Point
6:30 Wake up	
Get dressed	
Have breakfast	
Take meds	
Pack bag with reminders	
Morning chores	

General skills you noticed: _____

General stuck points you noticed: _____

Task: *Weekend Routine*	Skill Used or Stuck Point
10:30 Wake up (1 reminder)	
Free time (read, TV, see a friend, do homework)	
Eat lunch and do chores (make bed, take out trash, clear up your stuff from kitchen) 1:45–4:00 Practice	
Finish homework	
Family dinner	
Prep for next week	
Bed by 11:30	

General skills you noticed: _____

General stuck points you noticed: _____

Exercise 7.3 ANSWER KEY Morning Routine

Task	Skill Used or Stuck Point
6:30 Wake up	Skill: clear start time listed
Get dressed and brush teeth	
Have breakfast	
Take meds	
Pack bag with reminders	Stuck point: not specific about the number of reminders
Morning chores	Stuck point: not specific enough, no end time

General skills you noticed: *List is simple and to the point; the order seems to make sense because tasks that must happen before school come first.*

General stuck points you noticed: *Almost none of the tasks say if the teen is doing everything or gets any kind of support, and there doesn't seem to be any sort of reward for getting through the tasks on time.*

Exercise 7.3 ANSWER KEY Weekend Routine

Task	Skill Used or Stuck Point
10:30 Wake up (1 reminder)	Skill: specific time and number of reminders
Free time (read, TV, see a friend, do homework)	Skill: good list of examples
Eat lunch and do chores (make bed, take out trash, clean your stuff out of living room)	Skill: good list of examples Stuck point: may need set time if teen puts things off
1:45–4:00 Practice	Stuck point: may need details about getting there/who brings what supplies
Finish homework	Stuck point: may need details about check-ins, rules for completing homework
Family dinner	Stuck point: does not include details on what teen is supposed to help with
Prep for next week	Stuck point: may need details
Bed by 11:30	Skill: time listed

General skills you noticed: *Most tasks include examples and details; there are clear start and end times for some of the tasks.*

General stuck points you noticed: *Not much mentioned about what teen does solo versus with support; some tasks may need more details.*

TEST YOUR SKILL IN MEANINGFUL ROUTINES AND ACTIVITIES

In Exercise 7.4 are the sample morning and weekend routines from the previous exercise. Now, try creating your own version of the routines, making sure to think about the skills outlined in this chapter. There are a few extra lines for each routine in case you want to add in more tasks or detail. Of course, there are many ways to create effective routines with engaging activities. The example rewrites below each routine will outline a different option.

EXERCISE 7.4 TEST YOUR SKILL IN MEANINGFUL ROUTINES AND ACTIVITIES

Morning Routine Rewrite

Original	Rewrite
6:30 Wake up	
Get dressed	
Have breakfast	
Take meds	
Pack bag with reminders	
Morning chores	

EXAMPLE Morning Routine Rewrite

Original	Rewrite
6:30 Wake up	6:30 Wake up (1 reminder)
Get dressed	Get dressed
Have breakfast	Have breakfast (you make and clear dishes to sink)
Take meds	By 7:00 take meds (Mom will give)
Pack bag with reminders	By 7:15 have bags packed (check desk and grab lunch) with 1 reminder
Morning chores	Walk the dog, throw laundry in the hamper
	If done by 7:30, have 15-minute phone time
	7:45 out the door to catch bus

You might notice that this morning routine is not very different from the original, but it includes more detail. There are more time stamps, clearer descriptions of who does what task, and details about what some tasks involve. There is also a built in reward at the end. For a teen who does not struggle with attention, you may not need reminders or as much detail listed out.

WEEKEND ROUTINE REWRITE

Task	
10:30 Wake up (1 reminder)	
Free time (read, TV, see a friend, do homework)	
Eat lunch and do chores (make bed, take out trash, clean your stuff out of living room)	
1:45–4:00 Practice	
Finish homework	
Family dinner	
Prep for next week	
Bed by 11:30	

EXAMPLE Weekend Routine

Task	
10:30 Wake up (1 reminder)	Wake up by 10:30 (1 reminder)
Free time (read, TV, see a friend, do homework)	Free time till 11:30 (read, TV, do homework)
Eat lunch and do chores (make bed, take out trash, clean your stuff out of living room)	Chores (make bed, take out trash, clean your stuff out of living room)
1:45–4:00 Practice	Lunch and Free time until 1:45 (can see a friend until practice if you want)
Finish homework	1:45–4:00 practice (you grab bag, Mom will arrange carpool)
Family dinner	Snack and shower
Prep for next week	Finish homework
Bed by 11:30	6:30 set table and sit for family dinner
10:30 Wake up (1 reminder)	Prep for next week: throw down laundry, go through assignments and tell Mom if you need any help or supplies, text friends for plans
Bed by 11:30	Free time (walk, game, screens, etc.) *can go out if prep is done by 9:00. Must be home by 10:30
	Bed by 11:30

In this example, there was some significant rearranging to help set up natural rewards. In the morning, free time was split in two and chores were put in the middle. This allows the teen a little time to fully wake up before getting to work, and allows for a social reward if chores get done quickly enough. A snack was added after practice to help prevent any hunger meltdowns, and shower was moved earlier in the day to prevent late-night battles when teens (and parents) are already exhausted. These small shifts can be especially important for teens with mood and attentional difficulties, where their symptoms make it difficult to track body cues or follow-through with daily self-care. Prep included more detail, and there is another natural reward of free time if the teen finishes early enough before bed.

TRY IT OUT: MEANINGFUL ROUTINES AND ACTIVITIES

It is time to put routines and meaningful activities into practice in your own life. Worksheet 7.1 is designed to help you decide which parts of this skill to begin with over the next few weeks. There is no need to do a complete overhaul of your household schedule all at once. Start small and add on over time. Complete the exercise below to increase the likelihood of following through successfully this week. Next week, review your answers and decide if you want to keep them the same, or challenge yourself a bit more. Slowly build your skill over time.

WORKSHEET 7.1

1. Do you want to try creating a morning, afternoon, bedtime, or weekend routine?
   _____

   Is your family schedule consistent enough to use the same routine every day, or do you need to create different versions? _____

   _____

   Schedule a time in your calendar to create the routine you want to start with.____

   _____

2. Does your teen already have a range of meaningful activities, or would it be helpful to increase this in their schedule? _____

   _____

   If it would be helpful, schedule a time in your calendar to work through that exercise with them. _____

   _____

3. How will you remember to make time for these tasks (alarms, sticky notes, plan with partner, etc.)? _____

   _____

4. What barriers, including any of the common stuck points listed earlier in the chapter, do you think may interfere in using the skills, and how do you plan to troubleshoot them? _____

_____

_____

5. List three things that will help you complete this task and make sense of this skill. This could include reminders, skill review, social support, accountability measures, or other ideas you would find useful.

   1. _____

   _____

   2. _____

   _____

   3. _____

   _____

Helpful Support versus Unhelpful Accommodation

WHAT IS ACCOMMODATION?

For the purpose of this book, accommodation refers to a situation in which a parent or caregiver changes the normal routines or practices because of teen symptoms or behavior, in order to make things easier for the teen. Here are a few examples of what that may look like:

- A parent packs their teen's backpack daily because their teen struggles with organization.
- A caregiver writes a sick note to school on days when the teen has test anxiety.
- A teen is not asked to do any chores due to fear about how they might react.
- A parent makes excuses for their teen who lashes out at their family because of low frustration tolerance and never asks the teen to make a repair or work on better responses.
- Caregivers speak for their anxious child who is nervous about answering questions.
- Parents help set up extra supports in school for their teen who struggles to follow lessons.
- Parents agree to fold laundry a very specific way, as asked to do by their teen with OCD.
- During the week of the SATs, parents let their teen skip their homework so they can prep.

As you can see, accommodations come in many different shapes and sizes. They can be small changes that are only made once or twice or range all the way to systems-level shifts that result in changes over a sustained period. Whatever the scale, accommodations involve change specifically because of symptoms and no other reason.

WHY ACCOMMODATION MATTERS

Most parents of all teenagers, even those without mental health difficulties, use *some* accommodation. In fact, many adults receive forms of accommodation as well. They can be a useful strategy to help level the playing field for individuals with different types of difficulties. When mental health symptoms are in the picture, there is often an increase in the amount of accommodation that occurs. This matters, because it can have a huge impact on whether or not the teen feels supported, is given needed supports to thrive, and also has an opportunity to practice becoming more skillful.

What does this mean? Teens who are never given any accommodation may resent their parents. Perhaps they feel they are not being understood or given a voice. Teens who are given too much accommodation may get the impression their parents do not believe in them or that they are capable of doing hard things. Extra supports can also help make sure that all teens have an equal chance to show their strengths. For example, perhaps a teen with ADHD knows all of the material but struggles to focus on the test in a room of 30 kids. They will have a fairer chance of earning the grade they deserve if they get a quiet testing space accommodation. Accommodation also plays a role in how symptoms play out over time. Without any accommodation, teen distress can be so high that their urge to avoid hard situations is overwhelming. Kids with anxiety or depression may completely withdraw and find themselves unable to make any progress because the hurdles just seem too high. On the flip side, overaccommodation sets up a trap in which teens never have to push themselves to make progress. If the parent always steps in to save the day, there is little reason for teens to get out of their comfort zone to build new skills or learn through new experiences. This often leaves teens unable to solve problems or face adversity once outside the protective cocoon of their caregivers. With this in mind, it is important for parents to consider when and where accommodation is appropriate.

WHEN TO USE ACCOMMODATION

There are three main questions to consider that can help you decide when to use accommodation.

1) Does the accommodation align with your family values?
2) Is the accommodation one you are willing to offer without resentment?
3) Is this a temporary accommodation that will allow your teen to build skills?

Consider an example from earlier in this book: you have a teen who hates doing their math homework. Perhaps their ADHD symptoms make it hard to stay focused on the task or they become anxious and avoidant. As a parent, you have some ways you could accommodate your teen's distress. One option is to change the outcomes for doing math homework: make it really worth their while to get the work done through extra rewards and treats. Another option would be to switch up the context by asking school to change their homework policy, looking for a less intense math class, sitting with your teen to give them extra support while they do math, or getting your teen tutoring. You can likely think of other types of accommodation you could try as well. In trying to decide what (if any) of these options are worth putting into place, go back to the three questions:

1) Does the accommodation align with your family values? Perhaps your child would do math more easily if they got to eat their favorite takeout order every day while they worked. Some families may be completely fine with this. You might not be willing or able to offer that because you do not believe in ordering food that often or need to prioritize saving money by eating out less. That is okay; you do not have to pick this accommodation just because it would work. Maybe you are okay with a smaller version of this accommodation, like ordering take-out during their weekend math assignment if they got their weekday homework done

without an issue. Or perhaps you find a completely different way to make the math homework more interesting that is more in line with your values.

2) Is the accommodation one that you are willing to offer without resentment? You might be happy to stay in the room while your teen does their math homework so they do not feel quite so lonely and bored, but perhaps you draw the line at actually helping them write out answers. Or perhaps you don't mind checking in on them a few times but start to feel frustrated when they insist on doing math right when their siblings get home from school and make it impossible for you to be there for all of your kids. Again, consider if there is a version of accommodation that you can get behind without feeling like you are being taken advantage of.

3) Is this a temporary accommodation that will allow your child to build skills? If you told your teen they could skip math homework forever, they would never get better or know that they can get through hard tasks. If, instead, they got extra tutoring, they would be getting temporary help that allows them to build a skill. Perhaps you decide to give them a snack and fidget during math homework. Doing so would help meet their physical needs and give them a coping mechanism to make the task more tolerable, allowing them to get through some useful practice.

These are just guidelines to help you consider whether an accommodation might be okay. There might be some supports you do feel a bit resentful about, but overall recognize they are useful for your child and are willing to make that trade. Further, when it comes to the question about whether accommodations are temporary, there well may be situations in which accommodations last through one's lifetime. Some people have a true limit on their abilities that require accommodations in an ongoing way. For example, just as somebody with poor eyesight will always need glasses, it is okay if your teen always needs extra time on tests or access to a counselor for checking in during hard moments. The main points to consider are whether your teen is able to gain more skill and/or if there are any significant downsides to the accommodation. If the answers to these questions are yes, then it is often helpful to think about how to start with useful accommodations and then plan to lower them over time. A general rule of thumb is to wait until your child is about 80% successful before decreasing the amount of support. This number is used because *most* kids are not 100% successful 100% of the time. Eighty percent tells us they are making actively skillful choices most of the time, and are likely able to take on a bit more of a challenge when the accommodation is scaled down.

ACCOMMODATION SELF-ASSESSMENT

If you are not sure whether your style is overly supportive, not supportive enough, or just right, take the accommodation self-assessment in Exercise 8.1 to get a sense of where you fall on the accommodation spectrum. In each row, circle the description that you most relate to. Once done, check the results key to get more information on your style and tips you might find useful.

EXERCISE 8.1 ACCOMMODATION SELF-ASSESSMENT

1.	I find myself bending over backward to help make things easier for my teen.	I refuse to change how I do things at home just to make it easier for my teen.	I am willing to change a few things to make life easier for my teen, but I try to find a balance that works for everybody.
2.	It's not my problem if my teen is distressed or fails. They need to learn to figure it out.	I find that I cannot allow myself to sit by and watch my teen become upset or fail at something.	It is hard for me to watch my teen struggle, but recognize they need to do hard things in order to make progress.
3.	My teen is getting lots of negative feedback in areas that they seem to struggle with, but I want them to solve their own problems.	My teen would probably have a hard time taking care of things fully on their own, but they would have a good idea of where to start or get some things done.	My teen has major difficulty doing things on their own in at least one or two areas where I am giving accommodation.
4.	I do not think lowering supports will be easy, but I think I will be able to handle the outcome.	I am terrified of how my kid will respond if I take away some of the supports I am giving now.	I am worried my teen will become too dependent if I offer extra help or support when they are having a hard time.
5.	It seems like I do much more for my teen than other parents are doing.	I make sure my teen is much more independent than their peers. Parents are way too overinvolved these days.	I try to find ways for my teen to do things on their own when they can, but am okay to offer help while they are still learning.
6.	I make a point of letting my teen face challenges on their own and do not do much to clear hurdles when it comes to their emotions.	I can think of many, many examples where I step in to take care of problems or make things easier for my teen.	There are a handful of things I do to make things easier for my teen or help them solve problems.

Exercise 8.1 RESULTS KEY Accommodation Self-Assessment

1.	I find myself bending over backward to help make things easier for my teen. = 3 points	I refuse to change how I do things at home just to make it easier for my teen. = 1 point	I am willing to change a few things to make life easier for my teen, but I try to find a balance that works for everybody. = 2 points
2.	It's not my problem if my teen is distressed or fails. They need to learn to figure it out. = 1 point	I find that I cannot allow myself to sit by and watch my teen become upset or fail at something. = 3 points	It is hard for me to watch my teen struggle, but recognize they need to do hard things in order to make progress. = 2 points
3.	My teen is getting lots of negative feedback in certain areas, but I want them to learn how to solve their own problems. = 1 point	My teen has a hard time taking care of things fully on their own, but they can usually take some steps in the right direction. = 2 points	My teen has major difficulty doing things on their own in at least one or two areas where I am giving accommodation. = 3 points
4.	I do not think lowering supports will be easy, but I think I will be able to handle the outcome. = 2 points	I am terrified of how my kid will respond if I take away some of the supports I am giving now. = 3 points	I am worried my teen will become too dependent if I offer extra help or support when they are having a hard time. = 1 point
5.	It seems like I do much more for my teen than other parents are doing. = 3 points	I make sure my teen is much more independent than their peers. Parents are way too overinvolved these days. = 1 point	I try to find ways for my teen to do things on their own when they can, but am okay to offer help while they are still learning. = 2 points
6.	I make a point of letting my teen face challenges on their own and do not do much to clear hurdles when it comes to their emotions. = 1 point	I can think of many, many examples where I step in to take care of problems or make things easier for my teen. = 3 points	There are a handful of things I do to make things easier for my teen or help them solve problems. = 2 points

Score	Accommodation Style
6–9	*Underaccommodating.* Whether you are struggling to make time for accommodations, think they are unnecessary, or really want to help your teen learn how to face challenges on their own, it sounds like you may want to consider giving a little extra support. This does not mean overhauling your entire household to do everything for your teen, but consider what sorts of changes to your teen's life would make it easier for them to face hurdles without feeling overloaded or defeated.
10–13	*Just right.* Based on your responses, it sounds like you have found a good balance between giving support while letting your teen build their own skills and independence. This is really hard to do, so great work. Keep looking for ways to provide help that allows your child to reach their potential, without limiting their opportunities to work through problems they are capable of facing.
14–18	*Overaccommodation.* Your score suggests you may find yourself offering lots of extra support. This may be done with the absolute best intentions, but can become overwhelming for you as the parent or hide opportunities for your teen to grow. Use the tips in the chapter to create a plan to slowly lower how much support you are offering. Watching your teen become upset or struggle is difficult, but is usually only a temporary pitfall on their way to more skillful behavior.

COMMON STUCK POINTS TO HELPFUL ACCOMMODATION

There are many things that can get in the way of finding and using accommodations that work. In this section, read through the list of challenges that parents often experience when trying to find the right balance. Underneath each common stuck point, you will find tips and considerations that can help address each barrier. At the end of the chapter, you will have a chance to make note of any examples that would be helpful for you to keep in mind.

I try to take a step back, but it's just easier for all of us when I step in and take care of things.
Many parents find that scaling back their support comes at a cost. Teen symptoms flair and emotion and behavior dysregulation shoot up. This is hard enough, but is even more stressful when the teen actually falls short of certain goals without the extra push from parents. With all of this, it just seems easier for parents to either give into the teen or take care of the problem themselves. This is a very typical pattern and it is in everybody's best interest to break.

→ It is really hard to sit by as your teen becomes upset or starts to fail on tasks, especially if you can simply make it all go away by taking a more active role. Unfortunately, when parents do this over and over, symptoms tend to get worse over time. Whenever a symptom flare is rewarded by a parent who saves the day, that teen brain has learned that their symptoms are working for them. Whether it is anxiety, low mood, or something else, bigger shows of distress lead to bigger levels of support, so that symptom has good reason to increase over time. Additionally, when accommodation increases, teens miss out on opportunities to practice being skillful and feeling the success of doing something hard. Without those positive outcomes, it is much harder for them to make progress. Keep this in mind when you are trying to limit your accommodations but feel pulled to give extra support. Think about the long-term outcomes you want for your child. Doing so can help make it easier to put up with the short-term negative outcomes that may come up.

→ This is another opportunity to look back at Chapter 3 and review your parent coping skills. In-the-moment strategies can be really helpful when faced with a whining, negotiating, distraught, or argumentative teenager.

I think my teen needs to learn how to do things without extra help because that's what they'll face in the real world.
Some parents are hesitant to use accommodation because they believe they're being too easy on their teen. Caregivers worry that any accommodation will make it impossible for teens to learn how to manage challenges on their own.

→ There is a lot to be said about giving your teen time to work through problems independently. Overaccommodation is not helpful. However,

Helpful Support versus Unhelpful Accommodation

refusing to give accommodations when there are truly impairing symptoms can also set your teen up for failure because they are faced with a task that is impossible for them to manage. This can snowball into negative consequences with peers, teachers, and self-esteem.

For example, say your teen with low attention has a hard time completing tests in a single class period. You could ask the school to give your teen extra time, which is a typical accommodation for many kids, especially those with ADHD. But perhaps you think your teen really needs to figure out how to work more quickly. You don't bring it up with school and instead talk to your teen about moving faster through their work. Unfortunately, no amount of talking is going to magically change your teen's brain chemistry and structure. Even if they are really trying to move more quickly, they truly might not be able to. Now they get lower grades on their tests, are criticized by harsh teachers, and think badly about themselves for not performing.

→ Consider using accommodations to meet your teen where they are at while putting in place a concrete plan to help them build skills and remove the accommodations over time. In this example, this might mean getting extra time on tests while your teen starts to practice skills with a study coach or tutor, or meets with a doctor to consider medication options. Maybe the help will eventually allow your teen to move quickly enough that they do not need the extra time forever. Or you might find that the supports are helpful and the extra time is still a really useful addition to help your teen meet their full potential.

→ Whatever you decide, know that accommodations often provide opportunities for your teen to make progress, and they can be scaled up or down over time in a way that works for your family.

I never know how hard to push my teen who is struggling.
Many parents feel very guilty about taking away accommodations when their teenager is struggling with their mental health. They worry that asking their teen to do more will make them feel badly or worsen their symptoms.

→ This can be a very stressful situation for parents. You fear your choices will make your teen worse, and also see they cannot keep going on the path they are. In these cases, it can be helpful to plan out exactly how much you are going to reduce accommodation over time. Anytime somebody learns something new or faces a challenging situation, you can expect a certain level of distress. If you rate that on a zero to 10 scale, look for accommodations that will keep your teen roughly between a four and a seven. If the accommodation makes the situation *too* easy (distress from a zero to three), it is unlikely that your teen is having to practice skills or learn anything new. If the accommodation is too little and the situation is super hard (distress from eight to 10), your teen may go into panic mode. This is not necessarily harmful, but it is certainly unpleasant. You're likely to get pushback and they will be more resistant to trying similar situations in the future. When you think about how you want to start scaling down support, pick an option that might create a little bit of distress in your teen without going overboard.

→ If you have safety concerns about your teen and worry that reducing accommodation may lead to risky situations, speak to their pediatrician or mental health professional to have a safety plan in place. While it can be scary, many teens who have risk may still be in a situation where lowering accommodations is important. So, you want to have a concrete plan in place to address safety issues that come up for teens who get highly dysregulated with change or new challenges.

It's too hard to watch my teen fail.
When parents start to lower their accommodations, there is a big adjustment period where teen skills may not have caught up to the expectations placed on them. This can lead to distress and failures at school, in hobbies, with friends, or at home. Many parents worry that these bad outcomes will make things harder for their teen, or they will not be able to recover.

→ It is really hard to watch your teen struggle, especially when you know you could step in to help the situation turn out better. In some cases, the failure really may have big, negative consequences. However, failures are also lessons. As cliché as it sounds, people learn when things go wrong. If your child is going to have a misstep when their supports are lowered, it is in their interest to have the misstep earlier rather than later! Failing a class or getting fired from a job is typically much less of a problem for a 16-year-old than a young adult who is in college or at their first full-time job. Having a setback while under the protection and care of parents means they will have much more support in getting back up and recovering. Once teens leave the house and move more fully into adulthood, they are much less shielded when their symptoms interfere.

→ As is often the case, this is a good time for parent coping skills. Remember your long-term values for yourself and your child and use your in-the-moment coping skills to get through stressful periods.

I ping-pong back and forth between giving tons of extra support and then getting fed up and wanting them to do more on their own.
Many parents start with the best intentions as they add extra supports for their teen. At some point they get overwhelmed and try to scale way back. Their teen gets very distressed, and all the support goes back in place, only to lead to more parental frustration that results in overly demanding or harsh expectations. They bounce back and forth between two extremes because they are trying so hard to find an option that works!

→ If you find yourself in this situation, think about creating a clear pathway to scale down accommodation gradually. Create a ladder of different things you can do to reduce accommodation, starting small and growing bigger over time. Keep in mind the tip mentioned earlier in looking for steps that will keep your teen in that middle range of distress without going too low or too high. If you take it one step at a time, you lower the risk of becoming overly demanding and having a teen who loses control of their emotions and behavior and lower your own sense of burnout and resentment because you can see the pathway forward.

→ Make sure you are using your other parenting skills. Consider how to increase your reserves during this time, knowing that change can be difficult and you may need extra support. Look for ways to reward progress (either for yourself or your teen). Make use of your labeled praise and validation skills to emotionally support your teen as your interactions shift. Brush up on active ignoring so you are prepared when your teen becomes upset. All of these skills will help you make slow, steady progress over time.

I don't know what kinds of accommodation are helpful.
Unfortunately, there is no perfect accommodation roadmap you can use to know exactly when and how to support your teen who is struggling. It can be confusing to know what types of support are helpful, especially if you and your family are new to mental health struggles.

→ The first option is to talk with a guidance counselor, pediatrician, or mental health professional to get their input. Most of these individuals can provide suggestions about the types of supports that tend to be useful. It would be particularly useful to talk with a clinician who has training in Cognitive Behavioral Therapy or Parent Management Training, because they will have specific expertise on this topic. Of course, not every school has a guidance counselor well versed in scaling back parental accommodation, and you may not have access to a mental health professional in the community.

→ If you cannot get guidance from experts you trust, try to think about what is keeping your child most stuck and build a support ladder around that. Is there difficulty with organization (in which case supports may focus on reminders, organizational tools, and check-ins that are slowly removed over time). If the main pain point is anxiety, what supports help your teen feel brave or more willing to face worrisome tasks? If they struggle with mood, are there accommodations in place to temporarily lower the load they are facing or make it easier for them to access meaningful activities? Your knowledge of your teen is useful in answering this question, as is input from your teen.

> **I think I need to wait for my teen to get more skills before I start pulling back the extra supports I'm offering.**
> Lots of parents wait to see their teen making progress before they reduce accommodation. These caregivers, understandably, want to know their child can "handle" increased independence before putting them in a stressful situation. This is perfectly reasonable if your teen really wants to get more skillful and is actively working toward this! If they are in therapy or showing you how they are practicing coping and regulation strategies, it is okay to give that some time to build momentum before you scale down the supports.
>
> This strategy does not work for all teens. In some cases, the teen does not view accommodations as a problem and do not care about becoming more skillful or learning how to handle situations on their own. Other teens are very aware that their mental health symptoms are getting in the way, or that the accommodations are causing problems for them or you, but are too stuck in their symptoms to work on them. Building skills is hard work, and facing distress can be terrifying and exhausting, so the accommodations are overall worthwhile. For both types of teen, you can wait till you are blue in the face and your teen still may never gain an inch toward increased distress tolerance or independence.
>
> → For these teens, parents must make the first move. When the parents stop writing excused absence notes or ordering for their teen who is too shy, suddenly the balance between reinforcement and punishment has shifted. When this happens, teens start to feel the weight of their symptoms more, which can increase motivation to make change. This can be a scary leap of faith on the part of caregivers. However, in some cases it is the only way to get teens to start making forward progress.

TEST YOUR KNOWLEDGE OF ACCOMMODATIONS

In Exercise 8.2, take a look at sample accommodations parents are using. Put a check next to each accommodation that seems to be appropriate. Put an ✗ next to accommodations that seem to miss the mark and try to write down whether they are not enough support or are too much support.

EXERCISE 8.2 TEST YOUR KNOWLEDGE OF ACCOMMODATIONS

✓ or ✗	Consequence	Not Enough or Too Much
	Parent has made teen breakfast in bed every day for the last year to help make sure they wake up for school.	
	The teen's chore is to empty the garbage to earn allowance. The parents give numerous reminders and will still give most of the allowance even if the chore is not completed.	
	Teen procrastinates on homework and then panics when they cannot finish on time. Parents often write a note for the teen asking for extensions, giving made-up reasons for the delays.	
	Teen is very demanding that the family does things according to the teen's preferences. This usually involves parents bending over backward to rearrange schedules and ignore the other kids' preferences.	
	Parents agree to rearrange the Saturday afternoon schedule according to the teen's preferences, with the understanding that the morning is based on family preferences and the teen-determined time will decrease by 1 hour each week.	
	A teen has been refusing to go to school. The parents put in a request for complete remote learning for the rest of the year, feeling that this is easier than the battle every morning.	
	A teen has been refusing to go to school. The parents work with the school to put a gradual re-entry plan in place, so that the teen is on school grounds but slowly builds up their workload over a few weeks.	
	A teen has a hard time with interruptions and is trying to work on it. They have asked parents to give them a hand signal when they notice it happening. Parents think the teen should be aware enough to notice on their own, so do not agree to this.	
	A teen has been bullied by a peer in homeroom classroom all year. Parents ask the school to switch the teen to a different homeroom held at the same time.	

	A teen is working on reducing compulsive habits with their therapist who has suggested that the family slowly practice difficult situations. The parents are tired of the accommodation and decide to jump into the hardest practice areas all at once.	
	Teen needs lots of reminders to check the school portal for homework. Family agrees that parents will remind 3 times each night in September, 2 times each night in October, and 1 time each night in November. Will then decide what ongoing help is useful.	
	A teen is quite fearful of flying. They ask to sit in the aisle row of their upcoming flight so they are less likely to look outside the window. Parents think this is silly and say that the teen needs to take the window seat because they have to get over it.	
	Parents have been reading and rereading their teen's college essays because the teen is worried they are not good enough. This continues even after the essay looks good and the teen should really be shifting focus to other parts of their application.	
	A teen has a fear of throwing up and is terrified of eating foods nearing the expiration date. The caregivers have started to throw out food a few days before the expiration date to avoid any meltdowns.	
	There is a house rule that all kids must text parents if they are going to be home late. One teen struggles to remember to do this, so they offer to share their location with the parents so they always know where they are. Parents agree to this compromise.	
	A teen has been feeling depressed but is trying to stay involved in their activities. Parents think the teen is spending too much time "moping around" so refuse the teen's requests to have a low-key Saturday after a full week of trying to stay engaged in school.	
	A teen texts parents every few minutes while at school, asking for reassurance about things they are anxious about. Parents respond to each text, providing reassuring answers.	
	Teen's mood is getting worse and they are having a hard time making it to practice each day. Parents talk with coach so that teen can skip one day per week for a therapy appointment, and can skip the cool-down portion of practice to head home early so the task is not as overwhelming.	

Exercise 8.2 ANSWER KEY Test Your Knowledge of Accommodations

✓ or ✗	Consequence	Not Enough or Too Much
✗	Parent has made teen breakfast in bed every day for the last year to help make sure they wake up for school.	Too much
✗	The teen's chore is to empty the garbage to earn allowance. The parents give numerous reminders and will still give most of the allowance even if the chore is not completed.	Too much
✗	Teen procrastinates on homework and then panics when they cannot finish on time. Parents often write a note for the teen asking for extensions, giving made-up reasons for the delays.	Too much
✗	Teen is very demanding that the family does things according to the teen's preferences. This usually involves parents bending over backward to rearrange schedules and ignore the other kids' preferences.	Too much
✓	Parents agree to rearrange the Saturday afternoon schedule according to the teen's preferences, with the understanding that the morning is based on family preferences and the teen-determined time will decrease by 1 hour each week.	
✗	A teen has been refusing to go to school. The parents put in a request for complete remote learning for the rest of the year, feeling that this is easier than the battle every morning.	Too much
✓	A teen has been refusing to go to school. The parents work with the school to put a gradual re-entry plan in place, so that the teen is on school grounds but slowly builds up their workload over a few weeks.	
✗	A teen has a hard time with interruptions and is trying to work on it. They have asked parents to give them a hand signal when they notice it happening. Parents think the teen should be aware enough to notice on their own, so do not agree to this.	Not enough
✓	A teen has been bullied by a peer in homeroom classroom all year. Parents ask the school to switch the teen to a different homeroom held at the same time.	

✗	A teen is working on reducing compulsive habits with their therapist who has suggested that the family slowly practice difficult situations. The parents are tired of the accommodation and decide to jump into the hardest practice areas all at once.	Not enough
✓	Teen needs lots of reminders to check the school portal for homework. Family agrees that parents will remind 3 times each night in September, 2 times each night in October, and 1 time each night in November. Will then decide what ongoing help is useful.	
✗	A teen is quite fearful of flying. They ask to sit in the aisle row of their upcoming flight so they are less likely to look outside the window. Parents think this is silly and say that the teen needs to take the window seat because they have to get over it.	Not enough
✗	Parents have been reading and rereading their teen's college essays because the teen is worried they are not good enough. This continues even after the essay looks good and the teen should really be shifting focus to other parts of their application.	Too much
✗	A teen has a fear of throwing up and is terrified of eating nearing the expiration date. The caregivers have started to throw out food a few days before the expiration date to avoid any meltdowns.	Too much
✓	There is a house rule that all kids must text parents if they are going to be home late. One teen struggles to remember to do this, so they offer to share their location with the parents so they always know where they are. Parents agree to this compromise.	
✗	A teen has been feeling depressed but is trying to stay involved in their activities. Parents think the teen is spending too much time "moping around" so refuse the teen's requests to have a low-key Saturday after a full week of trying to stay engaged in school.	Not enough
✗	A teen texts parents every few minutes while at school, asking for reassurance about things they are anxious about. Parents respond to each text, providing reassuring answers.	Too much
✓	Teen's mood is getting worse and they are having a hard time making it to practice each day. Parents talk with coach so that teen can skip one day per week for a therapy appointment, and can skip the cool-down portion of practice to head home early so the task is not as overwhelming.	

TEST YOUR KNOWLEDGE OF ACCOMMODATIONS

In Exercise 8.3 are all of the example accommodations from the previous exercise that missed the mark. In this exercise, try to rewrite the accommodation to offer more appropriate support. There are lots of ways to give appropriate accommodations, but there are sample suggestions in the answer key.

EXERCISE 8.3 TEST YOUR KNOWLEDGE OF ACCOMMODATIONS

Consequence	Rewrite
Parent has made teen breakfast in bed every day for the last year to help make sure they wake up for school.	
The teen's chore is to empty the garbage to earn allowance. The parents give numerous reminders and will still give most of the allowance even if the chore is not completed.	
Teen procrastinates on homework and then panics when they cannot finish on time. Parents often write a note for the teen asking for extensions, giving made-up reasons for the delays.	
Teen is very demanding that the family does things according to the teen's preferences. This usually involves parents bending over backward to rearrange schedules and ignore the other kids' preferences.	
A teen has been refusing to go to school. The parents put in a request for complete remote learning for the rest of the year, feeling that this is easier than the battle every morning.	
A teen has a hard time with interruptions and is trying to work on it. They have asked parents to give them a hand signal when they notice it happening. Parents think the teen should be aware enough to notice on their own, so do not agree to this.	
A teen is working on reducing compulsive habits with their therapist who has suggested that the family slowly practice difficult situations. The parents are tired of the accommodation and decide to jump into the hardest practice areas all at once.	
A teen is quite fearful of flying. They ask to sit in the aisle row of their upcoming flight so they are less likely to look outside the window. Parents think this is silly and say that the teen needs to take the window seat because they have to get over it.	

Continued

Continued

Parents have been reading and rereading their teen's college essays because the teen is worried they are not good enough. This continues even after the essay looks good and the teen should really be shifting focus to other parts of their application.	
A teen has a fear of throwing up and is terrified of eating foods nearing the expiration date. The caregivers have started to throw out food a few days before the expiration date to avoid any meltdowns.	
A teen has been feeling depressed but is trying to stay involved in their activities. Parents think the teen is spending too much time "moping around" so refuse the teen's requests to have a low-key Saturday after a full week of trying to stay engaged in school.	
A teen texts parents every few minutes while at school, asking for reassurance about things they are anxious about. Parents respond to each text, providing reassuring answers.	

Exercise 8.3 ANSWER KEY Test Your Knowledge of Accommodations

Consequence	Rewrite
Parent has made teen breakfast in bed every day for the last year to help make sure they wake up for school.	Parent made breakfast in bed for the first few weeks of school, then shifted to waking teen up and having breakfast ready, then to waking teen up and setting out breakfast items, then knocking on the door as a reminder to get up, and then giving a reminder to set alarm for school the night before.
The teen's chore is to empty the garbage to earn allowance. The parents give numerous reminders and will still give most of the allowance even if the chore is not completed.	Parents help teen set an alarm on their phone to take out the trash, and will give one other reminder the night before. They will not give any allowance if chore is not complete.
Teen procrastinates on homework and then panics when they cannot finish on time. Parents often write a note for the teen asking for extensions, giving made-up reasons for the delays.	Parents tell teen that either the work has to be complete or the teen has to email the teacher asking for an extension or extra help. Parents will not write emails for the teen.
Teen is very demanding that the family does things according to the teen's preferences. This usually involves parents bending over backward to rearrange schedules and ignore the other kids' preferences.	Parents agree to set aside a few specific times of the week that the teen gets to have their way sometimes but will rotate other times of the week to make sure everybody's needs are met.
A teen has been refusing to go to school. The parents put in a request for complete remote learning for the rest of the year, feeling that this is easier than the battle every morning.	Parents get teen tutor and help shift teen's school schedule so some of the most difficult classes happen in the afternoon so mornings do not feel as overwhelming.

Continued

Continued

A teen has a hard time with interruptions and is trying to work on it. They have asked parents to give them a hand signal when they notice it happening. Parents think the teen should be aware enough to notice on their own, so do not agree to this.	Parents agree to give a signal for one month, only in situations where other people are around. They ask teen to practice self-monitoring when only the family is around.
A teen is working on reducing compulsive habits with their therapist who has suggested that the family slowly practice difficult situations. The parents are tired of the accommodation and decide to jump into the hardest practice areas all at once.	Parents work with teen to make a list of more and less stressful changes and agree to start small and then hop around the list. They do not promise to go in a specific step-by-step order but agree not to get above a 7/10 distress level until they meet with the therapist.
A teen is quite fearful of flying. They ask to sit in the aisle row of their upcoming flight so they are less likely to look outside the window. Parents think this is silly and say that the teen needs to take the window seat because they have to get over it.	Parents agree to let teen have the aisle for take-off and landing. They ask teen to take the middle or window seat for the middle portion of the flight so they can practice being brave, and so taller family members can have more leg room in the aisle.
Parents have been reading and rereading their teen's college essays because the teen is worried they are not good enough. This continues even after the essay looks good and the teen should really be shifting focus to other parts of their application.	Parents agree to give three rounds of edits and will not offer additional comments or reassurance after that.
A teen has a fear of throwing up and is terrified of eating foods nearing the expiration date. The caregivers have started to throw out food a few days before the expiration date to avoid any meltdowns.	Parents stop throwing out food before the expiration date but do not force teen to try it. After some time, they start to use these foods in baked or cooked dishes, and eventually shift to offering foods past the "best by" date that still seem fine to eat. Teen is not forced to eat them, but is responsible for making their own substitute if they want something different.

A teen has been feeling depressed but is trying to stay involved in their activities. Parents think the teen is spending too much time "moping around" so refuse the teen's requests to have a low-key Saturday after a full week of trying to stay engaged in school.	Parents are worried that sleeping all Saturday morning will set the weekend off on a bad foot. They ask the teen to be up before 11:00 a.m., but agree there will be no concrete plans or chores before 3:00 p.m.
A teen texts parents every few minutes while at school, asking for reassurance about things they are anxious about. Parents respond to each text, providing reassuring answers.	Parents agree to respond to texts during their lunch break and afternoon gap in meetings. They tell teen ahead of time they will no longer be responding to every single text. They tell teen they can send an SOS emoji if there is a true emergency so teen can be assured they will respond. Parents say they will remove this as an option if teen used the SOS emoji and there is not a true emergency.

As you read through this answer key and compare it to your own responses, remember that there is no perfect accommodation plan. How you choose to accommodate will depend on family values, your own feelings about the accommodation, how quickly you want to encourage change, and how much accommodation helps in the short term versus hurts over time.

TRY IT OUT: ACCOMMODATION

Now that you have completed each exercise in this chapter, it is time to put this tool into practice. Start by filling out the questions in Worksheet 8.1 to help clarify your plan for accommodations in your household. As with all skills, be patient with yourself as you make changes. Also know that it may take some time before you see your teen start to respond in skillful ways. Teens need to see that their parents are consistently sticking to their accommodation plan before they make changes of their own. Complete the worksheet below to increase the likelihood of following through on this task successfully and write down your attempts at setting up accommodations.

WORKSHEET 8.1

1. Do you tend to offer too much support, too little support, or just the right amount of support? If possible, ask your teen for their input on this.
   _____
   _____
   _____

2. What is one area of your teen's life where they are pulling for accommodation?
   _____
   _____
   _____

3. List out how you are currently responding. This might be ways in which you are giving into the asks for accommodation, ways that you are declining these asks, or both.
   _____
   _____
   _____

4. Thinking of the questions at the start of this chapter, make a list of possible accommodations that would align with your family values, be doable without creating resentment, and give your teen the support they need while they work on building skills.
   _____
   _____
   _____

5. List a few people you can ask for suggestions on how to support your teen in this area:

   _____

   _____

   _____

6. If you are going to try out some of the options you listed above, create a timeline so you have a general plan of how you want to shift accommodation over time (you may not need all phases, or may want to add extra):

   Phase 1 (most support):_____

   Phase 2: _____

   Phase 3: _____

   Phase 4: _____

   Phase 5 (least support): _____

7. When do you want to start this plan?

   _____

   _____

   _____

8. What barriers did you identify as potentially interfering, and how do you plan to troubleshoot them?

   _____

   _____

   _____

9. List three things that will help you complete this task and make sense of this skill. As a reminder, this could include reminders, skill review, social support, accountability measures, or other ideas you would find useful.

   1. _____

   _____

   2. _____

   _____

   3. _____

   _____

How to Set Up Consequences That Work

WHAT ARE CONSEQUENCES?

In this book, a consequence is a type of outcome put in place by the parent after a teenager takes action. If you recall from Chapter 4 on understanding your child's behavior, outcomes can either be reinforcing or punishing. Reinforcers feel good or positive in some way. Punishments are anything unappealing or unpleasant to your child. As a reminder, teenagers experience all sorts of different outcomes from all sorts of different places, including within themselves, from peers and teachers, from their environment, and from parents and caregivers. This chapter outlines how parent-driven outcomes, or *consequences*, can shape behavior.

WHY CONSEQUENCES MATTER

Consequences matter because they have a huge impact on how people choose to act in the future. Consequences that feel good lead to somebody repeating their choices. Consequences that feel bad usually make it less likely for those behaviors to occur. From a parenting perspective, this opens up an entire branch of options to help you encourage a teen's skillful behavior or lessen problem behaviors.

The early chapters of this book focus on tools like validation and routines. These skills can help you create an environment that makes it easier for your teen to be calm and skillful. Selective attention (labeled praise, positive attention, and active ignoring) help to encourage good behavior before it occurs *and* reward it after the fact. These are great options and can really help set your child up for success. However, *they are not always enough*. This is especially true for teens who are struggling with mental health symptoms. Sometimes, warmth, structure, and appreciation are not powerful enough to combat distress or impairment caused by anxiety, depression, ADHD, or other disorders. For kids with these concerns, consequences are a useful add-on to nudge them in the right direction.

From a practical perspective, consequences are important to talk about because so many families use them and they can easily go wrong. To be most effective in the long term, there are a few different factors to think about when putting consequences in place. This chapter will walk through some of the key principles to keep in mind.

WHEN TO USE CONSEQUENCES

Not all families need to use consequences. If your teenager is doing all the things they need and want to do at home, school, with friends, and in hobbies, you probably do not need consequences. If your teenager is really distressed by symptoms but is trying to be skillful and generally manages their impulses, a consequence system may not be worth it. However, most kids need some form of consequences, whether that is to reinforce steps in the right direction or punish inappropriate choices.

You especially want to use them if you can see that a child's symptoms and/or distress are making it difficult for them to progress on their own. In these cases, external motivation can be helpful. This is particularly true for behaviors that have nothing to do with your attention and can't be improved through things like labeled praise or ignoring. For example, you could probably use selective attention to increase polite tone of voice or decrease negotiating, because both of those things rely on your feedback. But what about behaviors like getting your anxious child to practice coping skills or getting your impulsive teen to stop sneaking out of the house? Your child isn't avoiding coping skills to get your attention; they are probably just hard to do. Similarly, teens are not sneaking out to see what your reaction is going to be, they just like to meet up with their friends. For these behaviors that have nothing to do with your attention, you likely need some sort of reward or punishment to help make the skillful choice appealing.

Because consequence systems can take a lot of practice and effort, it is important for you to carefully consider what sorts of behavior are really worth it. This makes it more likely for you to successfully following through with whatever consequences you put in place.

TYPES OF CONSEQUENCES

There are two main types of consequences that this chapter will discuss. Each have pros and cons, and it is up to you to decide which system will work best for your teen. Options include:

1. Logical consequences
2. Behavior plans:
   a. One-to-one consequences
   b. Point systems (also known as a token economy).

Logical Consequences

A logical consequence is a reward or punishment that makes sense given your child's behavior. Here are a few examples:

- A teenager returns the family car without filling up the tank of gas. Their logical punishment is to wake up early so they can fill up the tank before school.
- If a teenager went out of their way to do extra chores on a week when a parent had a lot on their plate, a logical reward might be to let them off the hook when it comes to doing dishes over the weekend.
- If a teenager does a great job checking in with their parent each time they get to their friend's house, a logical reward might be to give them more freedom to travel a little bit further or stay out a little bit later. Their responsibility leads to more independence.
- If a teen gets mad and breaks something in the house, they have to fix or replace it.

Pros of logical consequences: Logical consequences can be great because they just make sense. There is an obvious link for you and your teenager that connects their behavior to the outcome that happened next. You don't really have to justify or explain it because the reasoning is so clear. Logical consequences are also nice because you can be more flexible with them in real time. For many teens, behavior goes up and down day to day. As new behaviors come up, you can simply ask yourself, "What consequence makes sense for this situation?" Logical consequences do not involve rigid rules. You don't have to keep track of behavior over time. There are no tally marks to put on any charts. It's just a way to flexibly respond to situations that pop up in your household. Logical punishments are also helpful because they often give your teen a chance to repair a bad situation. Didn't fill up the tank? No problem, you can do it the next day. Abused the phone privileges and had it taken away for the night? That's okay, you can earn trust back by using it appropriately tomorrow. It is a nice way for your teenager to learn how to repair sticky situations.

Cons of logical consequences: While the flexibility of logical consequences is a strength, it can also make things more difficult. Without a specific behavior plan in place, this fly-by-the-seat-of-your-pants approach comes with two main problems. First, you must be able to think of a logical consequence on the spot, and that is much easier said than done. If your teenager hits their little brother, a logical punishment might be to let their little brother hit them back. But most parents recognize that this is not a good option. What then? Many parents struggle to feel comfortable and confident in coming up with a logical consequence quickly. Parents and caregivers can absolutely build this skill, but it is important to know that mastering logical consequences can take a lot of practice.

The other problem is that logical consequences do not always mean that much to teenagers who are struggling with their mental health. Taking the example where the teen hits their little brother, a possible punishment may be to send them to their room so they are separated from the family. That's logical, but your teen may not really care. Sure, your attention is generally important, but not so important that they change their ways just to avoid an hour of solo time in their room. Perhaps you know this and say, "Fine. Since you hit your brother, you don't get to go to your karate practice this weekend since obviously you can't control what you're learning there." This may work if your teen really loves karate, but many parents really struggle to follow through on consequences like this. You have already paid for the class, you really want your teen to have an activity on the weekends, and you see other benefits of your child going to their class. Come Saturday, you change your mind.

So even though the logical consequence makes sense, they are not always powerful enough to change teen behavior and can be hard for parents to follow through on.

Behavior Plans

A behavior plan helps parents pick a few specific behaviors they want their child to work on and links them to consequences (reinforcers and/or punishment). The consequences do not have to be logically linked to the behavior.

Pros of behavior plans: In general, behavior plans are helpful because you can plan them ahead of time when you are calm and have time to think. This makes it more likely for you to use appropriate rewards and punishment instead of making reactive in-the-moment decisions. Behavior plans allow your teen to give input on rewards they care about. They also create a set of expectations ahead of time so everybody in the household knows exactly what the rules and outcomes will be. As teens become more skillful on certain targets, you can simply swap them out for other behaviors they need to work on.

Cons of behavior plans: Behavior plans can be a lot of work for parents. Once you create a system, you have to stick to the system. If you don't, your kids will stop taking what you say seriously and will lose trust that their efforts have any meaning.

There are two main types of behavior plans. A one-to-one behavior plan links one behavior to one reward. Here are a few examples:

- If a teen does all of their chores for the day, they get $1 added to their allowance.
- Once a teenager finishes all of their homework, they have access to TV.
- If a teen hits their sibling, they lose phone access for the night.
- When a teen makes it to school on time they can hang out with their friends after school.

Pros of one-to-one plans: One-to-one behavior plans are nice because they are simple and work well for families who have one or two behaviors they want to target. It also allows you to make use of consequences that your teenager is really motivated by. You can use things like screentime, extended curfew, allowance, or decreased chores to motivate skillful choices, even if there is no logical link to the target behavior. There is also little tracking involved. Yes, you do have to check to see if the behavior did or didn't happen, but that's it. It is fairly straightforward and you can go one day at a time.

Cons of one-to-one plan: A one-to-one plan relies on daily rewards or punishment. This is fine for teens who want smaller things you can give day after day but does not work so well for those who are motivated by more expensive rewards (e.g., video game, clothing). Also, because there are usually only a handful of daily rewards teens care about (e.g., screentime, curfew, money), you are limited in how many behaviors you target at once. You can't ask your teen to meet six different goals if you only have one or two rewards they care about.

This leads us to our last option, which is a type of behavior plan called a point system. In a point system, teens have a few different target behaviors they can earn or lose points for. These points turn into rewards. Many people refer to this as a token economy, and it mirrors how most adults function in the world. Adults go to their jobs, do a whole bunch of different tasks, and then get paid. That money then gets turned in for things that we like or need.

Pros of points systems: A behavior plan like this is great because you have so many opportunities to personalize it for your teenager. If you have three or four behaviors that are important to you, you can fold all of them into one point system. You can also customize it so that harder behaviors earn more points and easier behaviors earn less.

You can also individualize the rewards. Some teens may have short-term rewards they really care about, like being able to stay up late, having more screen time, or getting to choose what your family watches on TV. Some teens only care about bigger ticket items, like the expensive clothing or having a sleepover with friends. You might be happy to offer those things sometimes, but not nightly. No problem. With a point system, bigger rewards are worth more points, so your teen can choose to save their daily credits and cash in for the larger rewards down the road. Importantly, for kids with things like ADHD, the daily points are still useful because they are a daily reminder of their progress and pitfalls. This helps to keep them accountable and on track.

Cons of points systems: The main con of point systems is that they can get really complicated really quickly. Parents are very tempted to throw in all sorts of behaviors because the plan can handle them, but doing so can make it overwhelming for teens and hard for parents to stay on top of. Every new behavior, reward, or punishment that gets added to the mix is another thing to track and follow through with. For many families, this level of organization is not a good fit.

TESTING YOUR KNOWLEDGE OF CONSEQUENCES OPTIONS

In Exercise 9.1, try to label each of the examples listed as a logical consequence, one-to-one behavior plan, or point system. Use the answer key to check your answer.

EXERCISE 9.1 TESTING YOUR KNOWLEDGE OF CONSEQUENCES OPTIONS

Situation	Type of Consequence Being Used
Teen has completed all chores on time so gets an extra $2 toward allowance	
Teen has completed all chores early, so has time to go see friends before bed	
Teen earns 3 points for completing homework and 5 points for going the day without cursing.	
Teen forgets to bring laundry to the washing machine, so parent does not do their laundry	
Teen did not get to school on time every day this week, so does not get a later Friday curfew	
Teen is working toward earning the ability to drive themselves to school. Needs to earn 100 points, which they can do by being ready to leave the house on time each day, staying under the speed limit when driving with parents, and texting parents when they plan to get home.	
Teen throws an object in anger and loses 5 points	
Teen gives parents phones whenever asked, so parents agree to remove app parental limits.	
Teen attends therapy session without a fight, gets to skip helping with dinner prep that night	
Each day teen gets outside for at least 20 minutes, they get to choose the music on the way to school the next morning	

Exercise 9.1 ANSWER KEY Testing Your Knowledge of Consequences Options

Situation	Type of Consequence Being Used
Teen has completed all chores on time so gets an extra $2 toward allowance	One-to-one behavior plan
Teen has completed all chores early, so has time to go see friends before bed	Logical consequence
Teen earns 3 points for completing homework and 5 points for going the day without cursing.	Point system
Teen forgets to bring laundry to the washing machine, so parent does not do their laundry	Logical consequence
Teen did not get to school on time every day this week, so does not get a later Friday curfew	One-to-one behavior plan
Teen is working toward earning the ability to drive themselves to school. Needs to earn 100 points, which they can do by being ready to leave the house on time each day, staying under the speed limit when driving with parents, and texting parents when they plan to get home	Point system
Teen throws an object in anger and loses 5 points	Point system
Teen gives parents phones whenever asked, so parents agree to remove app parental limits	Logical consequence
Teen attends therapy session without a fight, gets to skip helping with dinner prep that night	One-to-one behavior plan
Each day teen gets outside for at least 20 minutes, they get to choose the music on the way to school the next morning	One-to-one behavior plan

TIPS FOR MAKING CONSEQUENCES WORK

No matter what consequence system you use, there are a few tips you can keep in mind to help make sure it is as effective as possible.

All rewards and punishment must be at a reasonable scale. A teeny tiny reward or teeny tiny punishment has very little chance of getting your teenager to change their behavior. On the flip side, huge rewards feel almost silly to teens and are not sustainable for parents. Punishments that are too big can feel like an overreaction from the parent, causing teens to explode because they are so upset, or lose faith in their parents' judgment because the punishment was too harsh. Another tricky part is that excessive punishments are really hard to follow through with. Many parents have, at some point, taken away their teen's phone for entire week, only to give it back after two days when they can't stand the complaining any longer.

Focus on giving chunks of reward and punishment. Some parents are so eager to make a lasting impact that they use up their whole reward or punishment for one single behavior. For example, teens get their full TV time for completing one tough homework assignment. Or they may lose the phone for the night because the teen cursed one time. It's not that the consequence is so excessive on face value, but the problem is that you have used up all of your bargaining chips. If the teen gets to watch TV after the first tough homework assignment, there's not a ton of motivation to finish the rest. If they lose their phone after one cursing episode, they may as well keep cursing the rest of the night because they have nothing else to lose. A relatively easy fix to this problem is to take a consequence they care about and break it into smaller chunks. Give or take 15–20 minutes worth of a reward so that your teen still has some reason to turn their behavior around the rest of the day. Some parents worry that these small doses will not be motivating enough. However, you allow yourself much more flexibility to address lots of behaviors that pop up over the course of the day.

Pick a reward that is valuable to your child. There is often a disconnect between what parents want to give as a reward and what the teen really wants. This is a good time to think carefully about the types of things that really feel meaningful to your child. Is it spending money, time with friends, a later curfew, phone time, more independence, or something else? Perhaps they have wanted to redecorate their room, dye their hair, or get a piercing. While it can make sense for parents to nix those ideas if they go against a personal value, belief system, or are outside of the family means, many parents decline these types of requests for other reasons. Perhaps what the teen wants requires a lot of effort. Maybe it is a little impractical, foolish, or unappealing to the parent. But honestly, who cares? If there is no long-term harm, these are easy opportunities for you to get your teen's buy-in with relatively little cost to you.

Start small and build expectations over time. No matter what behavior you are looking to shift, you will almost always want to approach it in a gradual way. This is called shaping, and the idea is to reward small steps in the right direction until your teen eventually meets the goal. This strategy can help your teen build a sense of achievement and momentum. If the goal is set too high at the beginning, teens are easily demoralized. Tasks feel overwhelming, motivation tanks, and parents feel frustrated with the stalled progress.

There are a few concrete steps you can take to shape behavior. The first is to pick your target behavior. Ask yourself: What is the ultimate goal you would like to see? Then think about small steps your teenager will need to get there. For example, you may want your teenager to complete 100% of their homework on time, but right now they're only at 50%. You might set short-term goals where they work toward 60%, then 75%, then 100%. Once you have the benchmarks in mind, decide on what consequences to use. Remember, when you are shaping behavior, it is important to reward each small step along the way, rather than waiting until the end goal is met. As your child becomes more skillful, you'll move the benchmark and make the requirement slightly more difficult. Depending on your teen, you might be able to get rid of the consequence system altogether after enough progress. This can work particularly well for helping teens overcome anxiety, because rewarding them to face situations they have been avoiding will decrease the fear over time and rewards will not be as necessary. For other symptoms, like a learning disorder or ADHD, there may be some limit to how much symptoms can improve and some sustained rewards may be necessary.

To help increase the success of consequences, plan ahead. This means that you need to think through what sort of supplies or processes you have in place. If you are using a point system, how are you going to keep track of points? If you use logical consequences, how do you want to handle periods of time when you are not home to witness behavior (e.g., focus on times when you are home, or tap another caregiver). As you think through your plan, look for ways to stay one step ahead of your teenager. For example, let's say you are going to grant your teen TV time once homework is done. That is all well and good until your teen grabs the remote and turns on the TV while you are out for a walk. So, what do you do? If you have the type of kid who always looks for the workaround, you are going to plan for that. Pop the remote in your bag and take it with you, stash it in the laundry room, or put it in a lock box until you get home. In this same example, you may also need to plan to make sure you have access to your teen's school portal so you can check for homework completion instead of relying on their report.

For many parents, this level of planning may seem like too much. That is totally fine. If you do not have the type of teen who looks for all the loopholes, you do not need to be this strategic. However, many teens are amazingly clever at finding ways to wiggle out of punishment or sneak in rewards before they are truly earned. If this is your teen, and you are committed to shaping more skillful choices through consequences, planning ahead can go a long way. After all, as smart as teens are, parents can be smarter. For those who have teens that show some interest in change, have a conversation with them to lay out the goals and consequences (rewards and punishments) at stake. Be clear about the plan, give them a chance to contribute, and see if you can come to an agreement. If they are upset and unwilling to outright agree to the plan, you can still follow through with it. You have still set the stage for progress by being upfront and clear, and will help prompt change as long as you are consistent with the results.

Consequence systems should be reward plans first and only include punishment as a backup. This is crucial to keep in mind. It means that any sort of logical consequence or behavior plan you put in place should prioritize your teenager's opportunity to earn things and be reinforced for skillful behavior. Many times, behavior plans go wrong early on because they are set up to penalize teens being "bad" rather than acknowledging their skillful efforts. A punishment system sets up a family for a ton of conflict. It feels very discouraging, and it is easily abandoned by parents and teenagers alike. To avoid this, make sure there are lots of chances for your teen to be rewarded, and that any punishment on the table also comes with a chance for reinforcement. For example, you might punish your child for hitting their sibling (which is fine), but make sure to reinforce them for taking a break instead of lashing out.

TIPS FOR POINT SYSTEMS

Because point systems can be a bit more complicated, here are a few additional strategies to keep in mind beyond the ones listed on previous pages.

Begin with two or three behaviors and build as you go. One of the benefits of a point system is that you can target a few different behaviors at once. As you get started, settle on your top two or three. Once you get the hang of the program, you can add more. Try not to have more than four or five because things become too overwhelming.

Instead of using a point system, add as many tasks as you can to your teen's daily routine. A lot of parents want to create behavior plans that include daily tasks, like getting to school on time, showering, doing chores, or finishing homework. That is okay to do, but they take up valuable slots you may want to use for behaviors like practicing coping skills, accepting decisions, and staying in control of voice and body. Daily tasks can more easily be shifted to your teen's daily routine (see Chapter 7 on routines) than some of these more general emotion and behavior regulation goals.

Create a reward menu. Work with your teen to brainstorm a list of rewards they might want to earn with their points. This can be daily rewards, or bigger monthly rewards. As noted before, your teen can decide whether they want to spend rewards on daily items or save up for something over time. Not only does a reward menu keep things interesting, but it also is an important back-up plan for times when your teen earns some points, but not enough for a daily reward. For example, let's say your teen has to earn 10 points to earn an extra 20 minutes of daily screen time. On Monday, they only earn 8 points. Not enough for the screen time. But if you have a reward menu, they can simply bank those rewards for a weekly or monthly reward!

Points reset daily. No matter how many points a teen earns or loses, the points reset the next morning. If your teen earned more points than they could spend, they can simply bank them toward bigger rewards on the weekend or end of the month. This prevents them from earning tons of points on Monday and slacking off the rest of the week because they have points to spare. And if your teen goes into the negative, all "debt" is forgiven the next day and they start back at zero. Teenagers must feel that each day is a new opportunity to make progress. If they start the day with a negative point value, it is very demoralizing and will quickly create a point spiral your teen can never get out of. No matter how tempting it may be, the points start at zero each day.

TEST YOUR KNOWLEDGE OF CONSEQUENCES THAT WORK

In Exercise 9.2, take a look at sample consequences parents are using. Put a check next to each consequence that seems to be appropriate. Put an ✗ next to consequences that don't seem right, and then try to write down what the problem is. As a reminder, here are some of the general strategies to keep in mind when creating consequences: start small (both with expectations and the number of behaviors being changed); be specific (about the behavior being targeted and rewards); use rewards that are meaningful; use an appropriate scale (not too large or too small); and follow through consistently.

EXERCISE 9.2 TEST YOUR KNOWLEDGE OF CONSEQUENCES THAT WORK

✓ or ✗	Consequence	Notes
	Teen can earn points toward a new game console for good behavior.	
	Parents have a house rule where WiFi and cell data are shut off for one hour when teen is unwilling to leave the phone on the counter during dinner.	
	Once teen has fed and walked the dog after school, they can play video games.	
	Behavior plan states teens can earn getting out of dishes if they use coping skills 3x/day.	
	Teen earned getting out of dishes after coping 3x/day, then parents say they have to do dishes anyways due to disrespect at dinner.	
	Parents threaten to take away prom if teen keeps lying to them.	
	Parents have said teen is grounded from seeing friends this weekend due to lying about whereabouts last weekend, then feel badly on Saturday and say it is okay if teen sees their friends as long as they stick around the neighborhood.	
	Teen gets $10 for every A on their report card.	
	Teen gets a ticket for speeding. Has to pay the fine and parents have them take an online driver safety course.	
	Family uses a daily point system; parents tally points 2–3x/week.	

✓ or ✗	Consequence	Notes
	Teen with anxiety earns 3 points each time they use a coping skill and 5 points for every task they complete on their therapy goal ladder. After 150 points, they get concert tickets.	
	Parents have set up a point system. Behaviors include respectful language, finishing homework, safe body, accepting parent decisions, completing daily chores, and getting to activities on time.	
	Teen talks back and has phone taken away for the week.	
	Teen wants to earn money for shopping. Parents say teen has too many clothes, but could earn money for outings, like dinner or the movies.	
	Teen has ADHD. Parents have set up a point system where teen can earn a new pair of shoes at the end of the semester.	
	Teen can go to camp this summer if they get good reports from school.	
	Teen earns their weekly allowance if they make it to school on time Monday morning.	
	Teen throws a party while parents are out of town. When they find out, teen is made to pay for cleaning services and is not allowed to have friends over for two weeks.	

Exercise 9.2 ANSWER KEY Test Your Knowledge of Consequences That Work

✓ or ✗	Consequence	Notes
✗	Teen can earn points toward a new game console for good behavior.	Behavior isn't specific enough
✓	Parents have a house rule where WiFi and cell data are shut off for one hour when teen is unwilling to leave the phone on the counter during dinner.	
✓	Once teen has fed and walked the dog after school, they can play video games.	
✓	Behavior plan states teens can earn getting out of dishes if they use coping skills 3x/day.	
✗	Teen earned getting out of dishes after coping 3x/day, then parents say they have to do dishes anyways due to disrespect at dinner.	Parents not consistent; said reward would be earned for one behavior, and then took it away for something unrelated.
✗	Parents threaten to take away prom if teen keeps lying to them.	Not specific; will be hard to follow through with
✗	Parents have said teen is grounded from seeing friends this weekend due to lying about whereabouts last weekend, then feel badly on Saturday and say it is okay if teen sees their friends as long as they stick around the neighborhood.	Not consistent
✓	Teen gets $10 for every A on their report card.	
✓	Teen gets a ticket for speeding. Has to pay the fine and parents have them take an online driver safety course.	
✗	Family uses a daily point system; parents tally points 2–3x/week.	Not consistent

✓ or ✗	Consequence	Notes
✓	Teen with anxiety earns 3 points each time they use a coping skill and 5 points for every task they complete on their therapy goal ladder. After 150 points, they get concert tickets.	
✗	Parents have set up a point system. Behaviors include respectful language, finishing homework, safe body, accepting parent decisions, completing daily chores, and getting to activities on time.	Too many behaviors
✗	Teen talks back and has phone taken away for the week.	Too large of a consequence
✗	Teen wants to earn money for shopping. Parents say teen has too many clothes, but could earn money for outings, like dinner or the movies.	Not a meaningful reward
✗	Teen has ADHD. Parents have set up a point system where teen can earn a new pair of shoes at the end of the semester.	Probably too small of a reward that is too far off
✗	Teen can go to camp this summer if they get good reports from school.	Not specific enough and will be hard to follow through with
✗	Teen earns their weekly allowance if they make it to school on time Monday morning.	Too large of a reward
✓	Teen throws a party while parents are out of town. When they find out, teen is made to pay for cleaning services and is not allowed to have friends over for two weeks.	

TEST YOUR SKILLS OF CONSEQUENCES THAT WORK

In Exercise 9.3 is a list of all the consequences from Exercise 9.2 that had some problems. In this exercise, rewrite the consequence to correct those problems. There are many possible ways to come up with effective consequences, but you can see examples in the answer key on the next page.

EXERCISE 9.3 TEST YOUR SKILLS OF CONSEQUENCES THAT WORK

Problematic Consequence	Corrected Consequence
Teen can earn points toward a new game console for good behavior.	
Teen earned getting out of dishes after coping 3x/day, then parents say they have to do dishes anyways due to disrespect at dinner.	
Parents threaten to take away prom if teen keeps lying to them.	
Parents have said teen is grounded from seeing friends this weekend due to lying about whereabouts last weekend, then feel badly on Saturday and say it is okay if teen sees their friends as long as they stick around the neighborhood.	
Family uses a daily point system; parents tally points 2–3x/week.	
Parents have set up a point system. Behaviors include respectful language, finishing homework, safe body, accepting parent decisions, completing daily chores, and getting to activities on time.	
Teen talks back and has phone taken away for the week.	
Teen wants to earn money for shopping. Parents say teen has too many clothes, but could earn money for outings, like dinner or the movies.	
Teen has ADHD. Parents have set up a point system where teen can earn a new pair of shoes at the end of the semester.	
Teen can go to camp this summer if they get good reports from school.	
Teen earns their weekly allowance if they make it to school on time Monday morning.	

Exercise 9.3 ANSWER KEY Test Your Skills of Consequences That Work

Consequence	Rewrite
Teen can earn points toward a new game console for "good behavior."	Teen can earn points toward a new game console for following instructions on first ask (1 point), coming home by curfew (5 points), and having no teachers email parents about behavior (1 point each day).
Teen earned getting out of dishes after coping 3x/day, then parents say they have to do dishes anyways due to disrespect at dinner.	Teen has earned getting out of dishes after coping 3x per day. WiFi gets shut off 20 minutes earlier than normal because of disrespect at dinner.
Parents threaten to take away prom if teen keeps lying to them.	Option 1: Teen will have to cover $15 of prom expenses each time caught lying. Option 2 (if parents are really willing to take away prom): Teen will not be allowed to go to prom after 3 more instances where they are caught lying.
Parents have said teen is grounded from seeing friends this weekend due to lying about whereabouts last weekend, then feel badly on Saturday and say it is okay if teen sees their friends as long as they stick around the neighborhood.	Option 1: Teen can't go out Saturday; must keep location tracking on when out on Sunday. Option 2: Teen is allowed to leave house but must be picked up/dropped off by parents.
Family has a daily point system; parents tally points 2–3x/week.	Family has point system with daily alarm to tally.
Parents have set up a point system. Behaviors include respectful language, finishing homework, safe body, accepting parent decisions, completing daily chores, and getting to activities on time.	Parents have set up a point system and pick top 3 behaviors to work on.
Teen talks back and has phone taken away for the week.	Teen talks back and loses phone for an hour.
Teen wants to earn money for shopping. Parents say teen has too many clothes, but could earn money for outings, like dinner or the movies.	Parents say teen can earn up to 5 new clothing items (because this is what is most valuable to teen, and parents can still set limits on number of new items).

Consequence	Rewrite
Teen has ADHD. Parents have set up a point system where teen can earn a new pair of shoes at the end of the semester.	Parents have set up a point system where teen can save for expensive shoes at the end of the semester, and also has the option for daily rewards (like later curfew or more screen time) that are more immediate.
Teen can go to camp this summer if they get good reports from school.	Option 1: Teen can earn a weekend trip for improved behavior scores from teacher at the end of the semester. Option 2 (if parents are really okay skipping camp): Teen can go to camp if parents get no more than 3 calls about behavior for the rest of the semester.
Teen earns their weekly allowance if they make it to school on time Monday morning.	Teen can earn 1/5 of their allowance for each day they make it to school on time.

In the answer key, you can see that most of the original consequences started off right but just needed small tweaks to be more specific or a more reasonable scale. Of course, the exact scale depends on each child and situation. A good example of this is the teen who is earning summer camp through good reports from school. If it is January and the parent is getting calls from school twice a week, they will need to change the benchmark so the teen has a little more time to make improvements.

COMMON STUCK POINTS TO USING CONSEQUENCES

Read through this list of hurdles that parents often encounter when trying to use consequences. Underneath each common stuck point, you will find tips and considerations that can help address each barrier. At the end of the chapter, you will have a chance to make note of any examples that would be helpful for you to keep in mind.

My teenagers do not seem to care about any reinforcement or punishment I give them.

This is a common comment from parents who feel like they've tried absolutely every reward and punishment under the sun, and nothing really seems to work. There are a few possible things that might be going on.

→ The first thing to look at is whether the consequence you picked is meaningful to your teenager. For example, maybe you shut off WiFi from their phone, but they just use cell data or play games. Or perhaps you are trying to reward your teen with extra spending money but all they really care about is a later curfew. Make sure to use rewards that your teen really values, rather than something you wish had value to them.

→ The next thing to consider is whether your teen has found a workaround. Perhaps they lose allowance if they do not complete chores, but they just borrow money from their friends. Most teenagers will try their best to avoid the full weight of a punishment that has been given to them. If this is the case for your teenager, good for them! Very clever. Now it's time to consider what you can do ahead of time to help minimize the chances of your child finding a loophole. You may not be able to create a completely foolproof plan (again, teenagers are very clever), but there are usually at least a few things you can do to make it less convenient for your teen to escape the punishment being doled out.

→ With that said, the most common situation is that teenagers really *do* care about consequences. They are just either really good at pretending they do not care *or* will only start to care after they have gotten in trouble a few times. In the first case, a lot of teens know they can just wait out their parents. They pretend not to care about a reward or punishment and trust that their parent will eventually give up and get off their back.

In the second case, the teen may not care about the consequence until it happens a few times. For example, imagine you have told your oversleeping teen that if they get to school on time they can grab a smoothie with friends after school. Your child, who might be struggling with anxiety or depression or ADHD or something else, might not be in the most logical place in the morning. As they lie in bed, they are easily swayed by the cozy covers. They tell you they don't care about the smoothie and end up going late to school. But you are a smart parent. You picked that reward because you know your teen likes the sense of independence and social connection they get from those outings. Flash forward to the afternoon when you pick up your teen immediately after school, and suddenly the lack of smoothie (along with the independence and socializing) seems like a real bummer. Now maybe the same exact thing happens the next day. And the next day. And the next day. But perhaps after the fourth day (or sixth, or tenth), the loss of that reward will really start to make an impact. Over time their brain will start to figure out that it is in their interest to get to school on time, and they will start to change their behavior.

Keeping this in mind, it is usually not the case that a teen does not care about anything. Rather, learning from experience is key to behavior change, and it can take a few repetitions for the teen to build up that experience. No matter what consequences you are using, it is crucial to give it enough time for the lesson to sink in.

It is hard to be consistent with reward and punishment.
Consistency is a major barrier for most parents for a few main reasons. Sometimes parents go back and forth about what values they want to prioritize. For example, you might really want your teen to get their homework done, so you say they can't see friends until that happens. Come Saturday night, homework is not done, but you hate to see them being left out of the friend group. So you backtrack and let them go out. In some cases, two different caregivers have different priorities and are unwilling to back up the other parent on a reward or punishment because they do not agree with it.

→ In both cases, it is important to sit down and list out your long-term values for your teen. After you do that, try to order them from most important to least important. Hopefully, you will not have to choose between them. But being concrete about your priorities will help you make a decision and stick to it in cases when values do come head-to-head. If you decide that you care most about school, stick to your consequence. If you care more about your teen socializing, pick a different outcome to link to homework getting done.

If you and your partner cannot seem to agree on the overall order of values, compromise on specific behaviors. One person gets to make the call around prioritizing studying for tests over movies with friends. The other parent gets to prioritize birthday parties over completing every homework assignment. Both parents agree to back each other up, even if they do not personally buy-in to that specific expectation. This may not be ideal, but it is typically more effective for your teen to have coparents who compromise than ones who actively undermine the other's expectations or decision.

Another main culprit for inconsistency is the sheer exhaustion that comes with being a parent. Using logical consequences and behavior plans requires you to be fairly involved. This may mean tracking behavior, following through on rewards, and sometimes dealing with an angry teen who hates the consequence they got. When faced with all the negotiating, whining, and badgering, it is easy for parents to fall back and let their teenager get what they want in order to maintain some peace in the household. This is totally understandable. Unfortunately, it usually doesn't actually help much in the long term.

→ If this sounds like you, consider going back to the Chapter 3 on caregiver coping. Review ways to build your overall reserves and up the energy you have to keep up with consequences. You can also check out your in-the-moment coping plan to help you stay calm when your teen won't leave you alone. Importantly, make sure to think about your long-term values. If you are just choosing between taking your child's phone away because they didn't do their homework versus having an evening of peace, it's easy to pick the evening of peace and let them keep the phone. But if you know you are picking between helping your child build more skills so you don't have homework battles every night until they go to college *or* having one evening of peace, it's a little bit easier to take the phone away.

→ Another option is to set your expectations lower (so rewards are easier to access) or make your punishments smaller. Sometimes parents find it hard to follow through with behavior plans because the teen's reaction is so intense. It might be worth starting out more gradually so the reaction you get from your teenager is not quite so overwhelming. Over time you can build back up to the consequence that you think is truly appropriate.

Using consequences feels like a lot to stay on top of.
Whether you are delivering logical consequences or using some version of a behavior plan, consequences can be a lot for a parent to manage.

→ If this skill seems overwhelming to you, pick the absolute simplest version to start with. Even if that version does not give you a chance to work on every single target behavior you have for your teen, it is still a step in the right direction. You can always build your system over time as you get the hang of it.
→ Remember to use tools. Go online and print out a house rule worksheet. Download an app for a point system. Set daily alarms to check-in on progress. Add calendar alerts to hand out rewards. Make use of all the organizational tools you use at work, at home, or would want your teenager to try out when they are trying to stay on top of things.
→ Only use consequences if you have to. If using logical consequences or a behavior plan is more troublesome to you than your child's actual behavior, it is totally fine to skip this skill. It is okay for your teenager to have some problem behaviors. Focus on all the other strategies discussed in this book to make as much progress as possible, and then let it be.

I feel like consequences lead to too much conflict with my child.
Some parents find that consequences really add to the amount of negativity in the household. Caregivers feel like managers and kids feel like they are being nitpicked every single day.

→ When this happens, make sure that your consequence plan is rewards focused rather than punishment focused. Often, conflict pops up because opportunities to earn things have gone down over time, while punishment goes up. Parents accidentally slide back into focusing on the negative instead of the positive, which then understandably leads to more tension in the household. Instead, try to structure your teen-consequence plans like a contract you have at work. Start with outlining the expectations for the job (i.e., their behavior targets) and what they'll earn for meeting them (i.e., rewards). Include opportunities to earn a bonus, and make note of any key behaviors that would be hugely problematic. This way everything is clear and the frame is positive rather than negative.

I hate feeling like the bad guy.
Some parents really feel like consequences go against their natural parenting style or are too harsh to use for kids who are already struggling with their mental health.

→ Consider the previous tips from above. Consequence systems should focus on setting realistic expectations and delivering appropriate rewards. They should include reasonable, achievable standards and use consequences in proportion to your child's actual behavior. Remember the guidelines from Chapter 2 on basic principles of parenting: make use of neutral tone and language. If you follow this, there won't be anything mean about it.

→ More importantly, consequences can give parents the opportunity to preserve a positive relationship with their child. You might be wondering how that can possibly be the case when the parent is taking away a phone or serving as the gatekeeper to independence. But consider what happens *without* a consequence system. When a teen behaves inappropriately, most parents feel compelled to address it. The response may be a long-winded lecture, yelling, giving the cold shoulder, or somehow expressing your disappointment. *All* of those tactics come down to parents leveraging their relationship with their child in order to shape their behavior. Intentional or not, over time these strategies lead to more guilt, more resentment, and more frustration on both sides. This can really take a drastic toll on connection and trust.

If you have a consequence system in place, you can let the consequence be responsible for behavior change while you focus your efforts on being a warm, nonjudgmental parent to a child who is struggling. Once you deliver the consequence you can go right back to using labeled praise or positive attention to reinforce any appropriate behavior that was taking place at the same time as the problem behavior. You can use validation to support your child in their frustration, anger, anxiety, or sadness. External punishment or reward can free you from the emotional pull to "fix" the problem. The consequence will do this for you (or at least improve it). This is *such* an emotional relief for many parents.

My teenager tells me I always make up my own rules.
Many teens complain that their parents never told them about a certain house rule or didn't warn them about a potential consequence coming their way. While a lot of times this is not completely true, there *are* many instances in which parents shift the expectations on a whim. For example, maybe you say that you're going to take away your teenager's phone for the evening if they do not get the dishes done by 9:30. At 9:25 the dishes are not done, and you now say your teen is going to lose the phone the next morning as well if they do not finish their chore. So you started out with one consequence (dishes by 9:30 or no phone for the night) and then changed it up in the last five minutes. Another common occurrence is that a parent might take back an earned reward for an unrelated offense. For example, perhaps a teen earned a sleepover with friends for getting a good report card. Before the sleepover happens, they curse at their parent. To teach their teen a lesson, the parent takes away the sleepover.

→ When these sorts of switches happen, it undermines the teenager's faith in what the parent has to say. As far as the teen knows, there is always a chance that a parent is going to change things at any moment. If teenagers sense this might happen, they have no incentive to meet household expectations because there's no guarantee the parent will follow through with what they say. It can also lead to a teen losing respect for their parents because they no longer trust their word. For this reason, it is super important to stick with whatever rules you put in place. You cannot raise the bar the last second or change the consequence because of some new behavior that popped up. That does not mean you cannot address new behaviors, you just cannot do it in a way that undercuts what you have previously said. So if your teenager earned a sleepover for a report card and then curses you out, they still get the sleepover but has to put $5 in the swear jar.

I keep meaning to introduce the consequence plan, but it's hard to find time to iron out all the details and talk to my teen about it.
Parents are really eager to have a perfect reward or consequence system in place before they roll it out. In theory, this makes perfect sense. Why not give yourself the best opportunity for success? The problem is that there is no perfect consequence system.

→ You do not need to figure out every single detail of a consequence plan to get started. All you need to know is the type of consequence system you are using, a target behavior (or two) to focus on, and a reward (or two) to make use of. Along the way you can expand your list of behaviors or rewards. Consider your consequence system a living, breathing part of the household. Expect it to change over time. In fact, set a calendar reminder for two weeks after the start date to do a little review and make any tweaks you want. Two weeks will give you enough chance to see what goes well and find out the places where things are going wrong. You can always make things easier or harder or clearer. But first, you just need to get started and have a real sense of what your family needs most.

EXERCISE 9.4 CONSEQUENCE SELF-ASSESSMENT

If you have considered your options, the tips, and stuck points and still are not sure if there is a consequence option that is a good fit for you, take this self-assessment that follows for a little guidance on what consequence plan may work for your household. In each row, circle the item that best describes your family. Then, use the results key to tally up your points.

1.	I have a bunch of different behaviors I want to work on.	I do not have specific behaviors I want to work on, I just really need them to do what is being asked day-to-day.	I have 1–2 specific behaviors I want my teen to work on.
2.	I have a hard time staying on top of daily tasks.	I love to-do lists and spreadsheets.	I'm okay with remembering stuff I have to do, but it's not my favorite.
3.	My teen is really motivated by big-ticket items.	My teen cares a lot about things like screentime, curfew, and seeing friends on a daily basis.	My teen is pretty respectful of the punishments I use.
4.	I am good at thinking on my feet.	I do much better when I have a concrete plan.	I can be flexible, but can stick with a plan if I need to.
5.	My teen and I fight a lot about household expectations.	My teen may not like the house rules, but they know what they are.	My partner and I struggle to get on the same page with rules for our kids.

Exercise 9.4 RESULTS KEY Consequence Self-Assessment

1.	I have a bunch of different behaviors I want to work on. = 3 points	I do not have specific behaviors I want to work on, I just really need them to do what is being asked day to day. = 1 point	I have 1–2 specific behaviors I want my teen to work on. = 2 points
2.	I have a hard time staying on top of daily tasks. = 1 point	I love to-do lists and spreadsheets. = 3 points	I'm okay with remembering stuff I have to do, but it's not my favorite. = 2 points
3.	My teen is really motivated by big-ticket items. = 3 points	My teen doesn't seem to care about logical consequence, they're only motivated by things like screentime or allowance. = 2 points	My teen responds better to more immediate rewards and punishment. = 1 point
4.	I am good at thinking on my feet. = 1 point	I do much better when I have a concrete plan. = 3 points	I can be flexible, but can stick with a plan if I need to. = 2 points
5.	My teen and I fight a lot about household expectations. = 2 points	My teen may not like the house rules, but they know what they are. = 1 points	My partner and I have different priorities for what we want our kids to work on. = 3 points

Score	Suggested Consequence System
5–8 points	Logical consequences might be your best option. They minimize how much tracking you and your teen have to stay on top of, allow you to be flexible in the moment, and work well for kids who do better with immediate consequences.
9–12 points	A one-to-one behavior plan seems like it could be a good fit. They provide a bit more structure with a few hard and fast behavioral targets to focus on. This helps to ensure that you and your teen know what the plan is, without either side feeling like the other person was unclear or uninformed. It also allows you to make use of daily rewards that are meaningful for your teen.
13–15 points	A point system could be a great option for your family. It allows for a handful of behavior targets, creates clear expectations for your teenager, and gives them a pathway to earning longer rewards over time.

At the end of the day, you as the parent get to decide what plan (if any) makes the most sense for your family. It is okay to go with your gut and try something out, and you can always switch at a later point if you need to! It is also important to know that it is okay to mix and match plans. You might use a one-to-one behavior plan to target a few key behaviors, and make use of logical consequences from time-to-time as other issues come up. That said, really try to start with one option and make a point of considering how it will look in your household. Starting with one plan will make it less overwhelming for you to respond to behaviors and give you a clearer pathway for how to encourage change.

CONSEQUENCE OPTIONS FOR COMMON PROBLEMS

There are a few problem behaviors that come up over and over for families (such as teen clothing choices, bad attitudes, and picking up). Three of the most common fights happen over teens struggling to a) get off screens, b) get to school on time, and c) complete homework. Because they are so common, 9.1, 9.2, and 9.3 are examples of how you could approach them using consequences. As a quick reminder, consequences should not be the only strategy you use to address these issues. Make sure to look at the CAR model and think about contextual factors you may want to address or other outcomes you can take into consideration. If you have done that and are still struggling with the behavior, then turn to consequences. Every teenager's needs are different and these sample systems are not one-size-fits-all. If they will not work for your household, that is okay! If you have reviewed your CAR acronym and think some sort of consequence would be useful to shape your teen's target behavior, use the skills in this chapter to create one that is a good fit for you and your teen.

Box 9.1

SAMPLE CONSEQUENCES FOR ENFORCING SCREEN LIMITS

Consequence Type	Logical consequence: if the teen follows limit they earn more time, if they ignore limit they lose time.
Consequence Specifics	Teen has a set amount of time to use device (or a specific end time each day). If they turn off the device early, they get to bank that time for the weekend and earn an extra 5 minutes. If they go over the set amount of time, they lose double the next day.

How It Looks in Action:	Teen must turn in phone by 10:30 p.m. each night. On Monday, the teen turns it in by 10:25 (banks 5 minutes + 5 minutes extra). Tuesday goes over by 15 minutes (Wednesday end time now becomes 10:00). Wednesday, teen turns in phone at 10:00. Thursday teen turns in phone by 10:28 (banks 2 minutes + 5 minutes extra). Friday hands it in at 10:30. By Saturday, teen has banked 17 minutes, so can add that to their Saturday night screen limit. To help make it easier, stick a piece of paper on the fridge where you can jot down how many minutes were earned or lost or write it down in the notes app on your phone. This method is usually the best way to reward teens who are concerned about using every minute they think they are owed. If it is too complicated, a simpler version would be that your teen gets a point for every night they hand in the screen early, where each point = 5 extra minutes on the weekend. If they get at least 4 points, you add on an extra 10 minutes on top of what they've earned. This still makes sure they feel like they are getting a bonus for regularly handing time in early, without you having to track minute by minute. If a teen completely refuses to hand in the phone, parents have a few options. They can use parent controls to turn off WiFi, phone apps, or data at the end time. This allows the teen to earn and bank points for turning off the phone early, and the primary punishment is that the device simply turns off in the middle of what the teen was doing at exactly the pre-set time. If parents do not have access to any parental controls, they can keep phone chargers locked away, and only give access to teens in the morning before school if the teen has followed the pre-set limits. If the teen has gone over, they do not get the phone charger for that day.
Context to Plan For	Set alarms to help you or your teen remember the time limit. Decide where the device lives (in the teen's room, in the kitchen, with parents, etc.). If your teen tends to fight you on house rules and is unlikely to ever hand their phone in on time, look into the following: - Have an automatic end time *or* pre-set automated windows for teens to use screens. - If possible, get a parent control app that allows you to switch off/on devices from your phone. - If no auto-turn off options exist and your teen tends to sneak devices, find a lock box to keep devices, chargers, power cords, remotes, or other items needed to use the device.

Box 9.2

SAMPLE CONSEQUENCES FOR GETTING TO SCHOOL ON TIME

Consequence Type	One-to-One Behavior Plan
Consequence Specifics	The time teen gets to school = how much access to screens they have during the day. Getting to school on time = normal access to screens, but access to screens decreases by one hour for each class the teen arrives late to or misses.
How It Looks in Action:	The school day starts at 8:00 a.m. (first period) and ends at 3:45 p.m. If the teen arrives on time, they get regular access to screens. If they arrive after first period, they do not get access to screens until 4:45. If they arrive after second period, they do not get access to screens until 5:45, and so on. If the teen misses the entire day of school, they do not get access to screens during the school day or after school. This type of consequence can be useful because even if the teen does not make it on time, there is incentive to get to class as quickly as possible instead of skipping the entire day. Parents will need to be thoughtful about how to enforce this consequence. For teens who do not care about screens and want to spend the entire day sleeping in bed, this can be turned into a point system where the teen earns 1 point for every class they get to on time. Those points will then lead to a reward at the end of the day, week, or month (depending on what is motivating them).
Context to Plan For	• Post household expectations in a common area of the home. • Determine how teen can get to school if they do not leave on time. • If your teen tends to fight you on house rules and is unlikely to ever hand their phone in on time, look into the following:

	○ Have a pre-set end time OR amount of time to be used by teen. ○ If possible, set up screen limits to auto-turn off apps or devices. ○ If possible, get a parent control app that allows you to switch off/on devices from your phone. ○ If no auto-turn off options exist and your teen tends to sneak devices, find a lock box to keep devices, chargers, power cords, remotes, or other items needed to use the device.

Box 9.3

SAMPLE CONSEQUENCES FOR GETTING SCHOOL WORK DONE

Consequence Type	Point System (if a routine is not enough on its own)
Consequence Specifics	In the best case, you can use the routine plan to create structure for homework that is followed by some logical reward. For example, once the teen gets homework done, they can go see friends. If that logical consequence is not working for some reason, then parents can consider if shifting to a more involved point system would make sense. Specifics are flexible, but it may be that for each homework assignment completed by 8:00 p.m., the teen earns 2 points, and assignments completed after one reminder from parents earn 1 point. Points can be turned in for a pre-set weekly or monthly reward.

Continued

Box 9.3 *Continued*

How It Looks in Action:	A family whose teen has very interfering ADHD decides that the parents will check the school portal or paper assignments for completed homework at 8 p.m. They earn 2 points for every complete assignment. After that, the teen will have 30 minutes to complete any missing assignments. The parents will check again at 8:30 and assign 1 point for each additional assignment complete. At the end of each night, the teen knows exactly how much is earned. They can turn points in for a night reward, such as 30 minutes of extra screen time or time with friends, or save for a larger reward on the weekend like going out to dinner.
Context to Plan For	• Decide how you will check to make sure homework is done and let your teen know how you will determine if an assignment is complete. • Create a plan for situations when the teen cannot do the homework (for example, they either must have the homework complete, or email the teacher asking for help) • Agree on the standard of homework completion (does it count if it is all done, does it have to be done and completely correct, etc.). Families often get into fights because the teen met the bare minimum, but the parents really wanted more than that. • Decide if your teen needs any support (do they get reminders, are they allowed to ask for help, can they study with a friend, should they meet with a tutor, and so on).

TRY IT OUT: CONSEQUENCES

Now that you have completed each exercise in this chapter, it is time to put this tool into practice. Start by filling out Worksheet 9.1 to help clarify your plan. Be patient with yourself as you make changes. Also know that it may take some time before you see your teen start to respond differently. Teens need to see that their parents are consistently responding to behavior before they make changes. Complete the worksheet to increase the likelihood of following through on this task successfully, and write down your attempts at setting up consequences.

WORKSHEET 9.1

1. Which type of consequence system do you think would work best for you (can pick more than one): logical consequences, one-to-one behavior plan, or point system?

   _____

   _____

2. If you picked more than one, which type of plan do you want to start with first?

   _____

   _____

3. What target behaviors do you want to work on? Write between 3–5 and circle your top 2–3. Start with the first 2–3 and you can add or swap over time.

   _____

   _____

4. If you are using logical consequences, think ahead to the types of situations that tend to come up and what sort of logical rewards or punishments you might be able to use:

   _____

   _____

5. If you are using a behavior plan:
   a. Ask your teen what types of reward they would want to work toward:

   Daily: _____

   Weekly: _____

   Monthly (or
   longer): _____

   b. How will you keep track of your child's behavior or points?

   _____

   _____

   c. When do you want to start this plan?

   _____

   _____

6. What barriers, including any of the common stuck points listed previously, do you think may interfere in using the skills, and how do you plan to troubleshoot them?

   _____

   _____

7. List three things that will help you complete this task and make sense of this skill. As a reminder, this could include reminders, skill review, social support, accountability measures, or other ideas you would find useful.

   1. _____

   _____

   2. _____

   _____

   3. _____

   _____

10

De-Escalation

Lowering the Temperature in High Conflict Moments

WHAT IS DE-ESCALATION?

De-escalation is a set of skills that parents can use to respond to teenagers' big bursts of emotions in a way that helps everybody move forward. It helps parents think about how their teens' behaviors, emotions, and needs interact with their own behaviors, emotions, and needs so caregivers can better understand what patterns are helpful and which make situations worse.

De-escalation can be useful in a few different situations. This includes big outbursts when teens are yelling, cursing, throwing things, or slamming doors. It may also come in handy when teens are trapped in an anxiety disorder and so upset that they cry, beg for reassurance or accommodation, or cling to parents. It can even be useful for teenagers who are more withdrawn or depressed, and whose most problematic behaviors include shutting down in difficult moments.

No matter the behavior, parents can go through a wide range of emotions during major stand offs: anger, worry, annoyance, panic, hurt, exasperation, and so on. This makes sense. Kids are so hugely important to their parents, and their struggles can spark intense emotional reactions for the people who love them. While it is completely normal, this emotional rollercoaster can lead to parents making gut-reactions instead of planful responses. Often, parents tend to make choices they think will squash the conflict as quickly as possible. A parent may yell, bribe, threaten, beg, or give into their teen in moments of distress, because doing so gets their teen to back down and gives the parent a break from the distress. This may be intentional for some parents who think, "If I threaten to take the phone for a month, I know they will do what I need them to do," or the opposite, "This is not worth all of the crying, I will just drop this issue for now." But for many, everything happens so fast that actions kick in before there is a chance to think them through or opt for more skillful choices.

All in all, it can make for a completely overwhelming situation that leaves many parents confused about how they should respond. As with many of the skills in this book, de-escalation pays attention to the short and long-term outcomes of parent–teen interactions. The main goal is to find a way to encourage your child to make a skillful choice, while decreasing the chance that somebody does something to hurt the parent–teen relationship or teen's overall well-being.

Before getting into each of the skills that you can use during de-escalation, it is important to think about the pattern that usually occurs when people are upset. There are three phases:

1. *Build-up*: emotion starts to simmer and you see signs that your teen is getting worked up

2. *Peak*: emotion boils over and you see the most problematic behaviors
3. *Cool-down*: the temperature starts to lower and your child returns to their typical self

IDENTIFYING TEEN BEHAVIOR PATTERNS

It is useful to consider how your particular teenager behaves during each of the phases and you will soon learn about specific strategies to use in each. Because each phase comes with its own set of parent skills, you want to have a clear picture in your head of when your child is in build-up versus peak versus cool-down. In Exercise 10.1, write out the behaviors you see from your teen in each phase. To get you started, following are a few examples that commonly come up.

EXERCISE 10.1 IDENTIFYING TEEN BEHAVIOR PATTERNS

Build-Up
Examples: eye-rolls, fidgeting, tense, muttering, talking faster/louder, negotiating, reassurance seeking, predicting the worst, talking over you, attitude/saying no

_____

_____

Peak
Examples: yelling, screaming, cursing, crying, hurtful language, stomping, slamming doors, throwing items, threatening self/others, harming self

_____

_____

Cool-Down
Examples: rejoining group, relaxed body, normal volume/tone, physical contact, more flexible, makes conversation, appropriate language, apologizes

_____

_____

In looking at these behaviors, it is important to determine which ones are actively unsafe as opposed to those that may be highly problematic but will not lead to harm. If your teen is acting in unsafe ways, speak with their primary care physician or a mental health professional. It is important to have a family safety plan in place so that you know exactly what to do.

IDENTIFYING YOUR OWN BEHAVIOR PATTERNS

Because parents and teens impact each other, it is also useful to be aware of your actions as your teen moves through the three phases. Some of your choices may be helpful, while others need to be sidelined. Either way, being aware of patterns can make it easier to make skillful choices in the future. In Exercise 10.2 is a list of common behaviors that parents try while their teens are in the build-up, peak, and cool-down phases. Put a check mark next to any of the behaviors that you find yourself doing. There are a few empty boxes for you to add items that are not already in the list.

EXERCISE 10.2 IDENTIFYING YOUR OWN BEHAVIOR PATTERNS

Parent Behavior During Teen Build-Up	Parent Behavior During Teen Peak	Parent Behavior During Teen Cool-Down
_____ Hugging/cuddling/ physical contact	_____ Giving in/dropping it	_____ Hugging/cuddling/ physical contact
_____ Soothing words	_____ Suggesting skills	_____ Soothing words
_____ Bribing Example: I'll get you a smoothie now if you promise to do homework tonight	_____ Bribing Example: I'll get you a smoothie now if you promise to do homework tonight	_____ Pretending nothing happened
_____ Giving in/dropping it	_____ Pleading/negotiating	_____ Making conversation
_____ Removing obstacles Example: I'll tell school you're sick	_____ Removing obstacles Example: I'll tell school you're sick _____	_____ Apologizing
_____ Negotiating	_____ Ignoring	_____ Ignoring
_____ Ignoring	_____ Eye-rolling/angry gestures	_____ Giving the cold shoulder
_____ Persuading/using logic Example: Have you thought about _____?	_____ Tense body/clenched jaw	_____ Hurtful/shaming language Example: You still act like such a child
_____ Problem-solving	_____ Stomping/slamming doors	_____ Lecturing
_____ Minimizing concerns Example: There's no need to worry	_____ Walking away	_____ Giving a punishment

Parent Behavior During Teen Build-Up	Parent Behavior During Teen Peak	Parent Behavior During Teen Cool-Down
_____ Asking more questions Example: Why are you mad? What's wrong? What can we do?	_____ Raising voice	_____ Processing the situation
_____ Tense body/clenched jaw	_____ Yelling	_____ Explaining hurt feelings
_____ Eye-rolling/scoffing/muttering	_____ Hurtful language Example: You always ruin things	_____ Having a teachable moment
_____ Talking faster/louder Speaking over your child	_____ Threatening punishment	_____ Creating a plan for next time
_____ Shutting it down Example: We're not doing this now	_____ Knocking over/throwing items	
_____ Hurtful language Example: I can't believe you're acting like this. You're going to ruin this outing.	_____ Corporal punishment Example: Spanking, smacking, slapping	

In looking at the behaviors you put a check next to, think about which ones seem helpful and which seem unhelpful. To do this, you may want to go back to CAR (Context-Action-Response) and try to remember what usually happens in the short and long term when you act in a certain way. How does your child respond when you try to problem-solve versus using logic versus negotiate in build-up? How about during peak when you walk away versus yell versus threaten to punish? Not all the behaviors on this list are problematic; some are quite useful. Others may be useful, but only when you use them at a specific part of the interaction.

If you are not sure which behaviors keep you stuck, keep in mind the principles you learned in Chapter 5 on selective attention. Attention is rewarding, so generally you want to give attention during moments when your child is showing some appropriate behavior and removing attention when they are not. Unfortunately, often the reverse happens.

COMMON STUCK POINTS TO EACH PHASE OF DE-ESCALATION

Read through this list of obstacles that parents often encounter when trying to use de-escalation. Underneath each common stuck point, you will find tips and considerations that can help address each barrier. At the end of the chapter, you will have a chance to make note of any examples that would be helpful for you to keep in mind.

Build-up Phase Stuck Points

I think my teen's emotions are overblown.
It is common for parents to think that their kids are overreacting. When you see your teen starting to ramp up when faced with a seemingly small problem, the gut reaction is to try to get them to see how the situation is not so bad. You might say things like:

- *I'm not sure why you're so upset*
- *It's not that big of a deal, everything will be fine*
- *I think you're being a little too sensitive, you need to just calm down*

Unfortunately, these responses tend to make teenagers more upset, not less. Even though you may mean well, the message you send is that you either don't understand your teen's problem, or don't care. See Chapter 6 on validation to review how this can lead to even more distress.

I jump into action items or problem-solving too soon.
Parents often see solutions well before their teenagers do and try to offer up a handful of ideas so that everybody can move on. The thing is, if you start with problem-solving before you show your teen that you understand what they are going through, they won't trust any of your solutions. You could have the perfect suggestion, but it will not make a difference if your teen is not ready to hear it. Plus, most kids are

smart enough to find a solution if you give them the chance to, and benefit from finding their way on their own.

*I have limited patience.
During build-up, parents tend to be a bit impatient or annoyed when kids start to voice or act on their "negative" feelings, especially when paired with less-than-ideal behavior (example: they are expressing their feelings and keeping language appropriate but using a complaining tone). If this sounds like you, you might notice comments dismissing your teen's experience:

- *We're not doing this today*
- *I don't want to hear about it*
- *I know you're mad but it's too bad, we gotta go*

Like parents who think their kids are overreacting, impatient responses will leave your teen feeling invalidated. On top of that, your annoyance is going to show. This makes it more likely for your teen to get annoyed and head straight to peak. Over time, this pattern can impact how both you and your teen view your relationship.

I focus on the inappropriate behavior instead of what my teen is doing well.
During the build-up phase, your teen is going to have a mix of acceptable and unacceptable behaviors at the same time. They might listen to you without interrupting, but they roll their eyes. Or maybe they use appropriate language but grumble a bit under their breath. Maybe they are expressing their feelings to you, but do so in a tone that is rude or defiant. It is common for parents to jump on the "bad" behavior: "Excuse me, you do not speak to me that way." If you recall the selective attention principles, the behaviors you pay attention to will happen more often. Their eye-rolling, grumbling, rude tone, and defiance get a boost each time you comment. Meanwhile, the listening, appropriate language, and communication all go ignored and unrewarded. Long-term, this is not the trend you want.

*My anxiety or guilt for my teen impacts my behavior.
A pattern of anxiety-based behavior (like tearfulness, reassurance seeking, or pushing for more accommodations) can create guilt or sadness in parents that pulls them to make the problems ago away. This can help the teen feel supported in the moment. However, each time a parent bends over backward, it strongly reinforces the teen's anxious behavior without leaving much room for them to practice braver choices. It may not matter in the short term. In the long run you end up with teens who struggle to cope with problems on their own and parents who are resentful of how much they're doing for their kid (see Chapter 8 on accommodation).

Peak Phase Missteps

*I give in.
Peak behaviors are highly disruptive and can be distressing to watch. Many parents feel like they have no choice but to give into their teen's demands, especially when worried about worsening mental health symptoms. Whether it's caving on extra screen time, allowing a later curfew, or doing things for your child they were supposed to manage, giving in can put a pause to the problem behaviors. Unfortunately, it tends to make the peaks worse over time because the teen learns that bigger shows of distress are likely to get them what they want. In general, peak is the time to hold your ground rather than give in.

*My anxiety or guilt for my teen impacts my behavior.
As noted above, some parents find themselves really pulled to interact with their child during these difficult moments because they feel like they cannot "abandon" their child in their moment of need. This can be particularly true for teenagers who are anxious or depressed and whose peak behaviors may be more heartbreaking than they are annoying. The parental instinct to jump in and save the day is both valid and strong. Make sure to think about whether your behavior ends up paying off. Maybe it helps your child calm down in this moment, but can lead to more intense behavior over time and leaves little room for teens to learn self-regulation. If you have a feeling that it only helps in the short term, this is a good time to figure out what you will focus on during conflict so it isn't quite so hard to hold your breath.

*I lose my cool.
As teens go on their emotional rollercoaster, parents often experience their own. This is especially true during peak, when a teenager's emotions are the most intense and the behaviors are most problematic. A teen's behaviors (yelling, cursing, threatening, etc.) can trigger a fight or flight reaction in parents, prompting your own yelling, cursing, or threatening. You may lay out harsh punishment or say things you later regret. As mentioned in Chapter 5 on selective attention, these emotions and reactions are normal, but not super helpful. They tend to make conflicts worse in the moment while giving lots of attention to the problem behavior.

I feel like I have to gain control of the situation.
Parent and teen power struggles are common. Teenagers are trying to gain independence while parents are trying to set rules for their not-yet-adult child. In the middle of intense conflict, this often leads to parents to try to assert their control by

yelling louder, laying down punishments, or having the last word. When you take a step back, these choices tend to lead to higher escalation from teens, fail to change the problem behaviors over time, and can harm the parent–teen relationship. There is absolutely a time and a place for parents to use their authority, but the middle of peak tends not to be the most effective situation for it.

*I think I must do something when I'm in public.
The fear of judgment and shaming from friends, family, and strangers in public is very real for many parents. The second your teen starts to raise their voice, you can practically feel the eyes on you, waiting to see your next move. It is so tempting to respond to your teen, even when you know it probably will not help. Consider what your overall value is: Do you care more about showing other people that you are the boss, or do you care more about helping your teenager learn skillful behavior? If you care more about other peoples' reactions (which in some cases may be important), then responding to your teen during peak may work. If you care more about your child's long-term ability to regulate, it means doing your best to ignore the judgment from those around you. Having a plan for these moments can help.

I threaten or use harsh punishment.
Many parents fall into the trap of taking away a teen's favorite item for long periods of time: no phone for a week, can't drive the car for a month, no allowance for the rest of the summer, etc. Parents often hope that the threat of something so big will get their teen to step in line. The problem is that a teenager mid-peak is not thinking super logically. There are hormones to contend with, difficulty considering consequences, and struggles to control impulses. On top of that, to them it does not feel as if they are simply choosing between following your instructions or losing an allowance for three months. No, in that moment, their brain is telling them they are choosing between being their own independent person who can make their own decisions or being treated like a baby who never gets to have any control. In those moments, teens are willing to go scorched earth if it means they get to feel like they won the battle.

Cool-Down Missteps

*I'm still mad even though my teen is ready to move on.
Once the teen has gotten over their peak, many parents find they are still pretty salty about the battle that just played out. While their teen is back to acting like everything is normal, parents can be tempted to give the cold shoulder or try to shame their teen (e.g., "I can't believe you acted like such a child this afternoon"). In other instances, parents do not mean to be standoffish but are too hurt to forgive and move on. Unfortunately, these reactions can be punishing to teens who are finally showing some appropriately calm behavior. Teens can become angry that their parent cannot accept their apology, desperate for reassurance that everything is okay, or defeated

that they cannot move forward. After all, what is the point of regulating emotions if your parent just keeps bringing up the misbehavior?

I have to make sure my teen sees my point of view/has learned their lesson.
After an outburst, many parents want to make sure their teen understands just how problematic their behavior was. This makes total sense. Part of a parent's role is to teach their teen. However, neither parents nor teens are at their best a few minutes into cool-down. Parents are likely to give long lectures, while teens tune out once they get bored or annoyed. Both sides are frustrated, and nobody learned anything. It is okay to have a conversation with kids about how to improve behavior, but right after a fight is usually not the best moment.

I leave during peak and do not return during cool-down.
Some parents completely walk away when their teenager is in peak. This is typically a very good strategy (see below for more details), but it will become less helpful if you never re-engage once the intensity has cooled off. It is important to show how your response changes when your child's behavior changes. There needs to be a clear difference in your reactions when they are inappropriate vs. skillful.

GETTING UNSTUCK WITH DE-ESCALATION SKILLS

In looking at the list of all the stuck points, it is easy to feel like you have to walk on eggshells to avoid a major blow-up. The good news is that there are many strategies you can use to rework this negative pattern. You might have noticed that many of the stuck points have to do with parental emotions. In fact, all items with an asterisk (*) are centered around some feeling you might have during conflict. Whether it is anxiety, anger, guilt, or embarrassment, difficult emotions can lead to behavior that gets in the way. For these stuck points, turn to Chapter 3 on caregiver coping to review options for remaining in control of your feelings.

Beyond parent coping, there are several skills parents can make use of across the three stages of de-escalation. As stated before, the hope is to give you the best chance of settling the current conflict without sacrificing your relationship or your teen's long-term skill-building. Each phase has its own set of skills, all described as follows.

BUILD-UP

The build-up phase includes three main skills for parents to use:

1. Validation
2. Suggesting or modeling a coping skill
3. Reminding of outcomes

Validation is the first step-parents should take when teens start to ramp up. See Chapter 6 for a full refresher on all the benefits of this skill and how to master it. The main points to remember are that validation can help a teen feel understood, make it less likely for them to enter fight or flight, and make them more willing to be skillful later on. If parents can start with a heavy dose of validation during build-up, there is a decent chance peak can be avoided.

Most parents are willing to at least try validation, but stop too early. They think one validating statement should be enough before moving to solving the problem. It would be great if teenagers could cope with their emotions that quickly, but that usually does not happen. Even for adults, it can take more time to really feel understood and in control of intense feelings. When using validation during the build-up phase, aim for at least three to five validating statements before you try anything else. You will know if validation is working if your child seems to be getting calmer or staying at the same level, listens to what you have to say, or is able to talk with you. If these things are happening, you can continue validating for as long as you want.

There are some situations when validation is not going to be helpful. If you have a teenager who escalates very quickly or who is already pretty upset by the time you join the conversation, you may not be able to validate quickly enough for it to land well. This is particularly common for teens with ADHD who tend to become *very* distressed *very* quickly, or teens with overall higher baselines of anxiety who are almost always teetering on the brink of boiling over. In both cases, the teen's emotional intensity level is too high and is increasing too quickly for validation to avert the peak. You will know this is the case if your validation is met with yelling, complaints that you don't understand, or more escalated behavior. If this happens, there is no need to keep validating over and over again.

Assuming validation goes well (enough) and your teen has not entered peak, the next skill is to suggest or model a coping skill. The idea here is to remind your teenager that they have options to regain control of their emotions if they want to. And since being told what to do is often a major trigger for teens, it tends to work best to suggest rather than demand:

- *Hey, I know you're anxious right now. Sometimes you feel better when you draw for a few minutes. Would you like to try that?*
- *You've been working with your therapist on deep breaths. Is now a good time for that?*
- *I'm happy to bring the dog to sit with you for a few.*

If you already know that your teenager is particularly sensitive to these types of comments, you can skip the suggestion and move straight into doing the coping skill yourself. You might state out loud:

- *I'm feeling pretty stressed right now. I'm going to make myself a cup of tea.*
- *I can see we're both getting upset, I'm going to open the window to get some cool air.*
- *I think I probably need to take a few minutes to myself to calm down.*

Sometimes you can simply act without saying anything at all. Just make the tea, open the window, or step away for a few moments. You will feel better, and you will prime your teen's brain to think about skills they could use (without any sense of pressure to copy you). Even if your teen does not follow suit this time, the more they see coping skills the more likely they are to use them in the future. If your child opts not to use a coping skill, that's okay.

You can offer a skill one to two times and then drop it. This is not about badgering them into being skillful. It's just reminding them that it's an option; they can take it or leave it.

The final skill that you can use during build-up phase is to remind your teen of potential rewarding or punishing outcomes that will happen based on their behavior. When possible, focus on the positive outcomes they will get for appropriate behavior. Not only does it give them the concrete behavior to work on, but it can make the comment sound less like a threat. For example:

> *Threatening*: If you don't get your chores done you can't watch any TV.
> *Helpful*: House rule is that you are welcome to start TV time as soon as chores are done.

> *Threatening*: No way are you getting your curfew extended if you keep acting like this.
> *Helpful*: Just a reminder, if you can practice coping skills you can earn later curfew.

> *Threatening*: Well, I guess if you aren't getting out of bed it means you don't want your phone this afternoon. Fine by me!
> *Helpful*: If you can get to school on time, you can have your phone. If you sleep in, you'll lose time this afternoon.

Because you are aiming to keep your teen regulated instead of pushing them to peak, your tone is key. You can review Chapter 2 on the importance of being neutral, but here is your reminder to use your best restaurant server or flight attendant voice. Pretend that you have no attachment to what your teen chooses to do *or* the outcome. As hard as that is, you decrease the chance of a power struggle where they act up just to spite you.

Pro tip: do your best to think of these consequences before the fight even starts. If you and your teen run into the same battles over and over, decide ahead of time what they can earn for skillful behavior and what happens if they lose it. That way the consequence can be based on your calm, thoughtful judgment, rather than a rash decision in the heat of the moment.

Parents should only think about using this skill one or two times while their child is becoming worked up. Any more than that becomes annoying to a teenager and it can turn into a power struggle. Even if they end up following through, you basically did all the work for them. That might be fine short term, but in the long term you really want your teen to be the one who's willingly making skillful choices. There are also going to be times when you give the reminder and your teen still decides to make the inappropriate choice. That's a real bummer, but it's okay. View Chapter 9 on rewards and punishment for a review of how some consequences take time to be effective.

PEAK

If it's been a while since you brushed up on active ignoring, here's your opportunity to do so. Your main skill in peak is to actively ignore all the (safe) problem behaviors that your teenager is using. For example, if your teen is name calling, negotiating, or stomping around, you can act as if you do not even notice. That's it! That is the main skill to use in peak. Easy, right?

Maybe not so much—active ignoring is simple but *not* easy! Even though it is hard, you are going to do your best to disengage from the conflict so you can remove any accidental reward you may have been giving to unskillful choices. The only exception to this rule is if your teenager is engaging in unsafe behavior. If you are concerned for your child's safety or the safety of somebody else in your household, you are not necessarily going to disengage. Do what you need to do to keep everybody safe. As always, if this is a concern, talk to your child's primary care provider or a mental health professional to figure out a safety plan.

If there are no safety concerns but ignoring seems impossible, it can help to keep your long-term goal in mind. Do you want a better relationship with your child? Do you need them to learn how to manage big emotions without you jumping in? Is it crucial to create a calmer household? Active ignoring during peak can help get you closer to these outcomes. Even though the short-term distress may be high, thinking of the long-term gains can make this skill easier to stomach. Also remember that teen brains are in a period of rapid development that make peak behaviors more likely. The brain systems responsible for emotions are changing and the parts of the brain that manage impulse control and thinking ahead have years of development left. Through no fault of their own, this puts teens at a higher risk of saying and doing things that are unskillful and problematic. As noted previously, you can also review Chapter 3 on caregiver coping and brush up on your In-the-Moment Coping Plan and make sure you have made some progress on your domains of wellness. Try to put yourself in the best position as possible to ride out the wave of problematic peak behaviors. This will be your best chance to lessen peak problem behaviors as quickly as possible.

If you *still* cannot bring yourself to ignore (or are still practicing the coping skills to do so), you have a few options. You can start by picking two of the following skills during peak:

1. Use a when/then statement
2. Suggest or model a coping skill
3. Remind of outcomes

A when/then statement tells your child what will happen when they complete a particular task or behavior. The idea is that you are pairing a behavior you want to see with an outcome your teen wants. For example:

- *When you can lower your voice, you're welcome to come back into the living room.*
- *If you're able to change the topic of a conversation, I'm happy to keep talking with you.*
- *As soon as you've finished reading, you're welcome to have your phone back.*

This can sometimes be helpful because it cuts through the distress with one solid exit ramp for your child and is a pathway for them to get some of your attention back.

Your second and third skill options are the same as they are in the build-up phase: you can remind your child of a coping skill and/or potential outcomes. In peak, parents should only use these skills if they think their teen has forgotten they have coping skills, or that a reward or punishment is on the line. This happens sometimes when an outburst lasts a long time. Teens can get stuck in a distress loop and forget what they're even mad about. If you think this might be happening to your teenager, these options can be a lifeline. However, if you are pretty sure that your teenager is perfectly aware of coping skills but is actively choosing not to use them—save your breath. Ditto if they know what the outcome is going to be and decide they do not care. In these cases, giving the reminders is only going to make you mad that they refuse to listen and is likely to send them further into peak.

Even while making use of these options, do not lose sight of the overall goal to reduce attention during peak. Pick two things, total, to say out loud. Do not pick two categories of skills and repeat them over and over in hopes that something you say will finally stick. As always, your tone and word choice should be neutral and to the point.

COOL-DOWN

While it seems like peak never ends, it always does. Sometimes parents and teens are equally eager to move on, and simply go about their day without talking about the fight. This can be an effective strategy for some families. You avoid anything majorly punishing like a lecture or harsh punishment. Plus, everybody acting normally will (hopefully) involve giving your teen some general positive attention. This should reinforce their calmer behavior. Two possible downsides to this approach are a) missing a chance to praise any skillful behavior your teen tried, and b) parents becoming resentful because the problem behaviors are never mentioned. Other families take more time to talk through blow-ups. This can be okay too, as long as the teenager finds these conversations helpful rather than overly boring or critical. It is also important to make sure you mention what the teen did well instead of only focusing on what did not go well.

Some parents find the cool-down stage to be very difficult. Often, comments and behavior that happened during peak really sour the parents' mood and general family connection. While that is understandable, lingering annoyance or resentment toward your kid does not help improve the relationship or reward them for regulating. This is particularly concerning for teens with mental health difficulties who are more likely to end up in these situations repeatedly and are at greater risk of feeling criticized or alienated. To avoid those issues, try these skills:

1. Return attention without negativity
2. Praise any appropriate behavior
3. Use a compliment sandwich

The very first move parents can make in cool-down is to return attention to your child without negativity. Use your parent coping skills to manage your own emotions so you can go back to making eye contact, making conversation, and/or having physical contact when appropriate. The message you want to send is that you are noticing their behavior has changed so your response to them has changed. If you are not emotionally at a place where you can do these things, that is okay, but you need to own that. Try to avoid anything along the lines of "I can't believe you acted that way, I don't want to see you for the rest of the afternoon." Instead, you might say "I'm still pretty upset, I need 30 minutes to cool off." Then you can take the break and focus on getting back to your baseline.

Stating how much time you need is useful for kids who are anxious or self-doubting. Without that time estimate, kids with anxiety disorders or depression can get so frantic or self-defeating that they spiral into another peak. They think you're leaving for the rest of the day, assume you hate them, or convince themselves they're terrible. When parents are angry, it can sometimes feel satisfying to have your kids sweat it out. From a mental health lens, it is not worth the negative impact on self-esteem, the relationship, and symptoms. Feel free to take some space, but give your teen a heads up and take responsibility for needing to manage your emotions.

The next skill you can use is to praise any appropriate behavior that may have occurred over the course of your child's outburst. This is tricky because it is hard to compliment your teenager when they just made your life hell for the last 30+ minutes. Go back to Chapter 5 on selective attention. Remember that labeled praise is one of your best tools for shaping better behavior over time. This can include "expected" behavior that is really the bare minimum of what you need to see. Beyond that, there may have been points where your teenager tried to be skillful even if it didn't work completely. Were they able to listen to what you had to say even if they did not follow through completely? Or maybe they managed to keep their problem behaviors less intense, less damaging, or shorter than usual. Any of these behaviors are steps in the right direction and worthy of acknowledgment. Examples include:

- *Hey, I really appreciate you trying to take the deep breath.*
- *Thank you for picking up the books you knocked over.*
- *I'm glad you joined the family again. We missed you.*

In the middle of peak, it's possible that your teen did some highly inappropriate things that need to be addressed. This can be accomplished through a compliment sandwich. The compliment sandwich starts and ends with labeled praise. In the middle you can note the behavior that your teen needs to reflect on or take responsibility for. Examples include:

- *Thank you for rejoining us. You said some really mean things to your dad, and now might be a good time to apologize. I appreciate that you were able to calm down.*
- *Thank you for the apology. It wasn't okay that you dumped out your sister's backpack. I need you to pick that up. I'm impressed with how well you're staying focused right now.*
- *You did a great job of using your skills more quickly today. You weren't able to finish the chores by the time they had to be done, so no TV today. I know you'll do a better job tomorrow and I appreciate how much you're trying.*

A compliment sandwich lets your child know that you see beyond the "bad" behavior and recognize the good. It gives them feedback on the "bad" behavior in a way that is short and to-the-point (which makes it easier for them to take in). This is particularly important for kids with attentional difficulties who have a hard time staying focused during a parent's lengthy lecture. It is also easier for kids with anxiety who struggle to tolerate their feelings of shame when getting scolded. In all, a compliment sandwich makes it less likely for them to head back into peak and more likely for them to follow through on the repair or reflection you've asked of them.

There are some problem behaviors that call for more than just a compliment sandwich. Examples might be aggression, derogatory language, or breaking items. In these instances, a longer conversation, teachable moment, or repair could be appropriate. These will all go much better if you wait to have that conversation until later in the day or week. Even when your teen is in the cool-down phase, emotions are usually still a little rocky for everybody involved. Giving yourself (and your teen) more time to calm down will help you be more thoughtful about what you want to say and how you want to say it. It also makes it more likely for your teen to take in what you say without being defensive. For these moments, you can use the compliment sandwich to preview the conversation you're going to have later. For example:

I notice you used a coping skill your therapist taught you. That was really amazing. Sometime this weekend, let's talk about how to make sure you stay safe even when you're angry. I love you very much. I know you're doing the best you can right now.

TEST YOUR KNOWLEDGE OF DE-ESCALATION SKILLS

Read through the sample script in Exercise 10.3. In this example, the parent is responding to their teen's distress using skills. As you read, try to label each skill the parent is using. Here is a brief reminder of skills to look out for: validation; suggest or model a coping skill; remind of outcome (in build-up); active ignoring; when/then statement; remind of outcome (in peak); and return attention without negativity; labeled praise; compliment sandwich (in cool-down).

EXERCISE 10.3 TEST YOUR KNOWLEDGE OF DE-ESCALATION SKILLS

Statement	Skill
13-year-old (13): Dad I am freaking out. I'm going to fail my math test tomorrow!	
Parent (P): You care so much about your grades, I can understand why you're panicky.	
13: If I don't get the grade I want it's going to look so bad on my transcript!	
P: I know your school is really competitive, so no wonder you're thinking about that.	
13: I've just worked SO hard this year. It will feel like a total waste if I don't do really well.	
P: It makes sense you feel that way, right? You've given up a lot this year to focus on studying.	
13: It's just going to be for NOTHING! I can already tell!	
P: I know you're super anxious. You usually feel better if you take a walk or at least grab a snack.	

Statement	Skill
13: I don't even have time for that! I think you should just quiz me for the next hour or two!	
P: I'll tell ya what, if you're able to take a walk around the block, I'll help you organize your bag for tomorrow so you know you have all your notes ready to look over on the way to school.	
13: No! I just have to keep studying! Please just quiz me!	
P: I can see how worried you are about this. I don't think my answers are helpful at this point. I'm happy to take a walk or talk about something else. If not, I'm going to finish cleaning up.	
13: What!? Dad! That's so unfair. Please just quiz me!	
P: [no response]	
13: I'm going to fail and it's all your fault! I thought you wanted me to do well! [curses at Dad]	
P: [no response; makes tea with enough in the pot for two]	

Continued

Continued

Statement	Skill
T: [starts to get more frantic, tearful; pacing room for a few minutes before going to bedroom]	
P: [no response; drinks tea facing away from teen]	
T: [after 20 minutes, teen comes to sit at the table and slumps head into her arms]	
P: [pours cup of tea for teen] Thank you for allowing yourself to sit for a few minutes.	
T: Hmph.	
P: I know you're still upset and appreciate that you're trying to stay calm. You know that the house rule says cursing = $1 off of allowance for the week. I can see how much anxiety is getting in the way, and am really proud of you for being able to rein it in.	
T: Everything is just so much right now.	
P: I can see that. We're going to find some ways to get you more support.	

Exercise 10.3 ANSWER KEY Test Your Knowledge of De-Escalation Skills

Statement	Skill
13-year-old (13): Dad I am freaking out. I'm going to fail my math test tomorrow!	
Parent (P): You care so much about your grades, I can understand why you're panicky.	Validation
13: If I don't get the grade I want it's going to look so bad on my transcript!	
P: I know your school is really competitive, so no wonder you're thinking about that.	Validation
13: I've just worked SO hard this year. It will feel like a total waste if I don't do really well.	
P: It makes sense you feel that way, right? You've given up a lot this year to focus on studying.	Validation
13: It's just going to be for NOTHING! I can already tell!	
P: I know you're super anxious. You usually feel better if you take a walk or at least grab a snack.	Validation, Suggest coping skill
13: I don't even have time for that! I think you should just quiz me for the next hour or two!	

Continued

Continued

Statement	Skill
P: I'll tell ya what, if you're able to take a walk around the block, I'll help you organize your bag for tomorrow so you know you have all your notes ready to look over on the way to school.	Remind of outcome
13: No! I just have to keep studying! Please just quiz me!	
P: I can see how worried you are about this. I don't think my answers are helpful at this point. I'm happy to take a walk or talk about something else. If not, I'm going to finish cleaning up.	Validation and When/then
13: What!? Dad! That's so unfair. Please just quiz me!	
P: [no response]	Active Ignoring
13: I'm going to fail and it's all your fault! I thought you wanted me to do well! [curses at Dad]	
P: [no response; makes tea with enough in the pot for two]	Active Ignoring, Model coping skill
13: [starts to get more frantic, tearful. Pacing room for a few minutes before going to bedroom]	
P: [no response; drinks tea facing away from teen]	Active Ignoring

Statement	Skill
13: [after 20 minutes, teen comes to sit at the table and slumps head into her arms]	
P: [pours cup of tea for teen] Thank you for allowing yourself to sit for a few minutes.	Labeled praise
13: Hmph.	
P: I know you're still upset and appreciate that you're trying to stay calm. You know that the house rule says cursing = $1 off of allowance for the week. I can see how much anxiety is getting in the way, and am really proud of you for being able to rein it in.	Compliment sandwich
13: Everything is just so much right now.	
P: I can see that. We're going to find some ways to get you more support.	Validation, Return attention without negativity

TEST YOUR KNOWLEDGE OF DE-ESCALATION PITFALLS

Read through the sample script in Exercise 10.4. In this example, the parent responds in a way that is a little less skillful than the example in the previous exercise. Put a check next to each parent response that is skillful and an ✗ where the parent response misses the mark somehow. Then, see if you can label the skill or identify the stuck point. As an extra bonus, try to put a line to show where the conversation shifts from build-up, to peak, to cool-down.

Here is a brief reminder of skills to look out for: validation, suggest or model a coping skill; remind of outcome (in build-up), active ignoring, when/then statement, remind of outcome (in peak), and return attention without negativity, labeled praise, compliment sandwich (in cool-down).

And here is a reminder of stuck points to look out for: invalidating comments; jumping to action or problem-solving; parental emotions; parents' need for teen to accept parents' authority or point of view; paying attention to unskillful behavior instead of skillful behavior; overly harsh punishment.

EXERCISE 10.4 TEST YOUR KNOWLEDGE OF DE-ESCALATION PITFALLS

✓ or ✗	Statement	Skill/Stuck Point
	Parent (P): So I thought about the party you wanted to go to on Saturday, but it's just not going to work. We're supposed to be at your grandma's for dinner, and I don't feel comfortable having you go somewhere when we aren't even nearby.	
	16-year-old (16): What!?	
	P: I know, it's really frustrating . . . you wanted to go to that party so badly.	
	16: Wait, are you really serious?! I can't go just because you'll be at Grandma's?	
	P: Of course, I'm serious! I don't know the parents and I'll be an hour away!	
	16: You are being SO paranoid. Stop treating me like a baby. I'll be FINE.	
	P: I am your parent and it is my job to look out for you.	
	16: That's such BS. I'm not a kid!	

Continued

Continued

✓ or ✗	Statement	Skill/Stuck Point
	P: Okay, I think I need a minute to take a deep breath or two.	
	16: [takes deep breath] You have to let me go to that party. PLEASE.	
	P: The answer is no.	
	16: UGH! WHY ARE YOU TRYING TO RUIN MY LIFE JUST BECAUSE YOU DON'T HAVE ONE OF YOUR OWN!?	
	P: Excuse me? That is not how you speak to me. At this rate, don't expect to go to the next party either.	
	16: THAT IS SO UNFAIR! YOU ALWAYS DO THIS!	
	P: Well, I wouldn't have to do this if you would start acting your age. I would have *never* spoken like this to my parents.	
	16: Oh sure, you were SO perfect. SORRY I'M NOT YOU!	
	P: Stop being so dramatic. I'm not saying that. But you do need to grow up.	

De-Escalation 231

✓ or ✗	Statement	Skill/Stuck Point
	16: What's the POINT?! YOU'LL NEVER LET ME DO WHAT I WANT ANYWAYS. Everything ALWAYS has to be your way.	
	P: If you can lower your voice, I am happy to talk about other ways you can see your friends this weekend.	
	16: I DON'T WANT OTHER WAYS. YOU DON'T GET IT!!!	
	P: Okay I have had ENOUGH. Go to your room NOW.	
	16: Or what? You won't let me go to a party? OH WAIT—YOU WON'T LET ME ANYWAYS.	
	P: If you are not in your room in the next 30 seconds, no phone for a WEEK!	
	16: I HATE YOU! [storms away, slams door]	
	[60 minutes goes by, teen comes out to get a snack]	
	P: Hey, you.	

Continued

✓ or ✗	Statement	Skill/Stuck Point
	16: I'm just getting a snack.	
	P: Okay. Anything you want to say to me?	
	16: Not really.	
	P: I know you're mad. But you've gotta understand that you aren't an adult yet!	
	16: Can we just not do this right now?	
	P: I need you to understand that I have rules to keep you safe. You don't have to like them, but you have to respect them as long as you live under my roof.	
	16: I knoooow Mom. You tell me that literally every single week. Can I go now!?	
	P: Okay, fine! I would have hoped you would be grateful!	
	16: Whatever, Mom.	

Exercise 10.4 ANSWER KEY Test Your Knowledge of De-Escalation Pitfalls

✓ or ✗	Statement	Skill/Stuck Point
	Parent (P): So I thought about the party you wanted to go to on Saturday, but it's just not going to work. We're supposed to be at your grandma's for dinner, and I don't feel comfortable having you go somewhere when we aren't even nearby.	
	16-year-old (16): What!?	
✓	P: I know, it's really frustrating . . . you wanted to go to that party so badly.	Validation
	16: Wait, are you really serious?! I can't go just because you'll be at Grandma's?	
✗	P: Of course, I'm serious! I don't know the parents and I'll be an hour away!	Invalidating
	16: You are being SO paranoid. Stop treating me like a baby. I'll be FINE.	
✗	P: I am your parent and it is my job to look out for you.	Parent focused on teen accepting parents' point of view
	16: That's such BS. I'm not a kid!	

Continued

Continued

✓ or ✗	Statement	Skill/Stuck Point
✓	P: Okay, I think I need a minute to take a deep breath or two.	Modeled a coping skill
	16: [takes deep breath] You have to let me go to that party. PLEASE.	
✗	P: The answer is no.	Mom sticking to her plan is good, but she did not attend to skillful behavior
	16: UGH! WHY ARE YOU TRYING TO RUIN MY LIFE JUST BECAUSE YOU DON'T HAVE ONE OF YOUR OWN!?	
✗	P: Excuse me? That is not how you speak to me. At this rate, don't expect to go to the next party either.	Paying attention to unskillful behavior Overly harsh punishment
	16: THAT IS SO UNFAIR! YOU ALWAYS DO THIS!	
✗	P: Well, I wouldn't have to do this if you would start acting your age. I would have *never* spoken like this to my parents.	Paying attention to unskillful behavior Parents' emotions Parent focused on teen accepting parents' point of view
	16: Oh sure, you were SO perfect. SORRY I'M NOT YOU!	

De-Escalation

✓ or ✗	Statement	Skill/Stuck Point
✗	P: Stop being so dramatic. I'm not saying that. But you do need to grow up.	Paying attention to unskillful behavior Invalidating
	16: What's the POINT?! YOU'LL NEVER LET ME DO WHAT I WANT ANYWAYS. Everything ALWAYS has to be your way.	
✓	P: If you can lower your voice, I am happy to talk about other ways you can see your friends this weekend.	When/then statement
	16: I DON'T WANT OTHER WAYS. YOU DON'T GET IT!!!	
✗	P: Okay I have had ENOUGH. Go to your room NOW.	Paying attention to unskillful behavior Parents' emotions
	16: Or what? You won't let me go to a party? OH WAIT—YOU WON'T LET ME ANYWAYS.	
✗	P: If you are not in your room in the next 30 seconds, no phone for a WEEK!	Paying attention to unskillful behavior Parents' emotions Overly harsh punishment
✓	16: I HATE YOU! [storms away, slams door]	Active ignoring
⇨	[60 minutes goes by, teen comes out to get a snack]	

Continued

Continued

✓ or ✗	Statement	Skill/Stuck Point
✓	P: Hey, you.	Returned attention without negativity
	16: I'm just getting a snack.	
✗	P: Okay. Anything you want to say to me?	Parent focused on teen accepting parents' point of view
	16: Not really.	
✗	P: I know you're mad. But you've gotta understand that you aren't an adult yet!	Parent focused on teen accepting parents' point of view
	16: Can we just not do this right now?	
✗	P: I need you to understand that I have rules to keep you safe. You don't have to like them, but you have to respect them as long as you live under my roof.	Parent focused on teen accepting parents' point of view
	16: I knoooow Mom. You tell me that literally every single week. Can I go now!?	
✗	P: Okay, fine! I would have hoped you would be grateful!	Parents' emotions Parent focused on teen accepting parents' point of view
	16: Whatever, Mom.	

There are a few details worth pointing out in this answer key. One overarching positive behavior from the parent is that she did not back down simply because the teenager got really mad. She stood her ground because she felt her decision made the most sense based on the information she had. Sometimes teenagers share new information that might help a parent change their mind. For example, maybe in this case the mom did not know the parents of the teen throwing the party, but the teenager shares their older cousin will be there. Perhaps that would make Mom feel comfortable enough with the situation and she could change her mind. Either way, the key is that the parent does not give in simply to avoid their teen's blow-up. There are also many times when more than one stuck point comes up. Intense parental emotion may lead to invalidation or harsh punishment. It is useful to notice how these patterns show up for you in difficult moments so you can do your best to watch out for them in the future. One of the bigger overall issues with this example is that the parent remains engaged for nearly the entire peak. Unfortunately, her responses do not do anything to get her teen to calm down and add a lot of stimulation and attention to the mix.

TEST YOUR SKILLS: DE-ESCALATION

In Exercise 10.5 is the same script you just saw. The stuck points have been boldfaced. Your job in this exercise is to decide what skill you would want to use instead and rewrite the parent's responses based on that. In real life, it is very likely that a parent using skills during build-up could prevent the conversation from ever getting to peak. For the sake of you getting practice, this example will assume that the teen was going to lose their cool no matter what, so their responses are all the same as in the previous example. Keep in mind there are many ways to be skillful during conflict and there is no one "right" response, but you can see examples in the answer key later in the chapter.

Skills: validation, suggest or model a coping skill, remind of outcome (in build-up), active ignoring, when/then statement, suggest or model a coping skill, remind of outcome (in peak), and return attention without negativity, labeled praise, compliment sandwich (in cool-down).

EXERCISE 10.5 TEST YOUR KNOWLEDGE OF DE-ESCALATION PITFALLS

Script	Rewrite (Skill you want to use) Statement Example: (validation) It makes sense you're angry because you were really looking forward to the party
Parent (P): So I thought about the party you wanted to go to on Saturday, but it's just not going to work. We're supposed to be at your grandma's for dinner, and I don't feel comfortable having you go somewhere when we aren't even nearby.	
16-year-old (16): What!?	
P: I know, it's really frustrating . . . you wanted to go to that party so badly.	
16: Wait, are you really serious?! I can't go just because you'll be at Grandma's?	
P: Of course, I'm serious! I don't know the parents and I'll be an hour away!	
16: You are being SO paranoid. Stop treating me like a baby. I'll be FINE.	
P: I am your parent and it is my job to look out for you.	
16: That's such BS. I'm not a kid!	

De-Escalation

Script	Rewrite **(Skill you want to use) Statement** Example: (validation) It makes sense you're angry because you were really looking forward to the party
P: Okay, I think I need a minute to take a deep breath or two.	
16: [takes deep breath] You have to let me go to that party. PLEASE.	
P: The answer is no.	
16: UGH! WHY ARE YOU TRYING TO RUIN MY LIFE JUST BECAUSE YOU DON'T HAVE ONE OF YOUR OWN!?	
P: Excuse me? That is not how you speak to me. At this rate, don't expect to go to the next party either.	
16: THAT IS SO UNFAIR! YOU ALWAYS DO THIS!	
P: Well, I wouldn't have to do this if you would start acting your age. I would have *never* spoken like this to my parents.	
16: Oh sure, you were SO perfect. SORRY I'M NOT YOU!	

Continued

Continued

Script	Rewrite **(Skill you want to use) Statement** Example: (validation) It makes sense you're angry because you were really looking forward to the party
P: Stop being so dramatic. I'm not saying that. But you do need to grow up.	
16: What's the POINT?! YOU'LL NEVER LET ME DO WHAT I WANT ANYWAYS. Everything ALWAYS has to be your way.	
P: If you can lower your voice, I am happy to talk about other ways you can see your friends this weekend.	
16: I DON'T WANT OTHER WAYS. YOU DON'T GET IT!!!	
P: Okay I have had ENOUGH. Go to your room NOW.	
16: Or what? You won't let me go to a party? OH WAIT—YOU WON'T LET ME ANYWAYS.	
P: If you are not in your room in the next 30 seconds, no phone for a WEEK!	
16: I HATE YOU! [storms away, slams door]	

Script	Rewrite **(Skill you want to use) Statement** Example: (validation) It makes sense you're angry because you were really looking forward to the party
[60 minutes goes by, teen comes out to get a snack]	
P: Hey, you.	
16: I'm just getting a snack.	
P: Okay. Anything you want to say to me?	
16: Not really.	
P: I know you're mad. But you've gotta understand that you aren't an adult yet!	
16: Can we just not do this right now?	

Continued

Continued

Script	Rewrite **(Skill you want to use) Statement** Example: (validation) It makes sense you're angry because you were really looking forward to the party
P: I need you to understand that I have rules to keep you safe. You don't have to like them, but you have to respect them as long as you live under my roof.	
16: I knoooow Mom. You tell me that literally every single week. Can I go now!?	
P: Okay, fine! I would have hoped you would be grateful!	
16: Whatever, Mom.	

De-Escalation 243

Exercise 10.5 ANSWER KEY Test Your Skills: De-Escalation

First Example	Rewrite (Skill you want to use) Statement
Parent (P): So I thought about the party you wanted to go to on Saturday, but it's just not going to work. We're supposed to be at your grandma's for dinner, and I don't feel comfortable having you go somewhere when we aren't even nearby.	
16-year-old (16): What!?	
P: I know, it's really frustrating . . . you wanted to go to that party so badly.	
16: Wait, are you really serious?! I can't go just because you'll be at Grandma's?	
P: Of course, I'm serious! I don't know the parents and I'll be an hour away!	(validation) I am serious. I understand that you might be really upset about my choice because it doesn't make a whole lot of sense to you.
16: You are being SO paranoid. Stop treating me like a baby. I'll be FINE.	
P: I am your parent and it is my job to look out for you.	(validation) I can see why you would feel like I'm treating you like a baby because there are so many other things you can do on your own without me being around.
16: That's such BS. I'm not a kid!	

Continued

Continued

First Example	Rewrite (Skill you want to use) Statement
P: Okay, I think I need a minute to take a deep breath or two.	
16: [takes deep breath] You have to let me go to that party. PLEASE.	
P: The answer is no.	(labeled praise) I really appreciate you taking a beat, especially when this is so upsetting
16: UGH! WHY ARE YOU TRYING TO RUIN MY LIFE JUST BECAUSE YOU DON'T HAVE ONE OF YOUR OWN!?	
P: Excuse me? That is not how you speak to me. At this rate, don't expect to go to the next party either.	(active ignore) say nothing, focus on something else
16: THAT IS SO UNFAIR! YOU ALWAYS DO THIS!	
P: Well, I wouldn't have to do this if you would start acting your age. I would have *never* spoken like this to my parents.	(active ignore) say nothing, focus on something else
16: Oh sure, you were SO perfect. SORRY I'M NOT YOU!	
P: Stop being so dramatic. I'm not saying that. But you do need to grow up.	(active ignore) say nothing, focus on something else
16: What's the POINT?! YOU'LL NEVER LET ME DO WHAT I WANT ANYWAYS. Everything ALWAYS has to be your way.	

De-Escalation

First Example	Rewrite (Skill you want to use) Statement
P: If you can lower your voice, I am happy to talk about other ways you can see your friends this weekend.	
16: I DON'T WANT OTHER WAYS. YOU DON'T GET IT!!!	
P: Okay I have had ENOUGH. Go to your room NOW.	(remind of outcome) Just a reminder of our house rule: if you are able to stay calm or go to your room to cool off, you get to keep all of your privileges for the weekend.
16: Or what? You won't let me go to a party? OH WAIT—YOU WON'T LET ME ANYWAYS.	
P: If you are not in your room in the next 30 seconds, no phone for a WEEK!	(active ignore) say nothing, focus on something else
16: I HATE YOU! [storms away, slams door]	
[60 minutes goes by, teen comes out to get a snack]	[60 minutes goes by, teen comes out to get a snack]
P: Hey, you.	
16: I'm just getting a snack.	

Continued

Continued

First Example	Rewrite (Skill you want to use) Statement
P: Okay. Anything you want to say to me?	(praise appropriate behavior and engage without negativity) Got it. Thank you for heading to your room before to cool off. Do you want to watch some TV or something?
16: Not really.	
P: I know you're mad. But you've gotta understand that you aren't an adult yet!	(compliment sandwich) Fair enough. Thank you for responding calmly now. At some point next week, let's talk about how we can come to some compromises about you going out and help you manage decisions you don't like. I love how much you care about your friends and try really hard to spend time with them.
16: Can we just not do this right now?	
P: I need you to understand that I have rules to keep you safe. You don't have to like them, but you have to respect them as long as you live under my roof.	(praise appropriate behavior) No problem. Thanks for letting me know you're not ready to talk now. We'll talk later. I love you.
16: I knoooow Mom. You tell me that literally every single week. Can I go now!?	
P: Okay, fine! I would have hoped you would be grateful!	(engage without negativity) Of course. I'll see you for dinner.
16: Whatever, Mom.	

In reading though this answer key, you may have noticed that even though the teen's responses are exactly the same as the first script, the entire tone of the interaction seems to shift. There is understanding, support, and connection throughout. The parent makes it very clear that she is available for her child and loves them, even if that is not what the teen wants in this moment. Both in terms of short-term escalation and long-term relationship-building, skillful choices make a huge difference.

TRY IT OUT: DE-ESCALATION

Now that you have completed each de-escalation exercise, it is time to put this tool into practice. Start by practicing skills one phase at a time. Pick the phase you think will be easiest for you and plan to spend a few days to a week working on that before you add in skills from another phase. De-escalation includes many tools in one package, so there is no expectation to master them all immediately. As with all skills, be patient with yourself as you make changes. Also know that it may take some time before you see your teen start to respond differently. Teens need to see that their parents are consistently keeping their cool before they trust things are different and can react less intensely. Complete Worksheet 10.1 to increase the likelihood of following through on this task successfully and write down your attempts at validation below.

WORKSHEET 10.1

1. When will you try to use this skill during the week (are there any conflicts that come up routinely so you can plan ahead)?

   _____

2. How will you remember to practice this skill?

   _____

3. What barriers did you identify as potentially interfering, and how do you plan to troubleshoot them?

   _____

   _____

4. List three things that will help you complete this task and make sense of this skill. As a reminder, this could include reminders, skill review, social support, accountability measures, or other ideas you would find useful.

   1. _____

   _____

   2. _____

   _____

   3. _____

   _____

11
Putting It All Together

WHAT DOES PUTTING IT ALL TOGETHER MEAN?

At this point in the book you have been introduced to many different skills and have:

- Tools to help you understand the patterns that play out between you and your teen
- Strategies to encourage skillful behavior and help your teen feel supported
- Tips to stay regulated and calm so you can parent the way you want to
- Skills to address problem behaviors while helping your teen build their abilities

Now that you are more familiar with these different ideas and have had a chance to practice each one, you can start to use these skills in combination with each other. Instead of just focusing on one skill, like selective attention, for a week, you want to consider how to make use of selection attention *and* the de-escalation model (or validation, or behavior plans, etc.). This chapter is all about helping you see how to layer these skills in useful ways.

WHY DOES PUTTING IT ALL TOGETHER MATTER?

Each of these evidence-based strategies is useful on its own, but the whole is greater than the sum of its parts. No *one* skill is the cure-all for teen mental health or parent–teen conflict. In fact, sometimes one skill used in a vacuum can actually lead to more problems. However, when you start to understand how to put skills together, you will find a real balance in tools that help you build connection and your teen's self-esteem while managing problem behaviors and conflict. In a way, using these skills is a bit of a symphony. Different parts of the music may feature different techniques. All serve a function and have value. And then, at the climax of the music, you experience all of the threads working together to create a powerful, interconnected moment. Using all of your tools together will help you feel confident in creating meaningful, effective change.

HOW TO COMBINE SKILLS

There are a few steps you can take to most effectively combine skills:

1. Fill out the CAR acronym you were introduced to in Chapter 4. Write down what contexts, actions, and results are currently at play for your child.
2. For each action, decide what skills you can use to meet your goals. This will include:
    a. Skills that can help you change your child's context or empathize with them.
    b. Skills that can help you reinforce or punish appropriate and inappropriate behavior.

To help you with this, write out a list of all the skills you have learned so you can simply look at your options and plug them into the questions on previous page. If it is easier, take a picture of the word bank below, which includes every tool you have learned throughout this book.

CAR	Positive Attention	Active Ignoring	De-Escalation
Parent Coping	Labeled Praise	Routines	Logical Consequences
Accommodations	Validation	Setting Clear Expectations/Rewards	One-to-one Behavior Plan Point System

The point of these steps is to create a roadmap for yourself. Once you have a clear picture of the Context-Action-Results in question and what skills might be useful, you can start to combine all of your skills to help shift the pattern. Take a look at the sample situation below, and how a parent could use CAR and your skills word bank to create a plan. In order to give as many examples as possible, this outline showcases how to combine skills for multiple problem behaviors at once. As you work on this in your own life, it is much more likely that you would complete the steps (making use of CAR and using tools from your skills bank) for one target behavior at a time. There should be no pressure to tackle every concern in one sitting.

Jackson is a 14-year-old boy who struggles with ADHD and has been having a hard time with school. He gets up late in the mornings and usually needs a lot of prompting to get ready on time. In school he feels restless, and cannot focus in most of his classes. He has an easier time in history, where the teacher uses a lot of visuals to teach and checks in with each student once every two weeks. After school, Jackson usually comes home bored and restless. He has tons of energy from sitting in school all day long and can't seem to keep his body still. Homework is hard to focus on, and he often gets distracted doing other things. His parents get home from work around 6:00 p.m. and they have dinner together as a family. After dinner, Jackson usually has a lot of work left to do and he and parents get into fights about his procrastination. Jackson hates getting yelled at and spends most of his time in his room. Jackson is smart and cares about his academics, but cannot seem to get out of this rut.

Below is copy of the CAR table from Chapter 4, with details filled in about Jackson's life. See how Jackson's parents might personalize the chart based on the information above.

CONTEXT What is impacting your teen?	**ACTION** The specific behaviors your teen is doing.		**RESULT** Outcome of teen's actions
Environmental • Learning difficulties/mental health difficulties → ADHD • Others → We (parents) can't be home to help him stay on task	**Current Actions** Wake up late/slow moving Daydreaming in class	**Preferred Replacement Actions** Out of bed/ready on time Note-taking in class	**Reinforcement/Punishment of Current Actions** Reinforced with extra sleep. A little punished with parental annoyance. Avoids difficult effort required to focus, daydreams are more fun to think about than work. Punished much later when can't recall info on homework/tests

In-the-Moment • Structured vs. unstructured tasks → after school is unstructured • Type of task → worse with nonvisual material • Home vs. school vs. public settings → teacher matters, accountability matters • Parent-caretaker factors → tired after work	Procrastinating homework when home	Starting homework earlier, staying on task	Reinforced with enjoyment of nonhomework activities, punished much later when work isn't done
	Arguing with parents	Respectful language	Reinforced with stimulation, no concrete punishment but some emotional dip when yelled at
	Spending time solo in room	Spending more time in common areas	Reinforced with freedom to do what he wants, avoid being criticized, no punishment

Problem behavior 1: Waking up late/moving slowly in the morning

Skills I will use to change the context: *Help teen set alarm; create a clear morning routine with reward if completed on time; use a morning playlist to help energize teen and help him start to see how much time has passed.*

Skills I will use to build/show empathy: *Remember CAR model: at this age it is normal for teen bodies to stay up later and wake up later, validate that it is hard to get up so early.*

Skills I will use to reinforce the more appropriate behavior of getting up/ready on time: *Label praise getting up and showing any independence on morning tasks; reinforce finishing routine on time with a reward (TV before leaving the house, extra time to get a muffin on the way to school, etc.); decrease nagging in the morning when tasks are completed on time.*

Skills I will use to minimize the less skillful behavior: *Set very loud alarm to go off if he is not up on time; will no longer help teen pack bag if running late; he'll either be late to school or will forget items at home that I will not bring up.*

Problem behavior 2: Daydreaming in class

Skills I will use to change the context: *Get accommodations for teen to sit up at the front of the class; get visual aids in class; have regular check-ins with teachers so he feels more engaged.*

Skills I will use to build/show empathy: *Remember CAR model: attentional difficulties make it hard to attend and stay focused. Acknowledge that school days are long and some teaching styles may not be a great fit for him.*

Skills I will use to reinforce the more appropriate behavior of note-taking in class: Increase interest/attention given to teen when he can give details about his classes; set up a behavior plan for teen to earn rewards for taking notes in class; see if any teachers are willing to ask "attention questions" in class to help check that students are paying attention (example: who answered the last question? What was the last word I said?).

Skills I will use to minimize the less skillful behavior: Any days teen does not have notes/homework written down for a class, he has to message a friend/teacher for info (I won't do this for him).

Problem behavior 3: Procrastinating on homework
Skills I will use to change the context: Have teen stay after school to start homework in a less distracting environment; set up a tutor once or twice a week so a person is there to help him stay on task; on days teen is home solo we'll set up a daily routine for more structure, help him set alarms for when to start; ask for an update when he starts so he has more accountability; set screen time limits/limit access to electronics when I am not home.

Skills I will use to build/show empathy: Remember CAR model: attentional difficulties make it hard to complete difficult/less preferred tasks, especially during unstructured times. Symptoms also make time management more difficult. Validate to teen that school days are long and it's understandable to want to relax, validate that working on homework without oversight is hard given his symptoms.

Skills I will use to reinforce the more appropriate behavior of starting homework earlier and staying on task: Labeled praise any independence and task accomplishment; increase fun evening activities on days when homework is complete earlier.

Skills I will use to punish the less skillful behavior: Turn off WiFi after certain hour on nights when homework has not been started on time or has not been completed by a certain hour.

Problem behavior 4: Arguing with parents
Skills I will use to change the context: Create a conflict-free zone or one-on-one time as soon as I get home from work so first interaction is positive; use my parent coping strategies on the way home from work so I am more even and calm when I walk in the door; keep my tone/language respectful to reward his appropriate behavior; keep my statements short and sweet so conversations do not feel like lectures.

Skills I will use to build/show empathy: Remember CAR model: parent–teen conflict is normal at this age, and low frustration tolerance is common in kids with ADHD. Acknowledge my stress and worry for him is making me more reactive. Validate that feeling criticized every day probably makes things more difficult for him.

Skills I will use to reinforce the more appropriate behavior of respectful language: Labeled praise for any appropriate communication habits, especially respectful language, but also inside volume; letting me finish my sentences; staying in the same room as we talk.

Skills I will use to punish the less skillful behavior: Actively ignore disrespectful language so it does not get extra attention.

Problem behavior 5: Spending time alone in room

Skills I will use to change the context: Create conflict-free zones and one-on-one time so shared spaces are more enjoyable; set up a signal or phrase to alert teen to when a more serious conversation has to happen so he is not always worried he is going to get trapped into a fight if he comes out of his room.

Skills I will use to build/show empathy: Remember CAR model: at this age it is normal for teens to want more independence from parents. Validate that it probably does not feel good to constantly fight and it makes sense to want space.

Skills I will use to reinforce the more appropriate behavior: Give appropriate attention when teen is around us (not overbearing, but pleasant and engaged); help make common spaces more comfortable/fun when teen is around (music he likes, snacks he likes, TV shows he also enjoys, etc.).

Skills I will use to punish the less skillful behavior: Less accommodating when he is holed up in his room; won't bring him all his snacks/meals; won't clean up after him when he's been stuck in there all night.

As you can see from the examples, there are many different ways to combine skills in order to address different problem behaviors. There is no perfect pathway to follow, but it is generally helpful to consider how each of the tools available to you might play a role in promoting progress. You do not always have to combine skills, and it is reasonable to try out skills one at a time as you are getting comfortable with them. Still, in general, parents will often need multiple strategies to help support their teen as effectively as possible.

TEST YOUR KNOWLEDGE OF COMBINING SKILLS

In Exercise 11.1, you will complete the following True/False quiz to help you test your understanding of how to combine skills effectively. After writing if the statement is true/false, write a few notes explaining your answer. See the answer key to check how closely your responses match.

EXERCISE 11.1 TEST YOUR KNOWLEDGE OF COMBINING SKILLS

T/F	Item	
	1. When deciding how to manage a new behavior, it is always a good idea to start by making use of CAR.	
	2. It is always better to try one skill at a time to see if it works before moving onto the next option.	
	3. In general, it is faster and better to use punishment as the first line approach to shaping behavior.	
	4. When using punishment, it is a good idea to also validate your teen's experience.	
	5. Positive attention can be a skill used to change both the context and results surrounding your teen's actions.	
	6. You should not combine a logical consequence with a one-to-one behavior plan.	
	7. It is okay to make use of routines and point systems at the same time to target different types of behaviors.	
	8. Making regular use of positive attention, praise, validation, and routines will make punishment strategies more effective.	
	9. Skills will only work if you use them together, but not if you use them individually.	

T/F	Item	
	10. Parent coping is an important foundation for all other skills.	
	11. If you are good enough at labeled praise, you should not have to use behavior plans.	
	12. De-escalation combines labeled praise, active ignoring, validation, clear expectations, and consequences all in one skill.	
	13. The most important part of the CAR acronym is the results portion.	
	14. Active ignoring will be especially helpful when decreasing accommodations.	
	15. Active ignoring and labeled praise cannot happen at the same time.	
	16. Labeled praise and validation offer the same benefits, so you only need to do one or the other.	
	17. Active ignoring can be used to change the context and consequence surrounding behavior.	
	18. De-escalation can be most effective if you have already decided what logical consequences you are going to use in moments of distress.	
	19. Different actions that you identify in the CAR acronym may need different combinations of skills to address.	
	20. Using skills together gives you the most likely chance of creating progress.	

Exercise 11.1 ANSWER KEY Test Your Knowledge of Combining Skills

T/F	Item	
T	1. When deciding how to manage a new behavior, it is always a good idea to start by making use of CAR.	Making use of CAR will help you understand what is getting in the way of behavior change so you know where you can intervene.
F	2. It is always better to try one skill at a time to see if it works before moving onto the next option.	You can try to use one skill at a time, especially as you are learning the skills, but it is often appropriate to make use of multiple skills at once.
F	3. In general, it is faster and better to use punishment as the first line approach to shaping behavior.	Strategies like praise, routines, and rewards are the first line approach to help encourage new skills while keeping parent–teen relationships strong. Punishment can be used, but it is not recommended as the first option for most behaviors.
T	4. When using punishment, it is a good idea to also validate your teen's experience.	Using validation can help your teen feel as if their perspective is important and valued, even in instances where you are choosing to use punishment.
T	5. Positive attention can be a skill used both to change the context and results surrounding your teen's actions.	Positive attention can help to fill teen's attention cup and encourage skillful behavior, which can prevent problem behaviors from popping up. Positive attention can also be used after skillful behaviors to make them more likely to happen again.
F	6. You should not combine a logical consequence with a one-to-one behavior plan.	It is okay to use different consequence options to target different behaviors.
T	7. It is okay to make use of routines and point systems at the same time to target different types of behaviors.	Routines can be useful for making daily tasks easier to follow-through on, while behavior plans make target actions that do not fit into typical routines.
T	8. Making regular use of positive attention, praise, validation, and routines will make punishment strategies more effective.	These skills create more warmth and connection between parents and teens so that punishment is better tolerated by teens and less damaging to relationships, while still serving an important lesson.

Continued

Continued

T/F	Item	
F	9. Skills will only work if you use them together, but not if you use them individually.	Skills are often more effective when combined with other skills, but skills used individually can still be useful.
T	10. Parent coping is an important foundation for all other skills.	Parent coping makes it easier for parents to make thoughtful parenting choices instead of reactive decisions.
F	11. If you are good enough at labeled praise, you should not have to use behavior plans.	Labeled praise is useful, but many teens need additional motivation to change behavior because there are other outcomes (besides parent attention) that are important to them.
T	12. De-escalation combines labeled praise, active ignoring, validation, clear expectations, and consequences all in one skill.	This skill uses all of these tools within the three phases.
F	13. The most important part of the CAR acronym is the results portion.	Results give important information about why certain actions may happen over and over again, but context plays an equally important role in teen behavior.
T	14. Active ignoring will be especially helpful when decreasing accommodations.	Active ignoring will help parents stick to their plan to lower accommodation instead of responding to their teen's increased distress with attention.
F	15. Active ignoring and labeled praise cannot happen at the same time.	It is possible to actively ignore problem behaviors while praising positive things your teen is doing at the same time.
F	16. Labeled praise and validation offer the same benefits, so you only need to do one or the other.	Labeled praise recognizes teens for their strengths, while validation helps them feel their experiences are valued and understood. Both are important, but serve different roles.
T	17. Active ignoring can be used to change the context and consequence surrounding behavior.	A consistent household response to ignore minor problem behaviors can create a context in which teens know those behaviors serve no purpose and are not worth doing; active ignoring can also be used when problem behaviors show up in order to make them less likely to happen again.

T/F	Item	
T	18. De-escalation can be most effective if you have already decided what logical consequences you are going to use in moments of distress.	Having a consequence planned out can help with de-escalation because parents are not having to think of important outcomes in moments of high stress.
T	19. Different actions that you identify in the CAR acronym may need different combinations of skills to address.	Different skills are effective at targeting different types of problem behaviors.
T	20. Using skills together gives you the most likely chance of creating progress.	The skills build off of each other, and usually become more successful when used together.

TEST YOUR KNOWLEDGE OF COMBINING SKILLS

In Chapter 4 on understanding behavior, a sample scenario was used in Exercise 4.4 to help you practice identifying context, action, and results for 16-year-old Jordan, who lived at home with his mom and was starting to avoid school. At that point in the book, you had not learned enough skills to be able to think about how to address the problem behaviors. Having read through all of the chapters up to this point, you now have a better sense of what tools Jordan's mom could consider in helping her son. In exercise 11.2 that follows, you can test your knowledge of combining skills by rereading Jordan's story, thinking through CAR, and deciding what skills the parent could use. You will follow the format outlined earlier in the chapter: determining skills to help you change context appropriately, build and show empathy, reinforce a skillful behavior, and minimize unskillful choices. There are lots of different ways you could combine skills in this exercise, and the answer key will give you some examples.

Jordan is a 16-year-old junior living with his mom. His older sister recently went off to college. Jordan has struggled since transitioning back to school in person after the remote learning that took place during COVID. He feels awkward around classmates. Recently, he has been saying he does not want to go to school. When his mom asks what is wrong, Jordan says he has constant worry about difficult coursework and upcoming college applications. His anxiety seems to be spiraling, and his pediatrician thought he might meet criteria for an anxiety disorder. This week, Jordan has been refusing to get out of bed, staying under his covers when his mom tries to wake him, often sitting on his bed to rub his back. When Jordan stays hidden, his mom begins to remind him of how important each day of class is and how stressful it will be to miss it. Jordan gets more and more upset, eventually yelling at his mom to leave. Worried about arriving to work late, Jordan's mom eventually gives up and storms out of the room. As she is walking out the door for work, she tells Jordan that she expects him to get to school or he is going to be in trouble. Jordan decides to stay home. After a few more hours of sleep, he watches TV and scrolls on his phone for the rest of the day. When his mom gets home, she is exhausted and too tired to fight with Jordan. She tells him that they'll talk about it in the morning, but that he better be up for school the next day.

EXERCISE 11.2 TEST YOUR KNOWLEDGE OF COMBINING SKILLS

CONTEXT What is impacting your teen?	ACTION The specific behaviors your teen is doing.		RESULT Outcome of teen's actions
Environmental	**Current Behavior**	**Preferred Replacement Behavior**	**Reinforcement/Punishment** of Current Behaviors
In-the-Moment			

Problem behavior 1:
_____

Skills I will use to change the context:
_____
_____
_____
_____

Skills I will use to build/show empathy:
_____
_____
_____
_____

Skills I will use to reinforce the more appropriate behavior:
_____
_____
_____
_____

Skills I will use to punish the less skillful behavior:
_____
_____
_____
_____

Problem behavior 2:
_____

Skills I will use to change the context:
_____
_____
_____
_____

Skills I will use to build/show empathy:
_____
_____
_____
_____

Skills I will use to reinforce the more appropriate behavior:
_____
_____
_____
_____

Skills I will use to punish the less skillful behavior:
_____
_____
_____
_____

Problem behavior 3:

Skills I will use to change the context:

Skills I will use to build/show empathy:

Skills I will use to reinforce the more appropriate behavior:

Skills I will use to punish the less skillful behavior:

Problem behavior 4:

Skills I will use to change the context:

Skills I will use to build/show empathy:
_____
_____
_____

Skills I will use to reinforce the more appropriate behavior:
_____
_____
_____

Skills I will use to punish the less skillful behavior:
_____
_____
_____

Problem behavior 5:
_____

Skills I will use to change the context:
_____
_____
_____

Skills I will use to build/show empathy:
_____
_____
_____

Skills I will use to reinforce the more appropriate behavior:

Skills I will use to punish the less skillful behavior:

Exercise 11.2 ANSWER KEY Test Your Skill-Combining Skills

CONTEXT What is impacting your teen?	ACTION The specific behaviors your teen is doing.		RESULT Outcome of teen's actions
Environmental • Lives at home with Mom, who has limited bandwidth • Older sister at college • Hard time transitioning back to school in person • Hard time making friends • Overwhelmed with college applications • Increased anxiety **In-the-Moment** • Early morning • School day • Mom has to be at work	**Current Behavior** • Staying in bed • Stays under covers when Mom knocks/will not move when she comes in • Yells • Stays home from school	**Preferred Replacement Behavior** Gets out of bed on time Communicates with Mom Speaks appropriately Attends school	**Reinforcement/ Punishment of Current Behaviors** Attention from Mom, bed is nice, avoids facing the school day Attention/reminders of importance of school, bed feels good Frustration from Mom, ultimately left alone Extra sleep, TV, phone scrolling, no specific punishment from Mom

Problem behavior 1: Staying in bed

Skills I will use to change the context: Set nightly routine/turn off WiFi to make sure teen is not up late on devices; look into therapist to help manage teen's anxiety (which is making it harder to go to school) and/or a tutor to help with college apps so they are less overwhelming; encourage teen to join clubs so he may have an easier time connecting to other kids.

Skills I will use to build/show empathy: Remember CAR model: at this age it is normal for teens' body clocks to shift so they want to sleep later, this is a stressful year for high schoolers and pressure is intense, recent changes at home make it harder to cope. Validate that these contextual factors make it hard to enjoy school or feel your best. It makes sense that staying in bed seems more appealing.

Skills I will use to reinforce the more appropriate behavior: Morning routine that rewards getting out of bed on time; will need high stakes reward given how intense anxiety is; labeled praise any instances where teen gets up/out of bed; make morning extra comfortable (warm robe out of bed, preferred breakfast, upbeat music to help teen feel more awake.

Skills I will use to punish the less skillful behavior: Less attention when teen is in bed/under covers.

Problem behavior 2: Staying under covers/not responding

Skills I will use to change the context: Bring something of interest into the room; start with heavy validation and positive frame of mind (instead of focusing on how important school is, which may increase stress and avoidance).

Skills I will use to build/show empathy: Remember CAR model: anxiety can be difficult to cope with and lead to strong urges to avoid. Validate that having Mom check in may feel frustrating when all teen wants to do is sleep.

Skills I will use to reinforce the more appropriate behavior: Labeled praise responses; keep conversation light and brief so teen does not feel punished by lectures.

Skills I will use to punish the less skillful behavior: Less attention when teen is in bed/under covers; not going to use external punishment for teen not communicating.

Problem behavior 3: Yelling

Skills I will use to change the context: Use parent coping skills to stay calm and manage Mom's anxiety about teen missing school (so she doesn't lecture); will use agitation phase skills of the de-escalation model (validation, suggest/model a coping skill, such as coming up with a positive thought or putting on music); remind of potential consequences for not getting up on time or staying in bed (to make it easier for teen to make a smart choice).

Skills I will use to build/show empathy: Remember CAR model: teen wanting independence and control is normal at this stage. Also, people will often get more upset if others around them are also getting upset. Validate teen's irritability.

Skills I will use to reinforce the more appropriate behavior: Labeled praise appropriate responses.

Skills I will use to punish the less skillful behavior: Use peak phase skills of the de-escalation model: active ignoring (most helpful skill); use a when/then statement (when you lower your voice, we can talk about how to get through today); suggest a skill, remind of outcome.

Problem behavior 4: Stays home from school

Skills I will use to change the context: House rule that WiFi is shut off if teen is not in school; take TV remote to work; make sure teen knows that house will feel boring during hours teen would be in school.

Skills I will use to build/show empathy: Remember CAR model: staying home for a parent free day sounds much better than going to school. Validate how stuck teen must feel to want to avoid school this much, and how it is hard to go knowing he may feel worse in the short term.

Skills I will use to reinforce the more appropriate behavior: Reward teen for getting to school (access to phone/WiFi at school and TV after school); may use a point system where teen can earn bigger reward for making it to school over the course of the week.

Skills I will use to punish the less skillful behavior: Follow through on house rule, and limit access to devices if teen stays home from school; will make teen responsible for explaining absence to school and completing make up work.

Putting It All Together

Hopefully, after working through these examples, you can see how much knowledge and skills you have built over the course of this book. If you felt stuck during the exercise, or found that your answers did not seem to match up with the answer key, you may just need a bit more practice to help it all click. Take time to review the chapters and try skills out one at a time, before working to combine them again.

COMMON STUCK POINTS TO COMBINING SKILLS

While mastering each skill on its own is no small feat, combining them together takes it to a whole other level. Read through this list of obstacles that parents often encounter when trying to combine skills. Underneath each common stuck point, you will find tips and considerations that can help address each barrier. At the end of the chapter, you will have a chance to make note of any examples that would be helpful for you to keep in mind.

It's a lot to remember.
There are so many skills, and some skills have lots of different skills buried within them. It can be a lot to stay on top of! If you find yourself feeling overwhelmed or having difficulty remembering your skills, there are a few things to do.

→ First, slow it down and focus on getting comfortable with each skill individually. Of course, you want to be able to help your teen as quickly as possible, but it is okay to make slow, steady change over time.
→ Brains are great at many things, but memory is not what they are best at. Rely on other tools to help you keep skills at the top of your mind. Use visual cues around your home, set reminders on your phone, or keep a list of skills next to your bed or in your bag so you see them on a daily basis. These little prompts will help keep them present in your mind so they are easy to access when you need them.

It is easy to fall into old habits with skills use.
There were reasons why you developed the parenting style you did. Whether you had certain models growing up, had a lot on your plate, were influenced by your teen's behavior, or were prioritizing certain values—there is a lot of context to contend with when trying to make use of new tools that are outside of your typical pattern. Plus, behavior change is always hard.

→ Be patient with yourself. If you slip back into old habits you are not happy with, recognize that you are human and these things happen.
→ Make sure you are addressing any underlying factors that influence your parenting. If you keep mirroring unhelpful patterns you grew up with, make a clear case for yourself about why it is worthwhile to change course. If you are overwhelmed with all you have to juggle, make use of parent coping skills to give yourself enough emotional buffer to make progress. If that is not

enough, consider getting any personal or professional support you need to manage any symptoms that may bubble up when you interact with your teen.

I find myself favoring some skills and ignoring others.
Most people are likely to have certain skills they feel more comfortable with due to their own personality and style, background, or values. When there are heavy favorites (or skills you are still skeptical about) it is easy to end up with a lopsided approach to skills use. Some families might find this works well. Perhaps their teen thrives with positive attention and routine, and behavior plans are never really needed. If that is the case, then there is no need to complicate the situation by adding more tools. However, some families may notice that their current set of skills is not getting them where they would like to be.

→ When this happens, review the individual chapters and take a look at the stuck points for each skill. Do your best to address any barriers that are keeping certain tools out of favor.

→ If you have addressed all of the stuck points thoroughly and still find yourself favoring certain tools over others, set a goal for yourself! Give yourself a deadline to try out a new skill, or commit to using it a certain number of times a week. Sometimes being intentional with your plan makes it easier to follow through on.

I'm never quite sure what the right balance of skills are, especially when they seem counterintuitive (like validating a teen while giving them a punishment).

→ Unfortunately, there is no perfect fix for this. Parenting is not an exact science, and because each caregiver and teen are different, the right balance depends on the family dynamics. To help you figure it out, go back to your overarching values. Consider what you want and try to set a concrete marker of what progress would look like. Then experiment: as you try out new skills, go back to your goal to see if you are on your way to the benchmark you set. If so, great—you probably hit the right balance! If not, you may need to adjust.

→ Another important tool is the CAR acronym. Keep returning to it over and over again as new behaviors pop up. Oftentimes writing out your thoughts and seeing them visually can help you identify patterns and gain clarity. If you are able to pick out a handful of different tools to impact both the context and the result, there is a good chance you will be close to finding the right balance. If you notice your tools fall heavily to one side or the other, see what you can do to even out your strategy.

Putting It All Together

TRY IT OUT: COMBINING SKILLS

Now that you have completed each exercise, it is time to practice combining skills in your real life. To do this, work through CAR and answer the questions in Worksheet 11.1 on how you can use skills to address a current problem behavior you have noticed in your home. Then answer the questions at the end of the worksheet to increase the likelihood of following through on this task successfully, and write down your attempts at validation below.

WORKSHEET 11.1

1. What is a key problem behavior you would like to address this week?
   _____

2. Work through CAR (below) for that behavior.

3. Skills I will use to change the context:
   _____

4. Skills I will use to build/show empathy:
   _____

5. Skills I will use to reinforce the more appropriate behavior:
   _____

6. Skills I will use to punish the less skillful behavior:
   _____

7. How will you remember to practice these skills?
   _____

8. What barriers, including any of the common stuck points listed previously, do you think may interfere in using the skills, and how do you plan to troubleshoot them?
   _____
   _____

9. List three things that will help you complete this task and make sense of this skill. As a reminder, this could include reminders, skill review, social support, accountability measures, or other ideas you would find useful.

   1. _____

   _____

   2. _____

   _____

   3. _____

   _____

CONTEXT What is impacting your teen?	ACTION The specific behaviors your teen is doing.		RESULT Outcome of teen's actions
Environmental	**Current Behavior**	**Preferred Replacement Behavior**	**Reinforcement/Punishment** of Current Behaviors
In-the-Moment			

12

Maintaining Skills and Seeking Professional Support

WHAT IS MAINTAINING SKILLS AND SEEKING PROFESSIONAL SUPPORT?

It likely goes without saying, but for the strategies in this book to be useful for you and your teen, you have to use them! Some parents may find themselves needing support from somebody trained in mental health care. In this final chapter, you will find useful suggestions to make the most of this book after you have completed it. There will also be information on when you might want to seek professional support, and what questions to ask during your search.

WHY DOES IT MATTER?

You have put a ton of time and energy into reading, learning, and practicing these skills. They have hopefully helped you feel more confident and effective in supporting your child. To build on this, it is key to keep your tools active. If you are finding that the skills in this book are not enough, know that there is lots of evidence that professional care can make a huge difference in your teen's mental health and well-being, so it is worth looking into.

Maintaining Skills and Seeking Professional Support

EXERCISE 12.1 TEST YOUR KNOWLEDGE OF PARENTING SKILLS

The first step to using your skills over and over again is remembering them! In this exercise, fill out the following table with as much information as you can recall about each skill. This is a chance to really review each strategy you have learned using your own words. Feel free to review the chapters or exercises to respond to questions. You can then check your responses with the answer key to make sure you have a full understanding. If you feel lost or confused on some of the skills, simply go back and review the information from that chapter.

	As appropriate for each skill: • Write out the acronym • Describe the skill • Provide an example	What is this skill used for?	Give an example of a situation you might use it in.
Parent Coping Building Reserves In-the-Moment Coping Plan			
CAR			
Selective Attention Labeled Praise One-on-One Time or Conflict-Free Zone Active Ignoring			

Validation			
Routines			
Appropriate Accommodation (vs. over- or underaccommodation)			
Reward Plan Logical Consequences One-to-One Behavior Plan Point System			
De-Escalation Model Agitation Phase Peak Phase Recovery Phase			

Exercise 12.1 ANSWER KEY Test Your Knowledge of Parenting Skills

	As appropriate for each skill: • Write out the acronym • Describe the skill • Provide an example	What is this skill used for?	Give an example of a situation you might use it in.
Parent Coping Building Reserves	Creating a plan to improve one area of my life that would have a positive impact on my overall well-being. Example: Taking more time to connect with friends on a weekly basis.	Building in meaningful self-care so my overall baseline of stress is lower, making it easier to handle hard periods.	When I am feeling more exhausted, burnt out, or disconnected from myself or others. When I notice that my overall stress is higher or I am more reactive than I want to be.
In-the-Moment Coping Plan	Put together a list of tools to help me challenge stress in real time. Includes a grounding mantra, self-soothe skills, and using tools that have helped me cope in the past. Example: "He's only 16," putting on music, going for a walk.	To help me stay calm and make strategic choices (vs. reacting based on emotion).	Any time my teen and I start to get into a conflict.

CAR	Context-Action-Results: Context focuses on things happening in my teen's life that influence them. Actions include what my teen is currently doing and what I would like them to do instead. Results refer to the outcomes of my teen's actions. Results that are reinforcing will make actions likely to repeat, results that are punishing will usually decrease behaviors.	Finding the patterns that impact my teen's behavior. Once I know what context and results are influencing their actions, I can create an action plan to intervene.	Any time I notice a new problem behavior or am having a hard time supporting my teen through a current period of difficulty. Example: My teen is having a hard time getting out of bed on time, or recently started skipping their after-school club.
Selective Attention	Strategic use of attention: give attention to increase appropriate behaviors/remove attention from problem behaviors.	Shapes more skillful choices.	
Labeled Praise	Thanking or acknowledging teens for specific behaviors.	Build connections, reward teens for skillfulness, creates a cue for their brain to remember actions they can use in the future.	Teen does something helpful, like doing their chores unprompted.
One-on-One Time	A short period of focused attention on my teen doing things they enjoy.	Fills a teen's attention cup. Gives them chance to direct the interaction. Helps us enjoy each other's company/build connection.	Short daily walk around the block to chat about the day.
Conflict-Free Zone	A period of time during the day that is set up to minimize conflict.	Help us be in each other's company without fighting, increases connection.	20 minutes after dinner where I do not bring up stressful topics and focus on calm, pleasant interactions.

Continued

Continued

Active Ignoring	Removing attention from problem behaviors that are reinforced by a response from me.	Decreases problem behaviors over time because they are no longer being reinforced with my feedback.	Do not respond when my teen rolls their eyes or complains about having to come home by curfew.
Validation	Showing somebody that their experiences and feelings make sense based on their situation. Example: It makes sense that you are anxious about starting school this fall because it felt really overwhelming for you last year.	Builds connection and trust, decreases judgment so teen is more willing to share, minimizes sense of shame around emotions or choices.	Could tell my teen that their sadness over losing a friend is understandable, or that it makes sense they might be angry when they are grounded.
Routines	Put together a structured list of tasks or daily activities that help teens know what the expectations are while building in meaningful activities.	Decreases brainwork needed to remember tasks, clarifies expectations, makes a simple process for rewarding the completion of all items on the list.	Create a list of afternoon tasks my teen needs to complete before going out with friends for the evening.
Appropriate Accommodation (vs. over- or underaccommodation)	Finding ways to support my teen in the short term while they are building skills vs. shielding my teen from negative outcomes in a way that may make it difficult for them to build skills on their own vs. not providing support for my teen's difficulties/expect them to push through on their own.	Gives teen enough temporary support that they can focus energy on making progress (rather than being overcome with a sense of overwhelm or failure).	I might help my teen draft a letter to their teacher asking for an extension, but will not write it or send it on my own.

Consequences	The outcomes parents can use to shape behavior.	Consequences are used to shape behavior. Rewards make behavior more likely to occur. Punishment makes behavior less likely.	
Logical Consequences	Outcomes that make sense based on a teen's behavior.		When I prefer to have a simple, flexible consequence system that does not involve tracking behavior over time. Example: If teen trashes the house he can't leave until it is clean.
One-to-One Behavior Plan	Pairing one behavior with one desired outcome, even if there is no logical link.		When I have one or two behaviors I want to work on and my teen does not seem very motivated by logical consequences. Example: Each time my teen gets to school on time, they get to keep their phone for the day.
Point System	Picking a few different behaviors that teen can earn points for and then turn in for larger rewards daily, weekly, or monthly.		When I have several behaviors I want to work on, want to offer multiple kinds of rewards, or give different point values for different actions. Example: Give points for use of coping skills, homework, and keeping curfew. Teen can earn points toward later bedtime, spending money, and dinner out.

Continued

Continued

De-Escalation Model	A set of skills to help parents effectively respond to teens when they are upset.	Help teen regulate as quickly as possible/learn to soothe themselves, lowers chance of saying something that hurts the relationship.	Any time my teen has some sort of outburst or meltdown.
Build-Up Phase	When teens are starting to get upset I can validate, suggest/model a coping skill, or remind of a possible outcome.	Gives attention while there is some appropriate behavior happening. Increases the chances of helping teen and preventing peak.	When I can see my teen is starting to get upset.
Peak Phase	In peak, aim to disengage. If I have to say something: use a when/then statement, suggest/model skills, remind of possible results.	Minimizes any possible reward my teen's problem behavior might be getting from attention. Shortens peak as much as possible because I am not giving it more fuel.	When my teen is showing their most problematic behaviors (as long as they are still safe).
Cool-Down Phase	In cool-down: return attention without negativity, praise skillfulness, or use compliment sandwich to address problem.	Rewards teen for regulating, makes it more likely for your teen to listen to me without returning to peak.	When my teen is starting to calm down and return to their normal behavior.

COMMON STUCK POINTS TO USING YOUR SKILLS

Hopefully you found that you have a good recollection of all your tools. If not, it is always okay to go back to earlier chapters and brush up. Know that even if you have a great understanding of the tools in this book, there are certain stuck points that can make skills hard to keep up with. Since you are just now finishing this book, you may not know which stuck points (if any) are going to come up for you in the future. Read through the following barriers that some parents experience. Try to keep these in mind during the coming weeks and months so you can work on them sooner rather than later if they start to appear.

I backslide on how consistently I use the skills. This is very common. Parenting skills take a ton of work, and it's easy to let them slip.

→ The first option is to try to prevent the backslide with a concrete plan to help you remain intentional about skills use. See Worksheet 12.1 for full details. The main idea is to use reminders and schedules to regularly check-in with yourself on how skills are going, and set goals for yourself to keep tools fresh.

→ The second option is to remember why skills are *so* important. When skills start to work and behavior improves, it is easy to let the tools take a back seat. This is okay in some cases. Sometimes your strategies will have helped to create a new pattern or true shift in behavior that is lasting even when the strategies are taken offline. This is like using training wheels when you learn to ride a bike. You have supports while learning, and then no longer need the supports once the muscle memory has built up.

However, it is often the case that skills are the crucial scaffolding that allow for improved behavior to continue. For example, if you were training for a bicycle race and worked really hard building up your stamina for a few months, you couldn't just suddenly stop training in the weeks leading up to the race and expect to win. You would have to keep up with your practice to allow your body the best chance of success. Know that for kids who struggle with things like anxiety, depression, or ADHD, their brains often need regular support to stay on the right track. In addition, it can take these teens a long period of time to build up skills on their own. Using parenting skills for a few weeks while reading this book just won't be enough time for your teen to learn to fully manage their symptoms without support from their environment.

Remember why you picked up this book. What was so important that you needed to have tools in place? Then when things start to improve and you're tempted to shift gears away from active skills use, consider if your original goal is still important for you and your family, or if you're willing to let it slip.

→ Another option is to just be okay with the backslide. Skills are hard. Parents are busy. Sometimes you need to reprioritize. If your skills go down because you have to shift your efforts to other things, you just want to be planful about it. Write out a list of warning signs that tell you problem behaviors are really starting to ramp up. Once these signs appear, you want to get right back into consistent skills use. Do not wait until you reach a crisis moment because it will be much, much harder to right the ship. Also, try your best to acknowledge why the backslide is occurring (i.e., your skills use dropped). Some parents stop using their skills and then feel panicked when their teen starts to struggle again. They feel angry with their teen or anxious that something is terribly wrong, when in fact it usually makes perfect sense that things are becoming a little harder when the system stopped being as supportive.

New problem behaviors pop up and I do not know how to use my skills to work on them.

→ In most instances, whenever you feel stuck, go back to CAR. Map out the context and results of your teen's actions so you can look for patterns. As you get more comfortable with the skills, it is easy to go on autopilot. On the one hand this is good: the more automatic the tools feel, the more accessible they are. On the flip side, it's easy to take the skills for granted and you may not be as intentional as you need to be. If this may be happening to you, redo some of the CAR exercises and put together a solid strategy.

→ If you have tried working through CAR but just cannot figure out what strategies to use, it may be time for professional support (see more details later in this chapter).

It's really hard to use the skills when they don't seem to make a difference. In an ideal world, parents would use their strategies and behavior change would be immediate. That would be *so* reinforcing, and really make it worth your while to use skills. Unfortunately, that is not usually the case, and it can feel like all your efforts are wasted if you don't see progress.

→ In many cases, parents need to be extra patient. Changing long-standing patterns, especially when mental health is involved, is very, very difficult. It is hard for *adults* to shift their mindset and actions, and these efforts are certainly not always a top priority for teenagers. Sometimes teens just need to see enough evidence that their caregivers are truly sticking to the new tools before they start moving in the same direction. This is particularly true for parents who have started and stopped the use of parenting skills over and over. Kids do not trust that changes are going to stick, so they are hesitant to make any moves on their end. Keep up with the strategies, and over time you should see some benefit.

→ You may need professional support. Parents can go a long way on their own, but there is nothing like having a trained clinician to give guidance on your parenting. Not only may a professional see things from a different perspective, but they can give you little tweaks to help amplify your efforts. Many parents are 85% of the way there on their skills use, it just turns out that the extra 15% is *really* important to creating lasting change.

> → Your teen may need professional support. Mental health symptoms can be incredibly impairing. The good news is that there are some very effective treatments to help teens gain control over their symptoms, so they may be a helpful addition to your teen's care. Unfortunately, specialized mental healthcare is not an accessible option for all families. If that is the case for you, keep in mind that getting stuck is nobody's fault. Your teen is not trying to make their life harder, and you are doing everything you can to help. Do your best to be consistent with your strategies and give your family grace when there are barriers not under your control.

PLANNING FOR ONGOING SKILLS USE

There are a few tips to help you stick with your tools over time.

1. *Keep yourself accountable.* You found the time to make it through this book (even if it took a while), so do your best to keep that momentum going. It does not have to be a lot of time, but find a 5-minute block once every week to do a quick read through of the skills word bank you created in Chapter 11 on combining skills. The aim is to help keep your brain thinking about the strategies so they do not fade into the background.
2. *Be intentional.* Set a monthly 30-minute appointment with your partner (or with yourself) to focus on parenting topics. Have this book (or your skill bank) handy. During that meeting, ask yourself the following questions:
   a. Are we making progress on the problem behaviors we have worked on?
   b. Are there any new problem behaviors that we need to focus our attention on?
   c. What skills do we need to review?
   d. What skills are we going to prioritize this month?
   e. What do we need to do to follow through on our plan?

As needed, take a look back at old chapters to review. Even when you are pretty sure you remember most of it, there is almost always something that will have slipped your mind or is worth having a second look at. Redo exercises as needed, and do not hesitate to fully plot out the CAR acronym for any of the new behaviors that have come up.

If you are going through a particularly difficult period with your teen, move those 30-minute meetings to be more regular. They can be hard to make time for in the moment, but will save you time and frustration on the back end when you do not have to worry about improvising a plan in the middle of a stressful moment.

3. *Use your resources.* At the end of every chapter, you have been asked to write out what you can use to help you remember and use your skills. Continue to think about it. Use calendar alerts, reminders, planners, wall signs, signals from your family members, check-ins with your providers, and so on. Use everything you can to make the most out of these tools. Of course, this all takes time and effort to set up, but you will have greater confidence in making effective parenting choices and supporting your teen. Most parents will agree that the payout is worth the effort. Worksheet 12.1 will help you jumpstart this process.

WORKSHEET 12.1

Fill out the following questions to reflect on your skills use and try to set yourself up for success. Once you are done, take a picture of your answers or write out your own list to keep handy so you can stay on track.

1. Which skills were most helpful for me or my teen?

2. What skills do I need more practice with?

3. When are times and situations that I know I should be using skills?

4. How will I remember to use these skills in real time?

5. When I feel resistant or unmotivated to use the skills, what value will I keep in mind to help increase my willingness to practice?

_____

_____

_____

6. When is a good weekly time for a 5-minute skills check in?

_____

_____

_____

7. When is a good monthly time for a 30-minute skills check-in?

_____

_____

_____

8. How will you remember to practice your skills on a daily basis?

_____

_____

_____

9. What barriers did you identify as potentially interfering, and how do you plan to troubleshoot them?

_____

_____

_____

10. List three things that will help you keep up with your skills. As a reminder, this could include reminders, skill review, social support, accountability measures, or other ideas you would find useful.

    1. _____

    2. _____

    3. _____

SEEKING PROFESSIONAL SUPPORT

When you have a teenager who is going through a rough period, it can be very hard to know what changes are due to typical teen growing pains versus a more serious mental health concern. For some, it is important to move beyond your own efforts and pull in a health care provider. If you have a feeling that something more serious is going on, your teen asks for more support, or you have any concerns about their safety, try to seek professional help. This may include scheduling an appointment with a mental health professional, such as a psychologist, psychiatrist, social worker, psychiatric nurse practitioner, or licensed mental health counselor. All of these professions have an overall focus on mental health, but will have different levels of training and specific areas of expertise. Depending on where you live, your financial resources, access to insurance, and your family's schedule, mental health specialists may be difficult to find and access. If this is the case for you, you can schedule an appointment with a pediatrician to discuss your worries or try to meet with a school guidance counselor or school psychologist. If that is not an option, you could try calling a local help line. Even if your teen is not in crisis, these hotlines often have a list of referrals in the area they could provide you with.

For many parents, it is unclear whether or not they should try to get outside support for their teen. Unfortunately, there is no hard and fast answer. In fact, many of the red flags that clinicians look for (e.g., changes in sleep or eating, irritability, or shifts in normal routines or behaviors) can all be part of a typical developmental process for many adolescents. That said, there are a few things most clinicians will look for when deciding whether a teen's struggles would benefit from professional support: frequency, intensity, duration, and impairment of symptoms. These are jargon-y terms, but are ones you may hear if you talk with your child's pediatrician or a mental health provider. Here is what each one means.

1. *Frequency*: How often are the concerning behaviors happening? Did your teen skip soccer practice twice to hang out with their girlfriend, or are they skipping it almost every day? Is homework a battle every now and then, or a nightly fight? Are changes to their mood, emotions, or behaviors happening regularly, or only once in a while? You can ask yourself if the behavior happens almost every time your teen is in a certain situation (e.g., they have a panic attack almost every time they give a presentation), happening more often than not, or happening on a weekly or daily basis. If behaviors are happening quite often, it is a possible sign that something more significant is going on.
2. *Intensity*: Are the noteworthy emotions or behaviors happening at a high level of intensity? A typical teen may get annoyed at their parent, but it is less typical for a teen to fly into a rage that does not seem to let up. Perhaps their anxiety is all consuming and impossible to move past. Maybe they feel sadness, frustration, or disappointment deep within them in a way that seems to bowl them over. For teenagers trying to manage symptoms, behaviors like lying or sneaking out may become more pronounced or daring than those same behaviors in peers, and there may be an overall sense that their thoughts, feelings, or behaviors seem to be amplified as compared to other kids their age.
3. *Duration*: Are symptoms lasting over time? Teens come into constant contact with stressors. Between schoolwork, social life, hobbies, and household tasks, there are so many things that impact a teen's mood and actions day to day. If you

are starting to become worried about your teen, try to think about if the concerns come and go, or if they are lasting over the weeks and months. Typical teen mood swings or lapses in judgment should be somewhat temporary, but mental health concerns are less likely to disappear after just a week or two.
4. *Impairment*: How much are your teen's emotions or actions getting in the way of things that are important to them? This can mean lots of different things depending on the person and their specific context, but here are a few common examples:
   a. *Academic*: Missing or late assignments; difficulty getting to school or staying in class; trouble paying attention; ongoing procrastination; dropping grades
   b. *Social*: Conflict with peers; trouble meeting new people or making friends; difficulty initiating interactions; withdrawing from others; missing social cues
   c. *Hobbies*: Loss of interest in regular activities; avoidance of clubs or practice; difficulty keeping up with expectations when they used to be able to
   d. *At home*: Regular conflict; high-intensity interactions; consistent breaking of reasonable house rules; aggressive or unsafe behavior; pulling for lots of accommodations from parents or siblings

As you look over these areas, note that professionals are considering how *all* of the different pieces look together, rather than one or the other in isolation. It is very common for people to have some difficulty in some areas from time to time, and that does not mean there is a significant mental health concern in the picture. While your teen does not have to fall on the extreme end of this spectrum to get more help, most clinicians will start to take a closer look when a teenager seems to have a few markers across a handful of contexts. For example, there would likely be low concern for somebody who missed homework assignments frequently, but only for unimportant classes and only during the college application period. However, if somebody was missing homework assignments frequently for their key subjects over several weeks or months, there would be greater cause for worry.

Similarly, symptoms that bubble over into lots of different parts of a teen's life (i.e., school *and* friends *and* hobbies *and* home) would likely be evidence of a more serious concern. A good example would be a teen who is a little moody at home or with a teacher he doesn't like. This seems within the range of normal. On the flip side, there may be a teen who is irritable with parents and most teachers, having a hard time with coaches, and getting into fights with classmates to the point of friendships fading away.

FINDING THE RIGHT SUPPORT

Once you have decided that you would like to look into professional support, it can be hard to know where to start. As noted earlier, you could try speaking with a pediatrician or school guidance counselor. If you have insurance, you can look through your insurance website to search for mental health providers in your area. You can call a support or crisis line for local referrals or ask for recommendations through local community centers. Another possibility is to check any hospitals in your area. Some have psychiatric clinics where people can be seen for therapy or medication management on a weekly or monthly basis. Similarly, if you live in a town with a university, check out their psychology department website. Most programs that train psychologists offer some sort of community clinic where graduate students provide therapy under the supervision of licensed professionals. While some parents may be unsure about working with a student, this is often a great option. Graduate students are eager to be supportive and often have a bit more time and flexibility to work with families. Many teens also work well with graduate students, who tend to be in their mid-twenties or early thirties and can be approachable and relatable.

If you have a few different options of who your family can work with, there are a few other pieces of information to consider.

1. *Decide what you are looking for.* Would you like to find your teen somebody to provide general support? Are you hoping they can work through past difficulties, or learn specific tools? Would you like a provider who can give you information about medication options? Perhaps you have been told that parent focused services or family therapy may be a good option for you. Knowing what you are looking for will make it easier to sort through providers you find online or are referred to by your teen's doctor or school. If you do not know what would be most helpful, ask a clinician what their plan would be to help your child. Try to get information from them on whether there is research that shows their strategies are helpful and check in with your teen to see if they are comfortable with the recommendations.
2. *Ask about a clinician's background and training.* Do not hesitate to get information about a provider's training and experience. Sometimes provider websites use terms you are not familiar with or are vague about how much expertise they have in a particular area. It is okay to check how frequently they work with teens similar to your child or how many years of experience they have. New clinicians can be excellent, but you may feel more comfortable knowing they have had specialty training or certifications in certain areas. For example, you can see if they have any background in evidence-based treatments such as Cognitive-Behavior Therapy, Parent Management Training, Exposure and Response Prevention, Dialectical Behavior Therapy, Acceptance and Commitment Therapy, or other research-backed methods.
3. *Make sure it works for your family.* When you are eager to get help for your teen, it can be tempting to start treatment ASAP even when it isn't the right fit. Make sure that appointment slots, session fees, and typical length of treatment are feasible for your family. A provider might sound like the perfect fit, but it can create more problems than it is worth if they are too far away, too expensive, or too busy to provide care in a way that is comfortable for your family. While some flexibility on your part can be helpful to find the right person to work with your teenager, it is also important to be honest about what is reasonable for your family.
4. *Look for trust and connection.* Training and expertise matter, but so does having somebody your teen likes to talk to! Every provider is different, and not every teen will click with each therapist they meet. As they get started with somebody new, make sure your teenager feels like they can be honest in sessions. As a parent, you also want to make sure you can speak with the clinician in a way that feels respectful and collaborative. If you cannot be honest with your teen's provider or are not being taken seriously, it is okay to look for somebody new.
5. *Watch for improvement.* Being in treatment takes a lot of time, energy, and resources. You want to make sure these efforts are leading to improvement for your teen. Talk to your child's provider about how they monitor progress. Some

may use questionnaires or rating scales, others may ask for input on behavior or mood changes at home, and some may use objective measures like grades or attendance as a benchmark of improvement. Whatever the method, get on the same page so everybody can be on the lookout for signs of positive change. If you do not see progress, you may need to tweak the treatment plan. If there is still no change, the provider may not be the right fit.

Know that while it can take time to find the right fit for your teen, there are good options out there. All of the time and energy you put in can make a huge difference in your teen's life.

WRAP-UP

You have now reached the end of this workbook. It is my sincerest hope that the tools you have worked through have been helpful for you and your family. Parenting is such a mix of difficult, rewarding, confusing, beautiful, and overwhelming moments. While there is no exact recipe you can whip up to turn yourself into the perfect parent, there is lots of data out there to suggest that the strategies discussed in this book can be effective in supporting teens and their mental health. And while there is no expectation for you to use these tools perfectly in every interaction you have, I do hope you will take the time to review the exercises along the way so you can increase your confidence and skillset. Above anything else, trust that the love and care you have for your teenager is your biggest strength as a parent. Even though there are days where you yell or get annoyed and times where you forget an important date or forgot your skills, remember that you love your child in a way that nobody else ever could. Even if your teen will never admit it, they are lucky to have a parent who cares enough to read books like this, and I hope you are able to see all the amazing ways you are showing up for your teen.

REFERENCES AND RESOURCES

It is important to state that I did not invent the tools demonstrated in this book. These are skills I have learned over my years of training and practice through research articles, coursework, clinical training, manualized protocols, and supervision. Along the way I have developed my own way to present strategies so they are accessible to parents and families and have worked hard to put together practice exercises and examples to increase knowledge and skill. Within this book, I have tried to pull the most useful grouping of skills for teens experiencing a range of mental health difficulties, without hyperfocusing on one particular diagnosis.

To make sure that appropriate credit is given, I want to note that most of the strategies in this book stem from treatments called Parent Management Training or Behavior Management Training. Some principles are pulled from other types of treatment, including Parent–Child Interaction Therapy, Cognitive Behavioral Therapy, Behavioral Activation, and Dialectical Behavior Therapy. For example, I did not come up with the idea to create a roadmap for understanding behavior or using attention to encourage skillful choices. I did not develop the pathway for approaching a distressed teen or invent behavior plans. Many, many individuals have worked on the development of these tools over time. Many broader theoretical approaches, including but not limited to behaviorism, attachment theory, and family therapy, have been used to inform these practices. Beyond that, countless research studies have been conducted over the decades to help the field of psychology understand the connection between parents and their teens and inform the creation of effective treatments. While it would be impossible to list every person who has played a role in the development of these tools, I will name a few whose efforts were foundational in parent-focused interventions: Alan Kazdin, William Pelham, Russell Barkley, Matthew Sanders, Sheila Eyberg, Carolyn Webster-Stratton, and Eli Lebowitz. Beyond the individuals who have focused on parent-specific strategies, others have done work on the management of anxiety, mood, and emotion regulation difficulties. Some of those individuals include David Barlow, Michelle Craske, Phillip Kendall, John Weisz, Neil Jacobson, Christopher Martell, Sona Dimidjian, and Marsha Linehan. It should be noted that this book would not exist if not for the efforts of hundreds of individuals and I in no way want to take credit for their work. I simply hope that my presentation of these ideas will serve as an approachable and helpful support for parents and caregivers looking to support their teenagers.

If you are looking for additional resources, here are a few parent-focused books you may find useful:

1. *The Kazdin Method for Parenting the Defiant Child: With No Pills, No Therapy, No Contest of Wills* by Alan E. Kazdin (Boston: Houghton Mifflin Harcourt, 2008)
2. *Taking Charge of ADHD: The Complete, Authoritative Guide for Parents (4th edition)* by Russell A. Barkley (New York: Guilford Press, 2020)
3. *Your Defiant Teen: 10 Steps to Resolve Conflict and Rebuild Your Relationship* by Russell A. Barkley (New York: Guilford Press, 2013)
4. *You and Your Anxious Child: Free Your Child from Fears and Worries and Create a Joyful Family Life* by Anne Marie Albano and Leslie Pepper (New York: Avery Publishing, 2013)

ACKNOWLEDGMENTS

I am so appreciative of the many people who have been instrumental in the creation of this workbook. Thank you to OUP and Sarah Harrington for seeing the value of this book and bringing it into the world. Thank you to the countless families I have met with in my clinical practice. I cannot overstate how meaningful it is to work with you.

This book, and my career, would not exist without the many wonderful teachers, supervisors, and mentors who taught me how to be a good clinician, researcher, and colleague. In particular: Brian Chu, who changed the trajectory of my life and whose voice is a constant guiding light in my head; Sam Fasulo, who is unrivaled in his ability to champion teens' voices and lead with acceptance; and Shannon Bennett, who is the most amazing model of a working mom, clinician, and researcher for me to look up to and whose support has given me so much confidence. I am also so appreciative of my psychology friends and coworkers. One of the best parts of my job is working with kind, smart, endlessly supportive individuals who are generous with their friendship, time, and encouragement.

Thank you to so many friends who have loudly cheered me on at each stage in my life. An additional shout-out to all my parent friends, especially the women in my Moms Group, whose late-night texts and shared social media posts have fostered so much connection and humor and validation.

I am especially grateful to my own parents, who were using many of the skills in this book well before I ever knew PMT existed. Your unending support and love have meant the world. Thank you to my siblings for (mostly) listening to my parenting suggestions and (always) being there for me.

The biggest thank you to Jason. You never miss a chance to show your pride and belief in what I do, and I am forever in love with our amazing partnership. And to my boys, who I love to the moon and back, and who give meaning to every word in this book.

INDEX

academic pressure, 2, 32
accommodation
    coping skills and, 154, 156
    defined, 148
    expectations and, 156
    importance of, 148–149
    as just right, 150, 153
    overaccommodation, 149, 153, 154–155
    overwhelm and, 149, 153, 156, 160, 162, 166
    practicing, 169–170
    reassurance and, 160, 162, 165, 167–168
    self-assessment and, 150–153
    stress and, 149, 151–158, 167
    stuck points, 154–158
    testing knowledge on, 158–168
    underaccommodation, 153, 274, 277
    when to use, 149–150
accountability, 6, 18, 26, 174, 251–252, 282
action
    in CAR acronym, 31, 38–42
    defined, 31
    identifying, 39–42
    validation and, 108–109
active ignoring
    defined, 57
    overview of, 82–83
    as selective attention, 57, 82–91
    skills practice, 90–91
    stuck points, 84–86, 91
    testing knowledge on, 87–89
activity-based rewards, 126
advance caregiver coping, 23–26
anxiety
    building reserves, 20–21
    CAR acronym and, 46–47
    compliment sandwich, 220
    conflict-free zones, 68
    consequences and, 171
    de-escalation and, 211–214
    increasing rates of, 1–2
    maintaining skills with professional support, 280
    meaningful routines and, 124, 130–131
    validation and, 105, 107, 122
appropriate behavior, 57, 68, 72–73, 193, 211, 217, 219, 246, 251–253, 265–266, 279
areas outside control, 16
arguments, 24, 33–34, 39, 56–58, 108, 154
attention. *See also* selective attention
    bad, 56
    negative, 56
    positive, 57, 68, 74, 82, 85, 90, 171, 192, 219, 250, 254, 256, 268
    as response, 44
Attention Deficit Hyperactivity Disorder (ADHD)
    accommodation and, 149, 155
    conflict-free zones, 68
    consequences and, 172
    Context-Action-Result and, 31, 34
    de-escalation and, 216
    maintaining skills with professional support, 280
    meaningful routines and, 124, 130–131, 135
    parental confusion over, 1
    parental work and, 8, 10
    points systems, 174–175
    putting it all together, 250
    unstructured tasks, 34
    validation and, 105
attention-maintained behaviors, 82–84, 87, 101
attention-seeking behaviors, 82–84, 87, 101
Autism Spectrum Disorder, 1–2
awareness, 2, 14–16, 35, 37–38, 44, 54, 75, 104, 126, 158, 208, 218

backsliding, 280–281
bad attention, 56
bad behavior, 38–39, 212, 220
behavior. *See also* skillful behavior
    appropriate, 57, 68, 72–73, 192, 211, 217, 219, 246, 251–253, 265–266, 279
    arguments, 24, 33–34, 39, 56–58, 108, 154
    attention-maintained, 82–84, 87, 101

INDEX

attention-seeking, 82–84, 87, 101
bad, 38–39, 212, 220
caregiver modeling of, 13–14
changes to, 9
coping skills and, 41
cursing, 4, 38, 82, 86, 178, 193, 206, 208, 213
de-escalation and, 207–211
duration of, 286–287
expectations and, 31, 34, 44, 47
extinction bursts, 83–85
frequency of, 5, 58, 68, 286–288
good *vs.* bad, 38–39
impairment in, 171, 286–287
inappropriate, 4, 44, 47, 56–57, 63, 69, 90–91, 94–95, 212, 249
intensity of, 5–7, 10, 46, 83, 85, 105, 122, 124, 191, 206, 213–216, 220, 248, 286–287
overwhelm and, 37, 47
procrastination, 37, 39, 41, 126, 138, 159, 161, 164, 166, 250–252, 287
rudeness, 38, 212
stress and, 31–33, 35–36, 41, 48–49, 52
stuck points, 34–36
threats/threatening behavior, 8, 11, 39, 56, 206, 208, 211–214, 217
unskillful, 4, 45, 50, 56, 66, 228, 234–235
Behavioral Activation research, 134, 292
behavior plans, 172–175, 179–181, 183, 190–191, 249, 252, 256, 268, 293. *See also* one-to-one behavior plans
BIPOC populations, 2
bipolar disorder, 2
boring activities/tasks, 34, 70, 130, 219, 266
build-up phase of de-escalation, 206, 208–211, 215–217

calming activities, 24–25
caregiver coping. *See also* coping skills
in advance, 23–30
areas outside control, 16
building reserves, 17, 20–22
conflict and, 17, 25
defined, 12
importance of, 12–13
in-the-moment, 23, 29
modeling behavior, 13–14
overwhelm in, 17–18, 29
skills for, 12–14, 25, 266–267
stuck points, 29
successful interactions, 13
taking stock, 14

well-being importance, 14–16
well-being investment, 17–23
CAR model. *See* Context-Action-Result (CAR) model
changing what you can, 36–38
climate disasters, 2
compliment sandwich, 219–221, 224–228, 237, 246, 279
conflict
caregiver coping and, 17, 25
consequences and, 179, 192–193
de-escalation and, 206, 213–215, 217–218, 237
intensity of, 10
maintaining skills, 275–276, 287
management of, 3–6, 9–11
meaningful routines and, 124
putting it all together, 249, 252–253
selective attention and, 58–60, 67–69, 86, 96, 101
shaping and, 9
conflict-free zones, 67–69, 90–91, 96, 252–253
consequences. *See also* punishment; rewards
behavior plans, 173–175
CAR model and, 199
common problems, 199–203
conflict and, 179, 192
coping skills and, 172, 180–182
defined, 171
expectations and, 173–174, 178, 180, 190–193, 201
importance of, 171
logical consequences, 172–173
one-to-one plans, 174, 201–202
overwhelm and, 175, 178, 180, 191, 199
points systems, 174–175, 180, 202–203
practicing, 204–205
self-assessment over, 195–199
stress and, 171–172
stuck points, 189–194
testing knowledge on, 175–177, 180–188
tips for effectiveness, 178–180
types of, 172–175
when to use, 171–172
context
in CAR acronym, 31–38, 51–53
changing what you can, 36–38
defined, 31
environmental, 31–32
in-the-moment, 34–36

293

context (*Continued*)
  parental impact and, 35–36
  planning approach to, 51–53
  stuck points, 34–36
Context-Action-Result (CAR) model
  action in, 31, 38–42
  consequences and, 199
  context in, 31–38, 51–53
  de-escalation and, 211
  putting it all together, 249–250, 258, 268–269
  result in, 31, 42–47
  testing knowledge on, 49–50
  tracking patterns with, 54–55
  understanding of, 47–48
cool-down phase of de-escalation, 207, 208–210, 214–215, 219–220
coping skills. *See also* caregiver coping
  accommodation and, 154, 156
  behavior and, 41
  for caregivers, 12–14, 25, 266–267
  consequences and, 172, 180–182
  de-escalation and, 215–221, 228, 237
  in-the-moment, 23, 29, 218
  selective attention and, 58, 66, 84
  validation and, 107
COVID-19 pandemic, 2
cursing behavior, 4, 38, 82, 86, 178, 193, 206, 208, 213

daily resets, 25
daily routines, 124–127, 129–134, 180, 252
de-escalation
  behavior patterns and, 207–211
  build-up phase of, 206, 208–211, 215–217
  CAR model and, 211
  conflict and, 206, 213–215, 217–218, 237
  cool-down phase of, 207, 208–210, 214–215, 219–220
  coping skills and, 215–221, 228, 237
  defined, 206–207
  expectations and, 248
  peak phase of, 207, 208–210, 213, 217–218
  practicing, 248
  reassurance and, 206, 208, 212, 214
  skill-building, 215
  stress and, 206, 213, 216, 218, 221
  stuck points, 211–215
  testing knowledge on, 221–247
depression
  consequences and, 171
  Context-Action-Result and, 34
  increasing rates of, 1–2
  maintaining skills with professional support, 280
  meaningful routines, 135
  parental work and, 8, 10
  validation and, 105
difficult tasks, 34
distress. *See* stress/distress
duration of behaviors, 286–287
dysregulation, 4, 154, 156

eating disorders, 2
emotions/feelings. *See also* anxiety; overwhelm; stress/distress
  empathy, 5, 36–38, 48, 50–53, 106, 249–253, 258, 265–266
  impatience, 212
  judgment, 13, 38, 58–60, 104–105, 110, 178, 192, 214, 217, 287
  mood boosters, 25
  patience, 5, 9, 13, 15, 17, 20, 35, 109, 169, 204, 212, 248, 267, 281
  resentment, 149–150, 157, 169, 192, 219
  shame, 13–14, 105, 108, 131, 214, 220
empathy, 5, 36–38, 48, 50–53, 106, 249–253, 258, 265–266
environmental context, 31–33
expectations
  accommodation and, 156
  behavior and, 31, 34, 44, 47
  consequences and, 173–174, 178, 180, 190–193, 201
  de-escalation and, 248
  meaningful routines and, 124–127, 129, 133–134, 138–139
  routines and, 277
  selective attention and, 58, 68, 70, 73
  setting of, 5, 10
extinction bursts, 83–85

false appreciation, 72–73, 75
family values, 127, 149, 168, 169
freedom response, 44
frequency of behaviors, 5, 58, 68, 286–288
fun activities, 134

global instability, 2
goal setting, 5–6, 17–22
good behavior, 38–39
grounding mantra, 23–25
gun violence in schools, 2

INDEX

helpful thoughts, 23–24
household expectations, 127–129

impairment in behavior, 171, 286–287
impatience, 212
inappropriate behavior, 4, 44, 47, 56–57, 63, 69, 90–91, 94–95, 212, 249
independence response, 44
inequality awareness, 2–3
intensity of behaviors, 5–7, 10, 46, 83, 85, 105, 122, 124, 191, 206, 213–216, 220, 248, 286–287
intentionality, 38, 57, 59, 67, 192, 206, 268, 280–282
in-the-moment context, 34–36
in-the-moment coping, 23, 29, 218
invalidation, 212, 228, 233, 235, 237
isolation, 2, 117, 287

judgment, 13, 38, 58–60, 104–105, 110, 178, 192, 214, 217, 287
just right accommodation, 150, 153

labeled praise, 70–72, 74–82
learning disorders, 45, 179
LGBTQ+ individuals, 3
logical consequences, 172–173

maintaining skills with professional support
  backsliding and, 280–281
  conflict and, 275–276, 287
  defined, 272
  importance of, 272
  stuck points, 280–282
  testing knowledge on, 273–279
  tips for maintaining skills, 282–285
  tips for seeking professional support, 286–292
mass shootings, 2
mastery activities, 134
meaningful activities, 124, 134, 138–139, 146, 157
meaningful routines
  choosing and identifying, 136–137
  daily, 125–127
  defined, 124–125
  expectations and, 124–127, 129, 133–134, 138–139, 277
  household expectations, 127–129
  making time for, 134–135
  overwhelm and, 126, 129, 131, 138

  parental resistance to, 132–134
  practicing, 143–146
  stress and, 129, 131
  stuck points, 129–134, 139
  teen resistance to, 130
  tips for creating, 138
  understanding of, 138–141
misbehavior, 38, 56–57, 215
mismatched setting, 35
mood boosters, 25
mottos for coping, 24

negative attention, 56
negative interaction, 57–60, 66, 73
neutral interaction, 57–60, 66–67
nonpreferred task limits, 44

one-on-one time, 68–70, 101
one-to-one behavior plans, 174, 177, 198–199, 201–202, 250
overaccommodation, 149, 153, 154–155
overwhelm
  accommodation and, 149, 153, 156, 160, 162, 164
  behavior and, 37, 47
  in caregiver coping, 17–18, 29
  CAR model and, 265
  consequences and, 175, 178, 180, 191, 199
  de-escalation and, 206
  in-the-moment coping, 29
  meaningful routines and, 126, 129–132, 138
  validation and, 116, 120

pace of change, 9
Parent Child Interaction Therapy (PCIT), 68
parent work
  basic principles of, 8
  being specific, 10
  consistency as key, 9–10
  relationship importance, 8–9
  slowing pace of change, 9
  toning down big reactions, 10–11
patience, 5, 9, 13, 15, 17, 20, 35, 109, 169, 204, 212, 248, 267, 281
peak phase of de-escalation, 207, 208–210, 213, 217–218
physical activities, 134
points systems, 174–175, 180, 202–203
positive attention, 57, 68, 74, 82, 85, 90, 171, 192–193, 219, 250, 254, 256, 268
positive interaction, 57, 60, 66–67, 70, 73, 134

praise
    for expected behavior, 72
    false appreciation, 72–73, 75
    labeled praise, 70–72, 74–75
    positive interaction and, 73
    response to, 44
    selective attention and, 70–82
    tailoring to teen, 73–74
    validation and, 105
problem-solving
    de-escalation and, 211
    environmental context, 32
    validation and, 108
    well-being investment, 18–19
procrastination, 37, 39, 41, 126, 138, 159, 161, 164, 166, 250–252, 287
professional support. *See* maintaining skills with professional support
psychosis, 2
punishment. *See also* consequences
    backfiring of, 8
    chores and nonpreferred tasks, 45
    de-escalation and, 325
    defined, 42
    removing attention, 44
    removing preferred items, 44
    removing privileges, 45
    requiring apologies/repairs, 45
    as response behavior, 44–45
    scale of, 178
    stuck points, 189–190
    warnings and reminders, 45
putting it all together
    CAR model and, 249–250, 255, 268–269
    combining skills, 249–253
    conflict and, 249, 252–253
    defined, 249
    importance of, 249
    skillful behavior and, 249, 251–253, 256, 258, 265–266
    stuck points, 267–268
    testing knowledge on, 253–266

racism, 2–3, 33
reassurance
    accommodation and, 160, 162, 165, 167–168
    de-escalation and, 206, 208, 212, 214
    selective attention and, 68, 85–86
    validation and, 122
reflection, 3, 59–60, 67, 69, 72, 81, 91, 95, 100, 104, 220

resentment, 149–150, 157, 169, 192, 219
results
    in CAR acronym, 31, 42–47
    defined, 31
    impact on behavior, 45–46
    punishment and, 44–45
    reshaping behavior, 46–47
rewards. *See also* consequences
    activity-based, 126
    meaningful routines and, 126
    as response, 44
    scale of, 178
    stuck points, 189–191
    tangible, 44, 126
    value to child, 178
    well-being investment, 19
routines. *See* meaningful routines
rudeness, 38, 212

selective attention
    active ignoring, 57, 82–91
    building it in, 67
    conflict and, 58–60, 67–69, 86, 96, 101
    conflict-free zones, 67–68
    coping skills and, 58, 66, 84
    defined, 56
    example of, 91–100
    expectations and, 58, 68, 70, 73
    importance of, 56–57
    negative interaction and, 57–60, 66, 73
    neutral interaction and, 57–60, 66–67
    one-on-one time, 68–70, 101
    positive interaction and, 57, 60, 66–67, 70, 73, 134
    power of, 101
    practicing, 102–103
    praise and, 70–82
    reassurance and, 68, 85–86
    reflection and, 59–60
    responses, 60–65
    stress and, 58, 82, 85–86
    stuck points, 66–70
    use with teens, 57
self-assessment, 150–153, 195–199
sensory activities, 24
service activities, 134
shame, 13–14, 105, 108, 131, 214, 220
skill-building, 149–150, 155, 158, 215, 267, 277
skillful behavior
    consequences and, 179–180
    introduction to, 4

INDEX

putting it all together and, 249, 251–253, 256, 258, 266
selective attention and, 57
sleep reserves, 20
slogans for coping, 24
social accountability, 26
social activities, 134
social isolation, 2
social media, 1–2, 4, 21, 42, 135, 294
stress/distress
    accommodation and, 149, 151–158, 167
    behaviors and, 31–33, 35–36, 41, 48–49, 52
    causes of, 2–3
    consequences and, 171–172
    de-escalation and, 206, 213, 216, 218, 221
    meaningful routines and, 129, 131
    over accommodation and, 155–156
    selective attention and, 58, 82, 85–86
    skills for coping, 8, 10–17, 23–27
    toning down big reactions, 10–11
    validation and, 104–108, 111–112, 114–117, 120, 122
stuck points
    accommodation, 154–158
    active ignoring, 84–86, 91
    behavior and, 34–36
    caregiver coping, 29
    consequences, 189–194
    in context, 34–36
    de-escalation, 211–215
    defined, 4
    labeled praise, 74–75
    maintaining skills with professional support, 280–282
    meaningful routines, 129–134, 139
    punishment, 189–191

    putting it all together, 266–267
    rewards, 189–191
    selective attention, 66–70
    validation, 106–110, 113
substance abuse, 2

tangible rewards, 44, 126
threats/threatening behavior, 8, 11, 39, 56, 206, 208, 211–214, 217
time estimates/expectations, 126
time-of-day issues, 34–35
to-do lists, 17–18, 125–127, 134, 138
trust, 5, 67, 104, 106, 108–109, 157, 173–174, 189, 192–193, 211, 248, 277, 281, 288–289

underaccommodation, 153, 274, 277
unmet physical needs, 35
unskillful behavior, 4, 45, 50, 56, 66, 228, 234–235
unstructured tasks, 34
urgency considerations, 66

validation
    coping skills and, 107
    defined, 104–105
    goal of, 107
    importance of, 105–106
    overwhelm and, 116, 120
    practicing, 113–123
    reassurance and, 122
    stress and, 104–108, 111–112, 114–117, 120, 122
    stuck points, 106–110, 113
    understanding of, 110–112

weekly goals, 18
well-being, 2, 12–23, 206, 272, 275